The Taste of Summer

The Taste

INSPIRED RECIPES FOR

DIANE ROSSEN WORTHINGTON

of Summer

CASUAL ENTERTAINING

with wine notes by
ANTHONY DIAS BLUE

BANTAM BOOKS
TORONTO • NEW YORK • LONDON • SYDNEY • AUCKLAND

THE TASTE OF SUMMER
A Bantam Book / June 1988

Library of Congress Cataloging-in-Publication Data
Worthington, Diane Rossen.
The taste of summer.
Includes index.
1. Outdoor cookery.   2. Menus.   I. Title.
TX823.W67   1988   641.5′78   87-33377
ISBN 0-553-05273-X

Published simultaneously in the United States and Canada

Bantam Books are published by Bantam Books, a division of Bantam Doubleday
Dell Publishing Group, Inc. Its trademark, consisting of the words "Bantam Books"
and the portrayal of a rooster, is Registered in U.S. Patent and Trademark Office
and in other countries. Marca Registrada. Bantam Books, 666 Fifth Avenue, New
York, New York 10103.

PRINTED IN THE UNITED STATES OF AMERICA

DH   0 9 8 7 6 5 4 3 2

To my parents, Ruth and Allan Rossen,
who gave me the gift of
so many wonderful summers

Acknowledgments

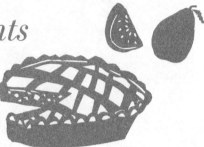

There are many people whose interest and assistance I have greatly appreciated and would like to mention: Don Cutler, my agent, for putting it all together; Coleen O'Shea for her belief in the project; Fran McCullough, for her skilled editing and her infectious laugh that helped me get through the longest days; Pamela Mosher, for her thoughtful copyediting; Anthony Dias Blue for his exceptional knowledge on pairing wine and summer food; Becky Champa, for her excellent word processing skills and general helpfulness; Joan Lenoff, for carefully testing the recipes; Kathryn Butterfield, for her food research; Laurie Burrows Grad, Janice Wald Henderson, Marlene Sorosky, and Jan Weimer for their professional wisdom; Bernard Jacoupy, for his innovative ideas; Denny Luria and Mary Rose, for their loyal friendship and thoughtful input; Kathy Blue, Barbara Windom, Pamela Singer, Connie Engel, Leslie Margolis, Joan Friedman, Robert Braun, Lucy Suzar, and Claudette Einhorn for their recipe testing and insightful suggestions; Dee Worthington, for her editorial assistance; Frieda Caplan, Judy Greening, Paradise Farms, and Taylors Herb Garden for their help in answering all of my questions; and finally, my husband, Michael, and daughter, Laura, for all their love and support.

Table of Contents

Introduction

Summer—with its balmy days, starry nights, bright flowers, and luscious fruits and vegetables—is reason enough to celebrate. This is a season for indulgence and spontaneity, a time for casual entertaining. When it comes to entertaining in summer, it's the food itself, with its vibrant colors and intense flavors, that becomes the focus. Precious free moments are meant for enjoying the outdoors, not polishing silver, arranging placecards, or toiling endless hours in the kitchen. It's much more fun to plan picnics, barbecues, and simple buffets—any meal that can either be prepared quickly or offer minimal last-minute preparation. The style of informal entertaining I present here gives you maximum time with family and friends, yet still allows you to serve exciting and elegant food.

The culinary treasures summer offers are, of course, the best of the year. Perfect produce, the cornerstone of summer cooking, is available everywhere and at its peak of flavor. It's so easy to create wonderful dishes with the inspiration of this extraordinary bounty. Any summer meal is automatically enhanced by fresh picked corn, so sweet you'll want to eat it raw, and tomatoes so red you'd swear they've been painted. And how can you resist a golden apricot, with its delicate balance between sweet and tart?

Fresh herbs also star in summer cooking. Fortunately, herbs are very accommodating—they grow as happily in tiny pots on apartment windowsills as they do in country gardens. One of my greatest everyday pleasures is stepping outside to snip fragrant basil leaves for pesto. Although herbs are available year round, the intensity and distinctive flavor they develop in the summer give a kind of magic to a dish; they are one of the signatures of the season.

Potted herbs serve as fragrant, appealing table decorations simply by being whisked from the windowsill to the dinner table. Their flowers—especially those of basil, thyme, chives, and society garlic—make tasty garnishes. And they can contribute charming notes of color to contrast or highlight the foods of the season. Lavender chive blossoms, for instance, can be sprinkled over orange-carrot soup or a yellow and green vegetable frittata—gorgeous.

Flowers are one of the easiest and most accessible garnishes; they can transform the simplest dish into a still-life of summer. Used as table accents, flowers in impromptu arrangements always look fresh and lovely. Pretty bouquets are easy to create. A drift of wildflowers freshly plucked from a meadow—or a bunch of daisies purchased from a supermarket—can look just as beautiful and more in keeping with the season than a sophisticated centerpiece.

Of course, what really showcases summer entertaining, the constant backdrop, is the pleasant weather. Gentle breezes, blue skies, and warm temperatures are guaranteed to spark a spontaneous gaiety among guests. Eating outdoors, whether it's on the terrace of a city apartment, a deck overlooking the beach, or a spacious lawn, is always a pleasure. It creates a lovely, school's-out atmosphere that seems to bring on high spirits.

In summer, great style can be achieved with a minimum of effort. Spreading a quilt on a patch of grass for a casual candlelight dinner for two can be as appealing as an elegant patio buffet. Even table settings take on less significance. There's no need to fuss over matching placemats and napkins; contrasting colors and patterns simply bring the table alive. At this time of year, anything goes; if there is one rule, it's Less Is More. Attractive, sturdy paper plates set inside wicker plate-holders can make an outdoor table look as festive as one set with china and crystal. In the summer, it's easy to be creative with what you have on hand—baskets, crocks, preserving jars—look at your house with a fresh eye and you'll see many possibilities.

The relaxed mood of summer should set the tone on special occasions too. Graduation and wedding parties may call for china and crystal, but these traditional celebrations also take on a more casual quality during this season. Fresh flowers, fresh produce, and mild weather combine to create a lighthearted atmosphere. You can serve dishes that are not complicated to prepare, like Spicy Lime Ginger Grilled Shrimp, Vegetable Platter with Grilled Red Pepper and Garlic Sauce, Cold Grilled Roast Beef with Sour Cream Herbed Sauce, and String Bean–Golden Pepper Salad. All these can be presented with nonchalant elegance.

The foods of summer should be fresh and colorful. They should not require long hours of preparation; in fact, a number of dishes in this book are basically *un*cooked. Grilling and sautéing replace more time-consuming cooking methods. Sauces are always made quickly, whether they are a reduction of a marinade or a combination of a few harmonious ingredients. Breads should either be quick and crisp or bought from the best bakery source—while it's a great pleasure in cool weather, making your own bread in summer seems unappealing. Cooking that generates heat in the kitchen is kept to a minimum; any necessary roasting or baking is completed in the early morning. The key is organization; the recipes are designed to help you think through the steps in advance to make it all easy.

Of course sensational summer foods are comprised of more than just time-saving techniques. I like to base new recipes on classical ideas, yet combine ingredients in slightly unusual ways to create an element of surprise. For example, in the first course chapter you'll find Guacamole Salsa. A combination of the best attributes of guacamole and salsa, this crunchy mixture of colorful vegetables and diced avocado is a perfect dip for tortilla chips or raw vegetables. An Indonesian-style satay is prepared with spicy pork tenderloin rather than chicken or beef. Instead of the traditional peanut sauce, it's accompanied by an orange cilantro cream, adding an unexpected taste.

A particular advantage of summer entertaining is that there is no need to plan the traditional fixed menu. On an exceptionally warm evening, three appetizers might make a complete meal. When a favorite vegetable, such as corn, is at its height of sweetness, you might plan an entire menu around it. One of my most successful dinner parties was a feast of Corn-Leek Cakes, Corn Soup, and Green Corn Tamales with Sour Cream Tomatillo Sauce. Or, you might opt for a communal feast and ask each guest to bring dishes based on prized items from their garden or the local produce stand.

The recipes in the book are arranged by courses; most are accompanied by menu and wine suggestions. Although the emphasis of this book is on entertaining, you will discover that many of these recipes are equally appropriate for family meals. Most are quickly assembled or the work can be divided into stages and prepared partially in advance. The boxes sprinkled throughout offer informal recipes and useful information.

This book is designed to be flexible. You can follow the menu suggestions given for most recipes or, you can combine your favorite recipes to create a menu tailored to suit a specific occasion. I have also included menus for such festive events as picnics, outdoor concerts, and buffets. You'll find these recipes are fun to prepare and even those that have many steps are easy to follow. Most of all, this food is designed to celebrate the splendid tastes of summer, while freeing you to enjoy the rest of its bountiful pleasures.

Cooking Over Open Fire

Cooking in the summer will more often than not find you standing in front of a barbecue. While we all know how to throw a steak on the grill, there are some fine points to grilling that will make all the difference in the final result.

TYPES OF GRILLS

There are three basic types of grills: the portable (the hibachi, for example); the open barbecue or brazier; and the covered barbecue. Portable barbecues are great for picnics and tailgate parties but don't have the flexibility to cook large portions of food or to cook thick pieces of meat without burning. Open barbecues are best for quick-grilling food that is no thicker than 1½ inches. Long slow cooking cannot be achieved on an open fire since there is no cover to trap the smoke and keep down the flame. Covered barbecues, which come in all shapes and sizes, provide the option of cooking the food covered or uncovered. There's usually an adjustable rack to allow you greater flexibility when cooking and timing the food. Certain foods, like butterflied leg of lamb, roast beef, and pizza (yes, pizza!) cook best covered.

There are some other distinctions to be aware of when shopping for a barbecue. Gas grills are a convenient alternative to regular charcoal grilling. While they may not satisfy the purist, they have become an acceptable alternative. These cookers are almost always equipped with a cover and usually have permanent "briquets" that are made of rock. A gas-fueled flame heats the rock in lieu of the standard charcoal briquets. The main disadvantage of these grills is that the food may not have the full smoky flavor we expect. This drawback can be partially overcome by adding wet, aromatic hardwood chips to the fire. The greatest benefits of gas grills are their quick heat-up time and ability to cook food on even heat for long periods of time.

FUEL FOR THE FIRE

There's an ongoing debate over which fuel is best for barbecuing. Not so long ago there was only one choice, the charcoal briquet. But times have changed and so has the fuel you can use to stoke up your barbecue. Hardwood charcoal is the new alternative.

Charcoal briquets were initially invented by Henry Ford for industrial purposes. But he sold out to the Kingsford company, whose name became synonymous with barbecuing. These briquets are made from wood scraps that have been burned into carbon. They are often mixed with fillers and additives, to keep them burning longer and faster. Some brands will even give the food an off taste. If you use charcoal briquets, let the coals reach an ashen gray state, which indicates that the chemicals have burned off. You don't want to cook over charcoal that is still the slightest bit black.

Hardwood charcoals are more expensive but contain no chemicals. They are chunks of wood that have been carbonized. The more common varieties include oak, maple, cherry, hickory, alderwood, and mesquite. Mesquite is the most popular hardwood today because it is plentiful and relatively inexpensive. A popular misconception is that mesquite charcoal will overwhelm the taste of the food. That's only true, however, of mesquite *wood*, which produces much more smoke and correspondingly intense flavor. Mesquite charcoal will add only a light, smoky sweet flavor. I particularly like to use it when grilling chicken and meat.

Wood chips, such as alder, hickory, cherry, apple, and oak, are another source of fuel and also a good flavoring agent. They are often used in addition to other fuel for the purpose of adding flavor. Soak the chips in water for ½ hour before tossing them over the coals. You can also place them in a small aluminum pan on top of the lava briquets in a gas grill to impart a smoky flavor to gas-grilled food.

Branches of fresh herbs, such as rosemary, fennel, bay leaves, or tarragon, thrown into the fire will add a wonderful aroma and flavor to the food. Soak the branches first to make them smoke slowly. Grape vine cuttings may also be used. Grape chips are now being marketed, if you want this particular taste.

HOW TO START THE FIRE

There are several ways to get your barbecue going. I grew up on charcoal fires lit with lighter fluid. While this gets the fire blazing, the after taste the fuel leaves on the grilled food makes it a less than desirable choice. A trickier way is to use hot air. My husband's favorite technique is to light crumpled newspaper placed under the briquets. He then uses a hair dryer on high to blow air onto the coals. Believe it or not, this really works. However, this would not be my first choice for a dinner party. The chimney starter, available in gourmet cookware and barbecue stores, is an easier and healthier way to ignite briquets because it eliminates the need for lighter fluid. You put the briquets in the top of the cylinder and crumpled newspaper in the bottom. You then place it in the barbecue and light the newspaper. The charcoal will ignite in about 15 minutes. Other methods include using an electric starter or kindling. Whichever you choose, try to avoid using lighter fluid.

WHEN IS THE FIRE READY?

Knowing just when to put your food on the fire is crucial to successful grilling. A fire that is too hot will char the outside of the food while leaving the center raw. If the fire is too cool, the food won't cook properly.

Charcoal and wood fires are ready 30 to 45 minutes after the initial lighting. For most foods, the coals should have a layer of gray ash. If there is a high flame the fire is not quite ready.

Medium-high-heat grilling: the fire should have red hot coals with just a thin layer of gray ash and an occasional flare-up. You can test the heat by holding your hand about 6 inches from the grid. You should be able to keep it there for only a few seconds. Medium-high-heat grilling is excellent for boneless chicken breasts or thinly sliced pieces of seafood, poultry, or meat.

Medium-heat grilling: The coals should be covered with a thick layer of gray ash and there should be no flames. This is a good way to cook thicker pieces of meat or poultry. You may want to use the cover to your grill for this lower temperature cooking.

GRILLING TIMES AND TEMPERATURES

These basic guidelines will tell you how long and at what temperature to cook, but remember that the food will continue cooking off the grill because it's so hot. You should remove it a few minutes before it is perfectly done.

Fish
Fish steaks and fillets are best cooked on an open grill over a medium-high heat since they do not require long cooking. Brush the fish liberally with oil before placing it on the grill to prevent sticking. If you're grilling a whole fish, a hinged basket is useful so that you can turn the fish without breaking it up. Cook whole fish on medium heat using a cover. Cooking times will vary according to the type of fish and its thickness. Check it with a fork; it should just begin to flake. Avoid overcooking fish as it will change not only the texture but also the taste.

Poultry
Cook most poultry on a covered grill over medium heat; it requires a longer and slower cooking time than fish or red meat. Boned chicken breasts and turkey slices are the exception; they need medium-high heat and quick grilling. Boneless chicken breasts require 6 to 8 minutes per side, while chicken

pieces require 8 to 14 minutes per side. Use these times as a guideline for other types of poultry.

If you don't have a covered grill, baste poultry often to retain moisture, and allow a slightly longer cooking time. Wait until there is a thick layer of gray ash on the coals before you begin cooking to ensure an even temperature.

Meats

An instant meat thermometer is handy when grilling large pieces of meat. General guideline temperatures for meat are: Beef and lamb should register 130°F to 135°F for rare, 135°F to 145°F for medium rare, and 150°F for medium. Pork roasts should have an internal temperature of 160°F; more than that and they tend to be very dry.

Steaks and chops can be cooked according to the thickness of the cut. Sear them on each side for 30 seconds and then cook as suggested below. The lower number indicates the time for rare and the higher number for well done. These times are for each side.

1 inch: 3 to 6 minutes
1½ inches: 4 to 9 minutes
2 inches: 6 to 10 minutes

Do not poke the meat with a fork to test for doneness as this will only dry it out. Season the meat with salt and pepper after it's cooked.

Vegetables

Clean the vegetables and slice them for the grill. Certain vegetables, such as pearl onions and summer squash, should be blanched in boiling water for just a minute to eliminate the raw taste that quick grilling might leave. Brush the vegetables with extra virgin olive oil or avocado oil before placing them on the grill. Sear them over a medium-high heat to seal in their juices and then move them to the side of the grill to finish cooking. Thinly sliced vegetables will take 6 to 10 minutes per side. Vegetables that fall apart easily, such as tomatoes or onions, should be placed in a grilling basket. All vegetables can be skewered on metal or bamboo skewers if desired, but remember to soak bamboo skewers for at least 30 minutes before grilling.

Fruit

Sliced apples, bananas, pears, peaches, nectarines, or pineapples may be threaded on skewers and grilled on medium-high heat for just a few minutes on each side. A basting sauce of lemon juice, melted butter, and a touch of brown sugar will give the fruit a pretty glaze.

SOME HANDY TOOLS

When barbecuing it's helpful to have these utensils on hand:

- Basting brushes, especially wide ones with long handles, are necessary for basting. Or you can use branches of fresh herbs, such as rosemary.
- An instant meat thermometer is very handy to check thick pieces of meat or roasts.
- A grilling basket with a long handle is indispensable for grilling whole fish or certain vegetables.
- A wicker basket is useful near the grill. Line it with a colorful napkin or tea towel and fill it with pot holders, a spray bottle of water for flare-ups, a flashlight, a long-handled fork, a large knife, and a spatula.

PREPARING AND CLEANING THE GRILL

It's untrue, unfortunately, that subsequent fires will burn off the residue from the last cookout, excusing you from cleaning the grill. In fact, you have to clean the rack—the cooking surface—every time you use it or the food will pick up strange tastes. To make it easier: Check the manufacturer's instructions for specific details. A crumpled ball of aluminum foil can be used to clean the rack while it is still lukewarm. Afterward, wipe the rack with a wet sponge or paper towels. Stiff barbecue brushes also come in handy, but check the manufacturer's instructions carefully because you could damage a chrome or porcelain rack. Occasionally, it is necessary to wash the entire grill with soapy water. As a preventive measure, I frequently brush the grid with a mild vegetable or olive oil to keep food from sticking and burning.

Marinades

Marinades are especially useful in the summer because they are made in moments and work wonders with grilled foods, tenderizing and adding flavor at once. They are usually made with a combination of an acid, such as citrus juice, vinegar, wine, or even yogurt, and vegetable or olive oil. A good ratio is 2 parts acid to 1 part oil. Salt should be kept to a minimum, since it can toughen the meat. Spices, herbs, and mustards are added for specific flavors. Always let the marinade rest for a few minutes before adding the meat to allow the flavors to develop. Use only glass, stainless steel, porcelain, or enamel vessels for marinating; aluminum will give food a metallic taste. Be sure all surfaces of the food are covered with the marinade.

There are a few general rules to remember when marinating: Thick pieces of meat can be marinated up to 24 hours without causing a change in texture. Generally, poultry needs less time, up to 6 hours. Fish should never be marinated for more than 2 hours if the acid content of the marinade is high because it will actually cook the fish.

A few other tips:

- If you are marinating food in the refrigerator, remove it ½ hour before grilling to let it reach room temperature.
- Use the marinade for basting during cooking to give the food extra moisture and flavor.
- Don't forget about marinating vegetables. They are excellent marinated and grilled.
- Pastes or herb coatings are other types of marinades that are used more to flavor than to tenderize.

Picnics

Picnics are certainly the most relaxed style of summer entertaining. The preparation can be as impromptu as stopping by the local deli and picking up what looks good, or as time-consuming as cooking pâtés, salads, entrées, sauces, and desserts for days. I enjoy both. My most memorable picnic took place high in the French Alps on a warm summer day with a cooking school group. We had prepared food for the picnic in class the night before and then bought fresh tomatoes and peaches from the local market. While the meal was superb, what made it unforgettable was the breathtaking mountaintop setting, the bright sunlight streaming down, and the warmth of the moment. It's good to remember that the food is only part of a picnic's appeal. The setting, the company, and the time of day each adds its distinct contribution.

My favorite picnics tend to be midafternoon lunches, wine and hors d'oeuvres at sunset, and outdoor concert dinners. While picnics may take place in a variety of settings—in a meadow filled with brilliant flowers, by a cold mountain stream, in a city park, on a sandy beach, or even on a boat—the secrets of all successful picnics are essentially the same.

Probably the single most important item to ensure a perfect picnic is a good food chest or cooler. There's such a large variety available today that you can choose one that will fill your particular needs. If you only go on picnics for two, a large cooler is probably unnecessary and cumbersome. If you usually picnic with a large group you may want to invest in a couple of different-sized coolers that will easily accommodate assorted

THE NO-COOK PICNIC

This extremely easy menu takes a little forethought, since the gravlax requires 3 to 4 days to cure in the refrigerator.

Chilled Avocado Soup with Cucumber Tomato Salsa

Basil Gravlax with Sweet Mustard Basil Sauce

Assorted Pumpernickel and Whole Wheat Rolls

Chilled Red and White Radishes, Carrots, and Cucumbers

A Wicker Tray of Fresh Goat Cheese, Mascarpone, Gorgonzola, and Sharp Cheddar

A Basket of Nectarines, Plums, and Apricots

Almond Cookies

shapes. It's also helpful to be able to separate the cold dishes from the warm ones. Different-sized packets of what I call blue ice—those rectangles of frozen blue jell that keep food chilled—kept in your freezer will allow you to picnic on a moment's

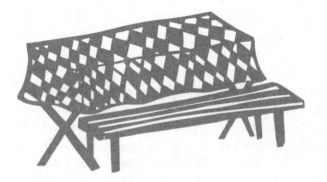

notice. Solidly frozen blue ice will usually keep already chilled food really cold for 3 or 4 hours.

A number of coolers for wine are on the market; some will hold two bottles and several glasses as well. I like to carry a double cooler filled with wine and sparkling water.

Make a menu ahead of time and keep it taped to your refrigerator. Check off each dish as you pack it into your basket. There's nothing worse than arriving with everything except that one important sauce or salad dressing.

A BARBECUE PICNIC

This high-spirited picnic is based on the exhilarating flavors of Latin food. It's easy to assemble once you solve the problem of bringing the grill along—a hibachi works fine. The beans, marinade, and fruit can be made a day ahead. Wrap the pot of hot beans in a tablecloth or in a few sheets of crumpled newspaper to keep it warm. The Guacamole Salsa and Papaya Salsa are best made the same day. Thread the shrimp on bamboo skewers that will fit into a plastic container and marinate them in the same container. If you have time, bake the cookies just a few hours before serving or choose your favorite packaged cookies. Mexican beer is great with this menu.

Guacamole Salsa

Tortilla Chips

Tequila Lime Grilled Shrimp

Cuban Black Beans

Tomato-Papaya Mint Salsa

Slices of Yellow and Red Seedless Watermelon

Almond Cookies with Lemon and Port

A Picnic Lunch

This light and easy picnic menu must be kept well chilled. Make up the pâté a few days ahead to allow time for the flavors to blend. Chill the interior of the thermos before adding the soup. Keep the salad dressing cold and add it to the potatoes just before serving.

Herbed Cucumber Soup with Walnuts

Picnic Pâté

*Cornichons, Dijon Mustard,
and French Bread*

Potato Salad Niçoise

Passion Fruit Caramel Custard in Individual Molds

Depending on your mood and the menu, you can take as little paraphernalia or as much as you like. The following is a detailed list of assorted items to help make your picnic easy and carefree.

- A picnic basket, hamper, or tote bag for carrying food and equipment
- Food chests to keep food hot or cold
- Frozen blue ice for chilled foods
- A tablecloth, quilt, sheet, or any other ground cover if you plan to eat on the ground
- Large cloth or paper napkins
- Wicker holders for paper plates
- Plates for appetizers, soup, main course, dessert
- Coffee cups, waterglasses, and wineglasses
- Flatware
- Serving pieces
- Bottle opener, corkscrew, and can opener
- Paper towels
- Plastic bags or plastic wrap for leftovers
- Large plastic bag for trash

- Large plastic bag for used dishes and utensils
- Small cutting board and knife
- Condiments: salt, pepper, sugar, cream for coffee, mustard, relish
- Fuel and matches if you are using a hibachi
- Ice, liquor, and mixes
- Thermos filled with hot coffee
- Soft drinks, sparkling water, beer, or wine
- Jug of cold water
- Whole lemons and limes
- Candles, candle holders, and matches
- Flashlight

AN OUTDOOR CONCERT PICNIC

This sensational picnic menu can be served as simply or as elegantly as you like. Prepare the cheese and the salsa the night before and pack separately so you can assemble the dish at the picnic. The soup can also be made a day ahead and, depending on the weather, served hot or chilled. The chicken tastes best served warm, so roast it right before leaving and pack the sauce separately. Place the chicken in a heavy duty plastic container and wrap the package in a tablecloth or several thicknesses of newspaper. The salad and asparagus can be assembled early in the morning. The tart may also be prepared in the early morning or the night before.

Double Cheese Spread with Zesty Italian Salsa

Minted Chinese Pea Pod Soup

Crispy Roast Chicken with Spinach Pesto Cream

Cracked Wheat Vegetable Salad

Chilled Asparagus with Red Pepper Vinaigrette

Hazelnut Plum Tart with Crème Fraîche

Packing and serving food on a picnic requires careful planning. These tips should help organize you so that your food arrives as fresh as when it left the kitchen.

- Pack the foods to be eaten last at the bottom of the bag or chest and the first on top, so that you don't have to unpack everything at once.
- Use vacuum-packed containers to avoid leaks and soggy bags; for extra reinforcement tape the lids with masking tape. Seal the containers in Ziploc plastic bags.
- Pack soft foods like deviled eggs, tomatoes, or fruit in hard plastic containers or egg cartons.
- If you are serving a hot soup, preheat the thermos with boiling water. For a cold soup, chill the thermos with ice water for several minutes.
- Divide or cut the portions in your kitchen. It's much easier to serve pieces or slices of grilled chicken or duck than to carve them on the ground.
- Pack garnishes in Ziploc plastic bags—parsley, basil, mint, and herb flowers should be sprinkled with water before packing. Keep them in the cooler.

S U N S E T   P I C N I C

Prepare the sauces and the eggplant the day before and assemble the dishes at the picnic. Baskets and serving trays decorated with herbs and herb blossoms will make this simple picnic fare special. To make a meal of it, add cold, sliced roast beef and sliced tomatoes with marinated sun-dried tomato garnish.

Smoked Trout with Roasted Garlic Mayonnaise

Vegetable Platter with Grilled Red Pepper and Garlic Sauce

Balsamic Roasted Eggplant with Niçoise Olives

Thinly Sliced French Bread

Champagne

An Elegant Picnic

This is a favorite picnic menu when I'm in the mood for something luxurious. The soup, the green bean salad, and the poached peaches can be made early in the day. Keep the eggs, lobster, and dressing very cold. Assemble the lobster salad right before serving. Start with the soup in chilled mugs and then serve the eggs and two salads together.

Golden Summer Soup

Smoked Salmon Deviled Eggs

Cold Lobster Salad with Caviar-Dill Mayonnaise

Green Bean, Mushroom, and Walnut Salad

French Rolls

Poached Peaches in White Zinfandel with
Fresh Raspberry Sauce

Toasted Hazelnut Cookies

And last but not least, strictly observe these practices to avoid food spoilage:

- Mayonnaise keeps well in a jar, but when added to a salad it can spoil quickly. As a precaution, dress salads or sandwiches at the picnic rather than at home. Keep the mayonnaise chilled in the cooler.
- Keep eggs, dairy products, and uncooked meat well chilled until just before serving.
- Make sure that there is breathing room in the cooler to keep the cold air circulating. Don't jam it full or the temperature will rise.
- Don't partially cook the food at home and finish it at the picnic site; during transportation the food is at the optimum temperature for bacterial invasion.
- Pack the food just before leaving for the picnic.

Buffets

The buffet is a casual, easy style of entertaining that seems especially well suited to summer. Guests particularly enjoy the unstructured feeling that a buffet creates; even if it's a relatively formal event like a wedding, serving buffet style will loosen things up. It's certainly the easiest possible style for the host and hostess, since only minimal last-minute preparation is necessary if the buffet is well planned. Depending on the budget and your intentions, you can hire bartenders and kitchen help, rent everything from glasses to the tablecloth, and host a nearly professional party. Or you can have an extremely simple buffet that is produced by only one pair of hands in the kitchen. Probably the most important element in planning any party is being able to think through the entire event in detail, so that you can avoid any pitfalls and leave yourself as free as possible to enjoy your guests.

THE FOOD

You can have a *grande bouffe*, an elaborate smorgasbord of dishes, or build the menu around a central dish supported by complementary dishes that won't overwhelm it. Choose foods that will not suffer if eaten warm rather than hot, or slightly chilled rather than cold. If you're not planning to have your guests sit down at tables, don't serve foods that need to be cut with a knife. Instead, choose fingerfood or precut bite-sized food. Remember your guests will already have a full plate of food, a napkin, and a wineglass to juggle.

Obviously, the more dishes you can completely prepare ahead of time, the better. Even if the main course is barbecued,

Serve little squares of the tart with drinks while the barbecued brisket and ribs finish cooking. All the side dishes
may be made early in the day; the Cole Slaw and Baked
Beans will taste even better if they're made the night
before. Dessert should be served on a separate table, with
the biscuits stacked on a pretty plate, the strawberries in a
glass bowl with a silver serving spoon, and the custard
sauce in a bowl with a ladle so the guests can assemble
their own shortcakes.

Eggplant Tomato Mushroom Tart

Barbecued Brisket of Beef

and/or

Sweet and Hot Spareribs with Apricot Plum Sauce

Two-Color Coleslaw

Baked Beans with Bourbon and Apple Cider

Garden Salad with Goat Cheese Thyme Dressing

Herbed Garlic Cheese Bread

Strawberry Shortcake with Raspberry Custard Sauce

consider grilling it a couple of hours in advance and serving it
at room temperature. If a dish won't reheat successfully, forget
it and choose something that will or that doesn't require heat-
ing at all.

Make up a prep sheet for the meal, including all the shopping information, which day you will prepare the dish, and
what it will be served on. Check everything off as you go. One

of the first things to check in planning your menu is the serving amounts—you need to know exactly how many times to multiply each recipe.

Remember that you'll probably need extra cooling space. If you can't use a neighbor's refrigerator, set up a cooler or ice chest and use it for foods that only need to be chilled. Greens can be prepared early in the day; clean, dry, and tightly roll them in tea towels so they'll take up less space in the crisper.

WHERE TO SERVE

Once you decide how many people to invite you'll know what size space will accommodate them. If you are going to serve outside, which is my preference during the summer months (weather permitting), examine the space and decide where the

---

A SOUP AND SALAD BUFFET

All of these dishes can be prepared well in advance to make a minimum of last-minute work. Serve the soup in a tureen or pitchers for pouring into plastic or glass mugs. For a tempting dessert presentation, scoop out vanilla ice cream balls a few hours before serving and place them on wax paper to freeze. Right before serving, arrange them in a glass bowl next to the pie.

Minestrone with Pesto Cream

Chicken Salad with Roasted Garlic Mayonnaise

String Bean–Golden Pepper Salad

Cherry Tomato and Hearts of Palm Salad

Lattice Crust Pie with Rhubarb, Peaches, Strawberries, and Plums with French Vanilla Ice Cream

---

buffet table would best be placed. Keep in mind that the closer to the kitchen the buffet table is, the easier it is to manage. Refilling platters, for instance, is much more convenient when the kitchen is nearby. One suggestion is to serve in the dining room or the living room even though people will then take their plates outside. This strategy will also avoid the problem of annoying insects hovering over the food and unreliable weather.

If you choose to serve on an outside buffet table you can either arrange the buffet table against the wall, in the center of the patio or deck, or, if it is an especially large party, you can put up two tables to avoid making your guests stand in a long line. You may want to set up a separate dessert table in a different location so that your guests who are finished with their entrées can move to another area. The dessert table should be near an electrical outlet so you can also serve coffee on it.

THE BAR

Designate a separate area away from the main buffet table to set up your bar. A bartender is an enormous asset for a large party but not essential; if the bar is self-service, though, it needs to be especially well organized. Arrange the mixers, liquors, red wine, glasses, garnishes, and napkins on a table or bar. An all-purpose wine goblet is a good choice for most drinks. You'll need a very large ice bucket with a refill source under the table in a cooler. I like to have a large pitcher or punch bowl of a mixed drink like Bloody Marys or Sangria available. There should also be a large washtub or cooler full of ice, soft drinks, white wine, or champagne for the guests to help themselves. Put out an appetizer or two on the bar as well. For more specifics on how to set up a bar, refer to the Summer Drinks section.

THE BUFFET TABLE

An important point to keep in mind is that there is no "right" way for the table to look. It is a matter of your own personal taste and what feels right to you. Mixing and matching old and new, complementary—not matching—napkins and tablecloths, dishes and serving pieces will create a warm and informal atmosphere. Thinking through all the elements of the buffet table can sometimes be confusing, so I am including some general guidelines to assist you.

Tablecloths and Napkins

If you would like to have a specific color scheme, start with the tablecloth and then match the napkins to it. I like to keep it simple by having one basic color predominate. Through the years I have collected an assortment of napkins in different colors and patterns that go with several solid-colored table-cloths. If you are serving barbecued dishes, nicely designed paper napkins may be preferable. Whatever cover you choose to place on the table, it should just barely touch the floor. Tablecloths for dining tables look pretty with an apron on them. First put a plain-colored tablecloth over the table, then fit either a square or a circular patterned cloth—or a lace tablecloth—on top. If you don't want to purchase or create your own tablecloths, remember your local party rental service.

Plates and Silverware

Matching plates are not any more necessary than matching table linens. Alternate the dishes to create an interesting pattern of color. If you want to invest in a set of buffet plates, I recommend large, plain white plates or clear glass ones because they adapt to any occasion and are inexpensive. Paper plates are sometimes more appropriate for a casual buffet. Choose a sturdy, attractive quality plate that can handle a full meal. Fitting paper plates into inexpensive wicker holders stabilizes them. Stack the plates at the beginning of the buffet line next to the silverware.

My favorite way to present the cutlery is to wrap it in a napkin and then tie a bow around it with either ribbon or jute. A fresh herb blossom or flower can be tucked into the bow. If this sounds too elaborate, skip the ties and arrange the napkin rolls in a basket. You can either pile them one on top of the other or stand them up with the handles on the bottom. Or just lay them neatly on the table.

Glasses

Mix and match whatever glasses you have on hand. For a large party, you might consider renting all-purpose wineglasses. Figure that you should double the amount of guests to arrive at the correct number of glasses. For a more informal party use thick plastic glasses. If you're serving champagne, use the right glasses, champagne flutes—buy them, rent them, or use plastic ones, but the shape is essential.

Serving Pieces

A variety of different serving platters will bring an added dimension to the table. You can mix pewter, glass, wood, china, and pottery in a variety of shapes. Using round, rectangular, square, and even sculptured bowls and platters will add dimension and interest to the table. You can also alter the height of some of the dishes by placing the bowls or platters on pedestals.

A HOLIDAY WEEKEND LUNCH

Almost everything can be made well ahead of time for this colorful, zesty menu. Slice the fruit shortly before serving.

Creamy Gazpacho Served in Icy Mugs

*Grilled Chicken Sandwich with Watercress and
Tapenade Mayonnaise*

Marinated Lentil Salad

or

Red Potato Salad with Celery Seed

Sliced Fruit Platter and Assorted Cheeses

Assorted Cookies and Fudgy Brownies

The main centerpiece on the table is the food—especially when it is attractively displayed and garnished with colorful, edible flowers and herb blossoms. Think of it as a still life. A basket of simply arranged flowers is always welcome, but make sure it is not too tall. You may want to have small vases of flowering herbs placed next to a dish that features the same herb. When you are deciding where to place the flowers, it is very helpful to first set up the table with all the necessary serving pieces so you won't have any last-minute surprises. Imagine what the colors of the various dishes will be and what type of arrangement would best complement them. Baskets of bright vegetables, such as red and golden peppers, orange and red tomatoes, and different shapes of green and yellow squashes make a striking presentation. Shallow bowls of freshly picked flowers floating in water along with floating candles are also very attractive. Assorted shapes and sizes of seashells scattered in the center of the table and interspersed with flowers make an unusual arrangement.

A SUNDAY BUFFET BRUNCH

Here's a hearty but easy menu to put together for a lazy Sunday afternoon.

Assorted Sliced Melon

Summertime Frittata

Lemon-Herb Roasted Potatoes

Grilled Chicken, Veal, or Italian Sausages

Raspberry Pound Cake

or

Fresh Fig Bread with Cream Cheese

Whether it's for a graduation, wedding, or birthday, this is a striking menu. Place the appetizers by the bar so your guests can help themselves. I've added the Tri-Color Vegetable Terrine and the Peach Brown Butter Tart for an especially large group.

Crudité Baskets with Buttermilk Garden Herb Dressing and

Ancho Chile Mayonnaise

Goat Cheese and Pesto Torta with Hazelnuts

Thin Toasts

Sautéed Chicken with Balsamic Vinegar and
Sun-Dried Tomatoes

Gratin of Summer Squash, Leeks, and Rice

Tri-Color Vegetable Terrine

Green Salad with Grapefruit, Baby Beets, and Avocado

Hot French and Sourdough Rolls

Apricot Mousse

Peach Brown Butter Tart

Chocolate Pecan Torte with Espresso Crème Anglaise

Summer Drinks

This is the season when beverages attract as much attention as food. Hot days require the contrast of the coolest and most refreshing drinks possible. In order to prepare a variety of interesting and classic drinks at a moment's notice it's best to have the necessary ingredients and assorted utensils within easy reach.

THE SUMMER BAR

A summer bar can be as simple or as elaborate as the occasion demands. Frosty drinks made with vodka, tequila, gin, or rum and tonic or club soda are always popular in the summer months. Chilled wines, sangrias, Campari, wine coolers, and beer are also welcome in the summer heat. Keep plenty of fresh juices and fruit nectars on hand to serve with sparkling water for a refreshing nonalcoholic drink. Icy herbal teas and thirst-quenching mineral water are crowd pleasers too.

A full bar includes vodka, gin, scotch, bourbon, whiskey, brandy, tequila, sweet and dry vermouth, Campari, various liqueurs—especially orange liqueur and amaretto, beer, and a selection of chilled white wine and red wine. Juices, soft drinks, tonic, sparkling water, bitters, grenadine, and sugar syrup will round out the supplies. You can estimate that you'll need about half a bottle of wine and/or 2 alcoholic beverages and soft drinks per guest. One liqueur per guest should be adequate.

Recommended utensils include a jigger, measuring spoons, a citrus squeezer, a citrus stripper, a paring knife, a blender, an ice bucket, tongs, a shaker, a corkscrew, glasses in assorted sizes and shapes, and perhaps a pitcher or a punch bowl.

Have on hand garnishes like lemon, lime, and orange slices and sprigs of mint. Sliced strawberries, peaches, nectarines, or kiwi also make attractive garnishes, adding a refreshing twist and a splash of color to your drinks.

SOME INTERESTING DRINKS

Certain drinks never go out of style. Here are some favorite classics as well as a few adaptations.

Pitcher or Punch Bowl Drinks

- Andy's Pink Sangria: Combine 4 parts White Zinfandel, 2 parts orange juice, 1 part lemon juice, 1 part Pimms Cup #1, and slices of lemons, oranges, limes, and peaches. Finish with sparkling water and a touch of sugar syrup, to taste. (You can also add frozen hulled strawberries as flavorful ice cubes. Freeze them on a cookie sheet and drop them in right before serving.) For a party, figure one bottle of Zinfandel for 4 people.
- Margarita: Combine 1½ ounces of tequila, 1 ounce lime juice, 1 ounce Cointreau or Triple Sec, and cracked ice. Shake it in a cocktail shaker and serve or blend it in a blender for a foamier drink. You can also add puréed fruit like strawberries and peaches or even crenshaw or honeydew melon. To serve this drink, first dip the rim of a balloon glass in fresh lime juice, then swirl it in coarse salt. Serves 1, and may be multiplied as needed.
- Strawberry Banana Daiquiri: Combine 4 ounces of rum with 1 cup strawberries, 1 sliced banana, the juice of half a lemon, 1 to 2 tablespoons sugar syrup, and ice cubes to cover in the blender. Blend until frothy, pour into a pitcher or balloon glasses, and garnish with mint sprigs. Makes 2 servings and may be multiplied as needed.
- Bloody Mary: First, prepare the mix as follows, then add the vodka to each drink. Combine 1 large can (46 ounces) tomato juice, ½ cup lemon or lime juice, ¼ cup Worcestershire, Tabasco sauce to taste, salt, and fresh cracked pepper in a large pitcher. Add 1 to 2 ounces of vodka for each glass and garnish with celery sticks with the leaves attached. Makes 12 servings.

Individual Drinks

- Kir: Pour ½ ounce crème de cassis into a wineglass and fill with chilled white wine.
- Kir Royale: Pour ½ ounce crème de cassis into a champagne flute and fill with chilled dry Champagne.
- Champagne Framboise: Pour ½ ounce Framboise Liqueur into a champagne flute and fill with chilled dry Champagne.
- Bellini: An inexpensive, slightly sweet, sparkling wine like Prosecco is recommended here. Use puréed unpeeled Babcock or other white peaches. Add ¼ cup peach purée to a champagne flute and top with sparkling wine.

Nonalcoholic Beverages

Juices and nectars mixed with sparkling water can be the perfect thirst quencher on really hot afternoons. Try these variations:

- Tropical Cooler: Mix 1 part guava nectar to 1 part fresh orange juice to 2 parts sparkling water. Float an orange slice on top.
- Peach Mint Sparkler: Mix 1 part peach nectar to 4 parts sparkling water. Wedge a peach slice and a mint sprig on the edge of the glass.
- Pink Honeydew Spritzer: Combine the purée of 1 medium pink honeydew melon with 2 tablespoons peeled and minced ginger, 1 teaspoon lemon juice, 3 tablespoons chopped mint, and 1 to 2 tablespoons sugar syrup. Add ⅙ of the mixture to each glass and fill with sparkling water. Garnish with a sprig of mint. Serves 6.
- For an added taste of fruit, make ice cubes out of fruit juice

and use them in your coolers or tea. Freezing pieces of fruit, such as chunks of peaches, nectarines, or whole berries, and using them as ice cubes makes a clever and pretty addition to your drinks.

- Citrus Mint Iced Tea: Combine equal parts orange, lemon, and mint tea bags together with a cinnamon stick and fresh mint leaves in a heatproof bowl. Pour boiling water over the tea and let infuse for 30 minutes. Strain out the tea bags and mint leaves and pour the tea into a large pitcher that will fit in your refrigerator. Add enough water to reach your preferred strength and then chill until ice cold. You can add different fruit juices or nectars right before serving. You can also add fruit slices to the tea.
- Iced Espresso: Prepare espresso coffee in your regular coffee maker, doubling the usual amount of coffee. Place a spoon in each glass to keep it from cracking, pour the glass half full, and fill it with ice.

MAKING AN ICE RING

When serving punch, to create a spectacular presentation that will also keep the punch cool, make an ice ring. Fill it with a colorful pattern of sliced fruits and mint leaves, freeze, and place it in the punch bowl just before serving. The secret to making a beautiful ice ring is to use distilled water for clarity and to freeze the ring in successive layers, trapping the fruit and leaves together in the middle layer so they won't escape into the punch as the ring melts.

Fill a ring mold with 2 inches of distilled water and freeze. When frozen, place fruit or leaves on top and add ½ inch of water. Replace the mold in the freezer until completely frozen. Fill the rest of the ring with distilled water and freeze completely. When you're ready to unmold it, dip the ring into a bowl of hot water or rub the outside with a hot towel.

The Wines of Summer

BY ANTHONY DIAS BLUE

Back in the dark ages of wine writing—about fifteen or twenty years ago—there was a lot of talk about rules. There were rules about which wine to serve with which food, rules about which glasses to use, rules about at what temperature the wines should be served, and rules about which wines should be served first. All of this was a manifestation of the basic insecurity Americans felt about choosing the "right" wine. People needed strict guidelines so that any possibility of making a serious oenological *faux pas* was eliminated.

Things are different today. Americans are surer of themselves when it comes to wine and food. We have discovered the brilliance of our own, indigenous modern cuisine and the consistent quality of our wines. We have a better understanding of foreign cuisines and imported wines. We are more confident about our own taste and much more relaxed about the choices that we must inevitably make.

There aren't any more rules. The choice of wine no longer depends on a rigid set of commandments. Today, the selection of a wine depends more on our own tastes and sense of appropriateness than any rigid doctrine.

If you hate Gewürztraminer, all the directives in the world dictating that variety will be useless. Why punish yourself by drinking something you just don't like? If you love drinking

Chardonnay with steak, go ahead and drink it. Enjoy yourself and don't feel guilty.

Pairing wine and food is a completely subjective exercise. Some people may like Sauvignon Blanc with salmon; others may prefer White Zinfandel or even Red Zinfandel with this rich, oily fish. None of those choices is wrong.

Appropriateness, on the other hand, is an important consideration. Let me give you an example: some years ago, my wife and I invited a group of friends to a beach party on a July weekend. As the day of the party approached, we threw ourselves into the preparations. We chopped, grated, kneaded, and sliced; we turned out pâtés, salads, and breads; we prepared meats for grilling. The question that most nagged at me, however, was which wine to serve my friends, many of whom were avid wine lovers. I finally settled on a great white Burgundy—an older Corton-Charlemagne.

The afternoon of the party was sunny and clear; our outdoor spread was resplendent; the guests were in great spirits. They exclaimed over the lunch and the wine, but my heart fell when I saw one of my most knowledgeable friends frown when he took his first sip.

"What's wrong?" I asked him. "Isn't the wine good?"

"Of course it is," he responded. "The problem is that the wine is too good."

He was right. I had served a rich, complex, serious wine that completely overmatched the food. Light summer meals are meant to delight the palate with simple pleasures and not-so-serious tastes. The wines that accompany them should do the same.

Fresh, snappy, youthful wines are the answer. They are especially appropriate as an accompaniment to summer food. There is no point in getting too serious; grand wines are suited for grand cuisine on grand occasions. Bright and active summer days, and the kinds of dishes Diane Worthington has created, call for young, full-flavored, unintimidating wines.

Here are some very general pointers: Gewürztraminer does very nicely when teamed with spicy foods. Try this assertive wine with seafood served in a peppery sauce or chicken with Mexican spices. Riesling or Chenin Blanc are wonderful picnic

KEEPING WINE

Often there are half-empty bottles of wine left over after entertaining. Don't just cork them and expect the wines to be drinkable the next day. The warm summer temperatures will oxidize your leftovers before you can say "vinegar barrel." After you have corked them, stick them in the refrigerator—yes, even the reds. When it's time to drink them, remove the wines from the refrigerator and let them return to room temperature—that should take about half an hour. There are a number of excellent and inexpensive devices on the market that pump nitrogen into the bottle and preserve the wine by protecting it from oxygen. Of course, the best way to make sure that the wine retains its freshness is to drink it up when it is first opened.

wines—lighthearted, fruity, and just a bit frivolous. Tangy, crisp Sauvignon Blanc has that steely quality that mates well with oysters or other seafood.

Chardonnay comes in a number of different styles. There are crisp versions, lush and fruity versions, and big, concentrated versions. This wide range makes Chardonnay a virtually all-purpose wine. The crisp style works well with seafood, pastas, salads, or light chicken dishes; the fruity style complements saucier, more highly seasoned dishes; and the heavy style should be matched with creamy sauces or with veal, pork, or even beef.

Zinfandel is a wonderful summer wine. It fills all the requirements: it's fresh, fruity, and at its best when young. Try a snappy, ruby-colored one with pasta, eggs, or meats—especially those served with spicy sauces.

Other reds—young Merlots, young Cabernet Sauvignons, spicy Beaujolais—are also appropriate for the season. Try them with meats or pastas, and try them slightly chilled.

Roses and "blush" wines are also suitable warm weather fare. Have a tangy White Zinfandel with picnics, with pizza, with sandwiches.

Also don't overlook the delightful crop of imports that fill the summer bill: Soaves, Frascatis, Orvietos, Bardolinos, Valpolicellas, Chiantis, and Dolcettos from Italy; Mâcons, White Bordeaux, Vouvrays, Beaujolais, and Alsatian wines from France; Chardonnays, Sauvignons, and Rhine Rieslings from Australia; crisp whites from Germany, Spain, and Portugal.

The wines of summer are all around us. They are breezy and charming, and they make the foods of summer just that much more enjoyable.

First Courses and Appetizers

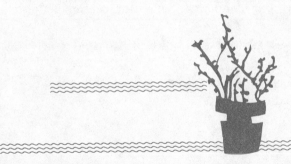

Smoked Trout with Roasted Garlic Mayonnaise

SERVES 4 TO 6

This dish makes a pretty presentation. Smoked trout slices are attractively arranged on a bed of lettuce with a small bowl of Roasted Garlic Mayonnaise in the center, surrounded by Niçoise olives and lemon slices. Toasted bread should be served on the side. I like to serve this with Champagne in the early evening as the sun is setting.

RECOMMENDED WINE: The smoky flavor of this dish pairs nicely with a well-structured Sauvignon Blanc from Napa or Sonoma.

> 1 head red leaf lettuce; cleaned and separated into individual leaves
> 1 pound smoked trout, skinned and filleted, cut into 2-inch slices
> ½ cup Roasted Garlic Mayonnaise (see page 345)
> 1 tablespoon fresh lemon juice
> 1 cup Niçoise olives or a combination of Greek and Niçoise Olives
> French or pumpernickel bread, thinly sliced and toasted

Garnish
> 1 medium lemon, thinly sliced

1. Arrange the lettuce leaves on a large, round platter, pointed end out in concentric circles. Place the trout fillets on top in a decorative fashion.
2. Combine the Roasted Garlic Mayonnaise and lemon juice in a small glass bowl and blend well. Set in the center of the platter.
3. Arrange the olives around the bowl of Roasted Garlic Mayonnaise.
4. Garnish the platter with lemon slices.
5. Serve toasted bread on the side.

ADVANCE PREPARATION: This platter may be made 4 hours in advance, covered with plastic wrap, and refrigerated. Take out of the refrigerator ½ hour before serving.

Basil Gravlax

SERVES 8 TO 12

Gravlax is usually marinated with dill, but this variation uses the stronger, more aromatic basil as the herb base for the curing element. The fish is actually cooked—or cured—by the marinade. Serve this on dark pumpernickel bread with Sweet Mustard Basil Sauce. You'll need to start curing the salmon four days before you plan to serve the gravlax.

RECOMMENDED WINE: A ripe, crisp, fruity Chardonnay will bring out the lovely basil flavor and neatly balance the salmon.

> 2½ to 3 pounds fresh salmon, filleted
> 3 tablespoons sugar
> 2 tablespoons kosher or coarse salt
> 2 teaspoons white peppercorns
> 4 large bunches fresh basil

Garnish
> Lemon wedges
> Basil leaves
> Sweet Mustard Basil Sauce (recipe follows)
> Dark pumpernickel bread

1. Lay the salmon on a sheet of wax paper. Combine the sugar, salt, and white peppercorns in a small bowl. Sprinkle the salmon with half the mixture. Turn and sprinkle the other side with the remaining mixture. Press down firmly on the salmon to coat it evenly with the seasonings.

2. Place 2 bunches of the fresh basil on the bottom of a large, shallow, nonaluminum pan. Place the salmon on top. Arrange the remaining 2 bunches of basil over the salmon.

3. Cover tightly with aluminum foil or plastic wrap, place a weight on top (use a heavy pot lid, brick, or large can) and refrigerate.

4. Turn the salmon twice a day for four days. Make sure the basil and peppercorns remain evenly distributed.

5. To serve, remove the basil and peppercorns. Lightly pat the salmon dry with a paper towel, making sure to remove all the salt and sugar. Slice very thinly on the bias and serve garnished with lemon wedges, basil leaves, Sweet Mustard Basil Sauce, and dark pumpernickel bread.

Sweet Mustard Basil Sauce

MAKES 1 CUP

This sweet mustard herb sauce has a texture similar to mayonnaise. It's great with ham slices, poached salmon, or Basil Gravlax.

¼ **cup Dijon or grainy mustard**
3 **tablespoons dark brown sugar**
2 **tablespoons cider vinegar**
1 **teaspoon dry mustard**
⅓ **cup safflower oil**
3 **tablespoons finely chopped basil**

1. In a food processor or blender, combine the mustard, brown sugar, vinegar, and dry mustard, and process for a few seconds.

2. With the machine running, pour in the oil in a steady stream and process until the sauce is thick and smooth.

3. Pour the sauce into a small bowl. Add the basil and taste for seasoning. Chill 2 to 3 hours or until ready to use.

ADVANCE PREPARATION: This sauce may be prepared ahead and kept refrigerated for several weeks.

Bruschetta with Tomato, Basil, and Mozzarella Relish

SERVES 6

Enjoy this rustic Italian appetizer while the rest of your dinner is cooking on the grill. Prepare the relish a few hours ahead and when the coals are at their hottest put the bread on the grill. Assemble just before serving. This is one of those dishes that can be addictive, so don't serve too many or your friends won't have room for dinner.

RECOMMENDED WINE: With mozzarella and garlic the answer has to be a young and fruity Chianti or Zinfandel, served at cellar temperature (60°F).

Relish
- 1 pound ripe plum (Roma) tomatoes, peeled and seeded
- 2 medium garlic cloves, minced
- 3 tablespoons finely chopped basil
- 1 tablespoon finely chopped Italian parsley
- 2 tablespoons extra virgin olive oil
- ½ teaspoon salt
- ½ teaspoon black pepper
- ¼ pound fresh mozzarella cheese, cut into ½-inch dice

    1 medium baguette, French, sourdough, or Italian bread, cut into ½-inch slices
    2 large garlic cloves, peeled
    2 tablespoons extra virgin olive oil
      Freshly ground black pepper

1. Dice the tomatoes into ½-inch pieces and drain over a bowl for ½ hour to remove excess liquid.

2. Combine all the relish ingredients except the cheese in a small nonaluminum mixing bowl. Stir well and taste for seasoning.

3. Prepare grill for medium-hot grilling. Place the bread on the grill and grill on each side just until marks of the grill appear. Remove from grill and place on a serving platter. Rub the bread on each side with whole garlic cloves.

4. Add the cheese to the relish, spoon the mixture onto each baguette slice, and then drizzle over a little more olive oil. Sprinkle with freshly ground black pepper and serve.

ADVANCE PREPARATION: The relish may be prepared 4 hours in advance through step 2 and refrigerated.

Summer Vegetable Guacamole Salsa

MAKES 4 CUPS

Sometimes the whole is greater than the sum of its parts, as in this cross between a spicy vegetable salsa and a traditional guacamole. Beware— you'll love this crunchy dip. When I first prepared it a few friends stopped by and we quickly consumed the whole bowl—and still wanted more. Crisp Tortilla Chips and some frosty margaritas or chilled beer or wine are just right with this, followed by Tequila Lime Grilled Shrimp and Cuban Black Beans.

RECOMMENDED WINE: If you're not having margaritas, something light and frivolous would be nice here. An off-dry Riesling, a Chenin Blanc, a Gewürztraminer, or a well-chilled bottle of beer.

> 2 large tomatoes (about 1 pound), peeled, seeded, and finely diced
> ½ medium sweet red pepper, diced (about ½ cup)
> ½ medium sweet yellow pepper, diced (about ½ cup)
> 1 large carrot, peeled and diced (about ¾ cup)
> ½ cup corn kernels (about 1 medium ear)
> 2 tablespoons finely chopped cilantro
> 2 tablespoons finely chopped Italian parsley
> 1 jalapeño chile, seeded and finely chopped*
> 2 tablespoons fresh lemon juice
> 1 teaspoon salt
> ¼ teaspoon black pepper
> 1 medium avocado, peeled and cut into ½-inch pieces

Garnish
    Extra cilantro leaves

1. Combine all the ingredients except the avocado in a medium mixing bowl. Refrigerate for 1 hour.
2. Spoon into a serving bowl. Right before serving add the avocado and taste for seasoning. Garnish with cilantro leaves and serve with fresh Crisp Tortilla Chips (see page 281).

ADVANCE PREPARATION: The salsa may be prepared up to 4 hours ahead through step 1 and kept in the refrigerator.

* When working with chilies, always wear rubber gloves. Wash the cutting surface and knife immediately afterward.

Summer Vegetable Guacamole Salsa

CRUDITÉS

The following is a list of raw vegetable possibilities to fill your basket or platter. Allow about ⅛ pound of each per person if you are serving a large variety of vegetables.

- Baby asparagus spears, tough bottom stalk removed*
- French green beans, ends removed, left whole*
- Broccoli, cut into florets*
- Green, purple, red, or yellow bell peppers, seeded and cut into strips
- Carrots, peeled and cut into sticks
- Celery, peeled and cut into sticks
- Chinese snow peas, cleaned, strings removed, left whole
- European cucumber, unpeeled, cut into sticks
- Jicama, peeled and cut into sticks
- Button mushrooms
- White and red radishes
- Sugar snap peas, strings removed, left whole
- Red and yellow cherry and pear tomatoes
- Zucchini, cut into sticks

*Immerse in boiling water for a minute and then chill

Some sauce accompaniments:

- Tapenade Mayonnaise
- Roasted Garlic Mayonnaise
- Buttermilk Garden Herb Dressing
- Tomato Cucumber Salsa
- Ancho chile sour cream sauce

Vegetable Platter with Grilled Red Pepper and Garlic Sauce

SERVES 8

These platters are perfect to serve when it's too hot even to think about cooking. Prepare the vegetables whole or sliced in an assortment of colors, textures, and sizes pleasing to the eye and easy to pick up for dipping into a variety of sauces. This combination works beautifully, but it is only a guideline for your own imagination. The red pepper and garlic dipping sauce has an almost mousselike texture. To make a meal of it, add poached chicken or seafood prepared in the cool morning hours. Other dipping sauces can accompany the vegetables: Pesto Cream, Buttermilk Garden Herb Dressing, or Ancho Chile Mayonnaise would be excellent. Add warm country French bread and finish with Poached Peaches in White Zinfandel with Fresh Raspberry Sauce.

RECOMMENDED WINE: A medium-weight Sauvignon Blanc or Chardonnay is ideal with this richly flavored dish.

Dip

- 2 medium sweet red peppers
- 2 medium garlic cloves
- ½ pound softened cream cheese
- 2 tablespoons fresh lemon juice
- 1 teaspoon finely chopped fresh thyme
- 3 tablespoons finely chopped basil
- 1 tablespoon finely chopped Italian parsley
- ½ teaspoon salt
- ¼ teaspoon white pepper

Vegetables

- 4 whole artichokes, cooked, chokes removed, and quartered
- 6 medium carrots, peeled and cut into 1 × 2-inch sticks
- 1 pound jicama, peeled and cut into 1 × 2-inch sticks
- 16 small white button mushrooms
- 16 cherry tomatoes

1. To peel the peppers, broil approximately 6 inches from the heat until blackened on all sides. Use tongs to turn them.
2. Close tightly in a brown paper bag and let rest for 10 minutes.
3. Remove from the bag, drain, and peel off the skin. Make a slit in each pepper and open it up. Core and cut off the stem. Scrape out the seeds and ribs.
4. Place the peppers in a food processor fitted with a steel blade and add the garlic, cream cheese, lemon juice, thyme, basil, Italian parsley, salt, and pepper. Process until the texture is almost mousselike. Taste for seasoning. Pour into a small serving bowl.

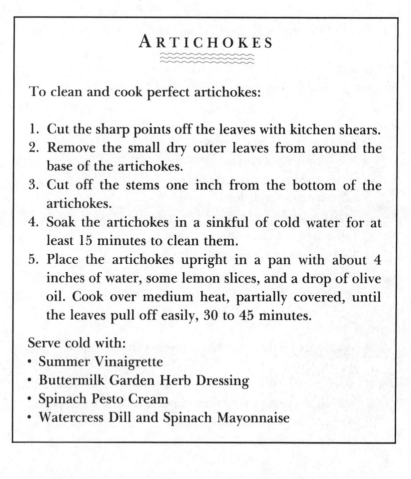

ARTICHOKES

To clean and cook perfect artichokes:

1. Cut the sharp points off the leaves with kitchen shears.
2. Remove the small dry outer leaves from around the base of the artichokes.
3. Cut off the stems one inch from the bottom of the artichokes.
4. Soak the artichokes in a sinkful of cold water for at least 15 minutes to clean them.
5. Place the artichokes upright in a pan with about 4 inches of water, some lemon slices, and a drop of olive oil. Cook over medium heat, partially covered, until the leaves pull off easily, 30 to 45 minutes.

Serve cold with:
• Summer Vinaigrette
• Buttermilk Garden Herb Dressing
• Spinach Pesto Cream
• Watercress Dill and Spinach Mayonnaise

5. Arrange the vegetables attractively on a large platter or in a basket. Place the red pepper and garlic sauce in the center and serve.

ADVANCE PREPARATION: The dip may be prepared 1 day in advance and refrigerated. The vegetables may be prepared 2 hours in advance. Cover the vegetables with wet paper towels to keep them crisp.

VARIATION: Remove the leaves from the artichokes and place them on a circular platter. Place a dollop of sauce on each leaf.

Vegetable Platter with Grilled Red Pepper and Garlic Sauce

Goat Cheese and Pesto Torta with Hazelnuts

SERVES 6 TO 8

This torta is constructed by layering softened goat cheese, sliced hazelnuts, and pesto into a loaf. I like to serve it with plain, crisp, thin crackers. It makes a pretty hors d'oeuvre to serve to company. Serve this as a prelude to Grilled Swordfish with Red Pepper Hollandaise Sauce and Grilled Japanese Eggplant. For dessert offer a platter of fresh peaches, nectarines, and Toasted Hazelnut Cookies.

RECOMMENDED WINE: A full-bodied Chardonnay will do well with this torta, or try a particularly spicy young Zinfandel or Chianti.

> 2 tablespoons sliced or chopped hazelnuts
> 8 ounces fresh goat cheese
> 4 ounces cream cheese
> ½ cup Spinach Pesto (see page 351)

Garnish
> Large red and green basil leaves
> Sliced hazelnuts

1. Preheat the oven to 350°F. Place hazelnuts on a baking sheet and toast until light brown, 3 to 5 minutes. Remove from the oven and let cool.
2. Oil a 3½ × 6 × 2½-inch loaf pan. Completely line the pan with plastic wrap, leaving enough excess to cover the finished torta. Tuck it into all the corners.
3. By hand or in a food processor fitted with a steel blade, combine the goat cheese and cream cheese until completely blended. With a rubber spatula, spread half the softened cheese in an even layer on the bottom of the pan. Sprinkle with a tablespoon of hazelnuts.
4. Carefully spoon an even layer of the Spinach Pesto on top. Sprinkle with the remaining hazelnuts.

5. With the rubber spatula, spread the remaining cheese evenly over the top; the pesto should not show through. Cover the torta with the plastic wrap and refrigerate for at least 4 hours or until well set.

6. To unmold, fold back the plastic wrap, remove the whole "package" from the pan, and invert onto a rectangular platter. Blot any excess pesto that has leaked down the sides of the torta with a paper towel. Press large, fresh basil leaves into the sides. Serve with slices of freshly toasted French bread.

ADVANCE PREPARATION: The torta may be prepared 1 day in advance through step 4 and refrigerated.

Double Cheese Spread with Zesty Italian Salsa

SERVES 6 TO 8

I like to serve this cheese and salsa at large parties because it can be easily multiplied. Choose a serving bowl in which you can mound the cheese and then decoratively surround it with the sauce. This salsa is rich with tomatoes—both sun-dried and fresh. It also makes a tasty condiment for grilled chicken or fish.

RECOMMENDED WINE: The word "zesty" brings to mind Zinfandel, Chianti, or Rhône reds. Although this dish calls for a spicy wine, if you must have a white, try a Gewürztraminer or a California Semillon or Sauvignon Blanc.

1½ cups ricotta cheese
7 ounces fresh goat cheese

Salsa
½ cup sun-dried tomatoes, dry packed
1 medium shallot
2 medium garlic cloves
½ pound plum (Roma) tomatoes, peeled, seeded, juiced, and chopped
½ cup basil leaves, medium packed
2 tablespoons olive oil
½ teaspoon salt
¼ teaspoon white pepper

Garnish
Small basil leaves

1. Combine the ricotta cheese and goat cheese in a blender or food processor fitted with a steel blade. Process until completely blended and softened. Mound in a small serving bowl, cover, and refrigerate.
2. *To prepare the salsa:* Pour boiling water over the sun-dried tomatoes and let soften for 15 minutes. Drain and set aside.
3. Finely chop the shallot and garlic cloves in the food processor. Add the drained sun-dried tomatoes, fresh tomatoes, and basil and pulse on and off until very finely chopped. Add the olive oil, salt, and pepper, and process just enough to combine. Taste for seasoning. Refrigerate in a small covered container.
4. When ready to serve, mound the cheese in a medium serving bowl (or larger if increasing the recipe). Spoon the salsa around the cheese, leaving the center uncovered. Garnish with a few basil leaves. Serve with thin slices of toasted French bread or very thin crackers.

ADVANCE PREPARATION: Both the cheese and the salsa may be prepared 2 days in advance through step 3. Refrigerate separately until right before serving.

- Smoked salmon with capers, lemon wedges, and softened unsalted butter on thin toast
- Belgian endive leaves spread or piped with mixed blue cheese and cream cheese garnished with bay shrimp
- Icy cold whole red and white radishes with coarse salt and unsalted butter
- Chilled shrimp with Summer Vinaigrette
- Smoked oysters on a bed of lettuce with a sauce of sour cream, dill, and fresh lemon juice
- Slices of melon or wedges of fig wrapped in prosciutto

Bluefish in White Wine

SERVES 6 TO 8

When I lived in Paris one of my favorite first courses was maquereau au vin blanc *(mackerel with white wine). Mackerel, however, is not always easy to find, so I came up with this adaptation. Bluefish in White Wine is a light and refreshing first course for a hot summer night. The small pieces of bluefish, offset by the bright orange sliced carrots and clear onion slices, make a very impressive platter. Serve this dish with lots of crusty French bread to soak up the sauce.*

RECOMMENDED WINE: A crisp white is ideal here but remember that bluefish is oily and requires a bit of substance in the wine. Chardonnay, a Sauvignon Blanc that has seen some oak aging, or a Premier Cru Chablis will do the job.

2 pounds fillets of bluefish, cut into 2-inch pieces with the skin on (12 to 16 pieces)

Sauce

2 medium onions, thinly sliced
2 medium carrots, thinly sliced
1 medium garlic clove, minced
4 large shallots, finely chopped
3 cups dry white wine
½ cup white wine vinegar
½ cup olive oil
½ teaspoon salt
¼ teaspoon black pepper
1 bouquet garni*

Garnish

Lemon slices
Parsley

1. Arrange the fillets slightly overlapping, in an oiled medium baking dish.
2. Combine all the ingredients for the sauce in a medium nonaluminum saucepan and bring to a boil over medium-high heat. Reduce heat and simmer until the vegetables are tender.
3. Preheat oven to 300°F. Pour the sauce over the fish and bake for 8 to 10 minutes, depending on the thickness of the fish. Cool to room temperature. Remove the bouquet garni. Cover and let come to room temperature.**
4. When ready to serve, arrange the fillets on a serving platter. Spoon the vegetable sauce over and garnish with the lemon and parsley.

ADVANCE PREPARATION: This may be prepared completely no more than 6 hours in advance if left at room temperature. It also may be prepared 1 day in advance and refrigerated. The sauce will be slightly jelled. Remove the dish from the refrigerator 2 hours before serving to allow it to reach room temperature.

* To make a bouquet garni, combine a bay leaf, parsley, and thyme in a cheesecloth and tie with a string.

** This must be served close to room temperature so that the olive oil and the gelatin from the fish do not jell.

Picnic Pâté

SERVES 8 TO 12

Pâtés are easy to master once you understand the special ingredients and basic techniques. A pâté is cooked like a meatloaf but at a lower temperature and is usually wrapped in either caul fat or back fat, which bastes it and gives it extra moisture. The thin, lacy caul fat is my preference. Back fat is thinly sliced pieces of pork fat that your butcher usually keeps on hand; you may have to special order caul fat. Weighting the pâté with a heavy object like a brick makes it denser than a meatloaf and easier to slice.

Several years ago, a friend and I established a cottage industry making pâtés, which we sold to local restaurants. Picnic Pâté was our biggest seller. Making this recipe in 100-pound batches quickly lost its glamour. Nevertheless, I still enjoy making a good pâté in small quantities. This one makes an excellent first course, especially when garnished with cornichons and served with a variety of Dijon-style mustards. Or take it on a picnic along with an assortment of cold salads, such as String Bean–Golden Pepper Salad and Cherry Tomato and Hearts of Palm Salad. A platter of minted melon slices makes a light and refreshing finish.

RECOMMENDED WINE: This rich pâté would do nicely with a fresh red, but a full-flavored white is probably more appropriate. Try a ripe and lush Chardonnay.

1 pound pork stew meat, ground
1 pound veal stew meat, ground
½ pound pork fat, ground
1 cup cooked ham, cut into small pieces
½ cup brandy or Cognac
4 medium shallots, finely chopped
2 medium garlic cloves, minced
¼ cup all-purpose flour
2 eggs
⅓ cup whipping cream
½ cup finely chopped parsley
¼ pound chicken livers, ground
1 tablespoon salt
½ teaspoon finely ground black pepper
¾ teaspoon chopped fresh savory, or ¼ teaspoon dried
¾ teaspoon chopped fresh oregano, or ¼ teaspoon dried
1½ teaspoons chopped fresh thyme, or ½ teaspoon dried
¾ teaspoon allspice
¾ teaspoon cinnamon
¾ teaspoon freshly grated nutmeg
¼ cup shelled pistachio nuts
½ pound caul or back fat, thinly sliced
1 bay leaf

Garnish

Parsley sprigs
Cornichons
Dijon mustard
Sliced French bread

1. Preheat oven to 300°F. Combine the pork, veal, pork fat, ham, brandy, shallots, garlic, and flour in a large mixing bowl. Add the eggs, cream, parsley, and ground chicken livers. Add all the seasonings and mix until the ingredients are well combined. Add the pistachio nuts and mix well.

2. Line a large (11½ × 5½-inch) terrine or loaf pan with the caul or back fat, making sure that the pan is completely covered and that the fat hangs generously over the edge. Put the meat mixture in the pan, carefully patting it down

so there are no air bubbles. Cover with the overhanging caul or back fat and place a bay leaf in the center. Cover with aluminum foil.

3. Place the terrine in a larger pan and add enough warm water to come halfway up the terrine. Bake for 3½ hours.

4. Remove from oven and let cool. When cool, drain off the fat and remove from the pan onto a board or platter. Blot off all the excess fat. Wrap the pâté in aluminum foil and place on a baking sheet or pan. Place a brick or other weight on top of the pâté to press it down for at least 12 hours. Refrigerate. It can be served when completely cooled but tastes best if kept refrigerated for at least 2 days before serving.

5. *To serve:* Cut into ½-inch slices and present on plates, garnished with parsley sprigs, cornichons, and sliced French bread. Pass the mustard separately.

ADVANCE PREPARATION: This may be prepared completely 5 days in advance and refrigerated. Remove from the refrigerator 1 hour before serving.

Roasted Eggplant with Balsamic Vinegar

SERVES 6

Balsamic vinegar is made from the boiled-down must of white Trebbiano grapes and comes from Modena, Italy. By Italian law, balsamic vinegar must be at least 10 years old before it can be sold. It varies greatly in strength, so taste it before you cook with it. The older the vinegar, the more concentrated and full-bodied it becomes and the less you will need. The sultry Mediterranean taste of this appetizer comes from its combination of deep flavors: balsamic vinegar, shallots, and fresh basil, combined with extra virgin olive oil. The soft, roasted eggplant absorbs these robust flavors without losing its own unique taste. A border of sliced, roasted red peppers and Niçoise olives on the serving dish looks particularly attractive. Serve with Toasted Pita with Parmesan or crisp crackers.

RECOMMENDED WINE: Serve with a barrel-fermented Chardonnay.

> 6 pounds eggplant (4, each about 1½ pounds), peeled and cut into ½-inch pieces
> 2 teaspoons salt

Marinade
> 6 medium shallots, finely chopped
> 2 medium garlic cloves, minced
> ½ cup balsamic vinegar
> ¼ cup extra virgin olive oil
> ½ teaspoon black pepper
> 1 bunch basil leaves, finely chopped

Garnish
> 2 sweet red peppers, roasted, seeded, peeled, and cut into ¼-inch slices and marinated in 2 tablespoons olive oil and 2 tablespoons balsamic vinegar
> 16 Niçoise olives
> Fresh basil leaves

1. Preheat oven to 400°F.
2. Place the eggplant pieces in a large colander and sprinkle with the salt. Drain over a bowl for 30 minutes, tossing once or twice.
3. In a large roasting pan, prepare the marinade by combining the shallots, garlic, vinegar, olive oil, and pepper.
4. Dry the eggplant with paper towels. Place in the marinade, tossing to coat evenly.
5. Place the eggplant in the oven and roast until soft, about 45 minutes. Toss with a large spoon every 15 minutes to cook evenly.

6. Remove from the oven and let cool. Add the basil and taste for seasoning.
7. Mound onto a serving dish. Garnish with the red pepper slices, Niçoise olives, and basil leaves.

ADVANCE PREPARATION: This may be prepared 1 day in advance through step 6 and refrigerated. Remove from the refrigerator ½ hour before serving.

Spicy Lime-Ginger Grilled Shrimp

SERVES 6 TO 8

Pretty to look at and fun to eat, this shrimp is spicy but also slightly sweet. For an appetizer, each skewer of grilled shrimp is served on a plate of shredded cucumber, carrots, and lettuce and accompanied by a little bowl of the light lime-ginger dressing. If the shrimp are served as a first course, remove them from the skewers and place them atop a mound of the fresh vegetables. To preserve the flavor balance of the marinade, use plain charcoal briquettes rather than the stronger-tasting hardwood charcoal. Gas grilling is a good solution. This substantial first course is best complemented by a light main course, such as Roasted Sea Bass with Herbs and Sautéed Tomatoes with Basil Cream.

RECOMMENDED WINE: A nearly dry California or Alsatian Gewürztraminer is called for here, or you might try a crisp Soave, Mâcon, or a fairly lemony Chardonnay.

 ¾ cup fresh lime juice
 1 tablespoon minced fresh ginger
 2 medium garlic cloves, minced
 2 small shallots, finely chopped
 2 tablespoons finely chopped cilantro
 ½ teaspoon salt
 ⅛ teaspoon black pepper
 ⅛ teaspoon crushed red pepper flakes, or to taste
 2½ tablespoons lemon or lime marmalade
 ⅓ cup olive oil

 1½ pound large shrimp or 4 to 6 per person, peeled and
   deveined with tails left on
 1 large European cucumber, halved and seeded*
 4 large carrots, peeled
 1 head red leaf lettuce
 2 tablespoons finely chopped cilantro

1. If using bamboo skewers, soak in cold water for at least 1 hour. This will prevent them from burning when grilled.
2. Combine the lime juice, ginger, garlic, shallots, cilantro, salt, black pepper, red pepper flakes, and marmalade in a small mixing bowl. Whisk until all the ingredients are well combined. Slowly add the olive oil, whisking until thoroughly incorporated. Taste for seasoning.
3. Thread the shrimp on short wooden skewers (4 to 6 to a skewer), and lay them flat in a shallow, nonaluminum dish. Pour half of the marinade over the shrimp and marinate for ½ hour, turning once or twice.
4. Meanwhile, shred the cucumber and carrots with the shredder blade of a food processor and place in a medium mixing bowl. Add enough of the remaining marinade to moisten the vegetables; reserve the rest for dipping.
5. When ready to serve, prepare the barbecue for medium-high-heat grilling and place the skewered shrimp flat on the grill. Baste each side with the marinade and grill until just cooked, about 3 minutes on each side.

6. Arrange the red leaf lettuce on a 12-inch platter and mound the cucumber and carrot mixture on top. Place the skewered grilled shrimp on top of the vegetables and let guests help themselves, using small plates. Or arrange each serving separately, placing a lettuce leaf on each plate, adding the vegetable mixture, and then the shrimp, off their skewers and arranged in a circular pattern. Garnish with the chopped cilantro and pass the remaining marinade for dipping.

ADVANCE PREPARATION: The marinade may be made a day in advance and refrigerated. The vegetables may be shredded and lightly dressed up to 4 hours in advance.

*It's not necessary to peel the thin-skinned European cucumbers.

Spicy Grilled Pork Tenderloin with Orange Cilantro Cream

SERVES 4 TO 6

These piquant brochettes were inspired by Indonesian satay, a delectable grilled skewered meat or chicken. Usually satay is served with a peanut sauce, but in this variation the Orange Cilantro Cream combines the tang of citrus with Hot Pepper Oil for a summery barbecued appetizer.

RECOMMENDED WINE: This dish goes nicely with a medium to heavy weight Chardonnay or—if you are feeling daring—try a young, slightly chilled Zinfandel.

Marinade
½ cup fresh orange juice
2 tablespoons fresh lime juice
1 teaspoon chopped fresh oregano, or ½ teaspoon dried oregano
1 teaspoon finely chopped cilantro
1 teaspoon marjoram or ½ teaspoon dried marjoram
¼ teaspoon cumin
2 tablespoons oil
½ teaspoon salt
¼ teaspoon pepper

1 pound tenderloin of pork cut into 1-inch pieces or thin horizontal slices while partially frozen

Orange Cilantro Cream
½ cup sour cream
3 tablespoons marinade
1 orange zest, finely chopped
2 tablespoons finely chopped cilantro
1 teaspoon Hot Pepper Oil or to taste (see page 367)

Garnish
Fresh cilantro leaves

1. If using bamboo skewers, soak them in cold water for at least 1 hour. This will prevent them from burning when grilled.
2. Whisk the marinade ingredients together in a medium bowl. Reserve 3 tablespoons.
3. Skewer the pork and place in a shallow, nonaluminum dish. Pour the marinade over and marinate for 6 to 12 hours.
4. In a small bowl combine all the ingredients for the Orange Cilantro Cream, add the reserved marinade, and mix well. Taste for seasoning. Cover and refrigerate until ready to serve.
5. Prepare the barbecue for medium-heat grilling. Grill the pork about 3 inches from the flame, 5 to 7 minutes on each side. Test a piece; the meat should not be pink inside.

6. Arrange the skewers on a large plate. Garnish with fresh cilantro, and serve with the Orange Cilantro Cream.

ADVANCE PREPARATION: The marinade and Orange Cilantro Cream may be prepared 1 day in advance and refrigerated.

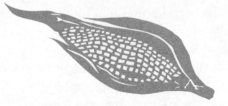

Corn-Leek Cakes with Caviar, Smoked Salmon, and Crème Fraîche

SERVES 8; MAKES 32 TO 34 SMALL PANCAKES

These delicate onion-flavored corn mini-cakes look especially inviting on a large round platter decorated with watercress or dill sprigs and, if available, tiny white corn-on-the-cob. These are a perfect way to start a formal dinner such as Barbecued Leg of Lamb with a Mustard Sage Crust and Semolina Gnocchi with Pesto. Finish the meal with Frozen Praline Mousse with Bittersweet Hot Fudge Sauce.

RECOMMENDED WINE: Serve a soft, off-dry Johannesberg Riesling or a crisp Alsatian white. If you are feeling more festive, a snappy Blanc de Blanc or Brut Champagne would be lovely.

> 1 cup fresh corn kernels (about 2 medium ears)
> ½ cup (1 stick) unsalted butter
> 2 medium leeks, white part only, very finely chopped
> 1 cup half-and-half
> 2 eggs
> ¼ teaspoon salt
>   Pinch white pepper
> ½ cup fine cornmeal
> ½ cup all-purpose flour

Corn-Leek Cakes with Caviar, Smoked Salmon, and Crème Fraîche

½ cup Crème Fraîche (see page 369)
2 ounces caviar
2 ounces smoked salmon
   Fresh watercress or dill sprigs

1. Place the corn kernels in a food processor fitted with a steel blade. Pulsing on and off, process just until the corn is coarsely chopped. Set aside.
2. In a medium skillet melt ¼ cup butter over medium heat and reserve 2 tablespoons. Add the leeks and sauté until softened, about 10 minutes. Set aside.
3. In a blender combine the half-and-half, eggs, reserved melted butter, salt, and pepper, and blend. Add the cornmeal and flour and blend until it become a smooth batter.
4. Add the coarsely chopped corn and sautéed leeks and blend just until mixed.
5. Heat the remaining ¼ cup butter in a large non-stick skillet or on a griddle on medium heat.
6. Using a small ladle or measuring cup with a pouring spout, pour about 1 tablespoon of the batter into the skillet for each cake. Cook until they bubble and are just set, approximately 2 minutes. Then flip the cakes and cook another minute. Turn out onto a paper-towel-lined baking sheet to absorb any excess oil.
7. *To serve:* Place the cakes on a large serving platter and garnish each with a dollop of Crème Fraîche, caviar, a small piece of salmon, and a sprig of watercress or dill. Serve immediately.

ADVANCE PREPARATION: The batter may be made up to 1 day in advance, covered well, and refrigerated. The corn cakes may be made up to 2 hours ahead and kept warm in a very slow oven. Remove the paper towel liner before placing the cakes in the oven for reheating.

Sparkling wine always seems to put people in a good mood. A chilled glass of bubbly in warm weather can turn an ordinary meal into a special occasion. Americans have fallen in love with sparklers, and domestic wineries have obliged with a torrent of lively wines in every price category. A good sparkling wine can usually be purchased for the same price as a still wine, and it can be substituted in most instances where a white wine is appropriate.

Sparkling wine is best when chilled in an ice bucket, but if this procedure is too cumbersome, half an hour in the refrigerator should do the trick. Champagne (a word that legitimately should only be applied to sparkling wines made in the Champagne district of France) and other sparklers should be served at 50°F to 55°F. Champagne prices rise and fall with the dollar—when it's high, a good nonvintage Brut is affordable. Champagne *is* incomparable; if you're willing to settle for something less extraordinary, look for a sparkling wine from the Spanish, Italian, and other French regions, where there are some good buys.

The perfect glass for sparkling wine is the "flute" or "tulip." These long, tall glasses preserve the bubbles, and the chimney shape neatly concentrates the wine's delightful perfume so that the aroma can be appreciated while the wine is being sipped. The curiously popular saucer-shaped glass, on the other hand, totally defeats the purpose of the bubbles and dissipates the aroma. Too shallow to allow the bubbles to rise gracefully, and too wide at the top, it allows both the bubbles and the aroma to escape too quickly. This awful glass can turn Champagne flat in a very short time.

Stuffed Baby Red Potatoes with Eggplant, Tomato, and Peppers

Tiny new potatoes, the size of medium apricots, make great appetizers because they are easy to pick up and they absorb the flavor of any filling, making variations almost endless. This provençal-style filling of peppers, tomatoes, and eggplant is classically robust. The filling is cooked until meltingly tender, creating a wonderful textural contrast with the crunchy potato shell.

RECOMMENDED WINE: Balance these rich flavors with a fruity Chianti Classico or Beaujolais served at cellar temperature (60°F).

Filling
- 2 tablespoons olive oil
- 1 small onion, very finely chopped
- 1 medium eggplant, peeled and cut into ½-inch dice
- 1 sweet red pepper, seeded and cut into ½-inch dice
- 1 yellow pepper, seeded and cut into ½-inch dice
- 1 green pepper, seeded and cut into ½-inch dice
- 2 pounds plum (Roma) tomatoes, peeled, seeded, and finely chopped
- 2 medium garlic cloves, minced
- 2 tablespoons finely chopped basil
- 1 teaspoon salt
- ¼ teaspoon pepper

Potatoes
- 1½ pounds baby red potatoes (approximately 12 to 16), unpeeled
- 2 tablespoons olive oil
- ½ cup freshly grated Parmesan cheese

1. Preheat oven to 475°F. *To prepare the filling:* In a large skillet heat the olive oil over medium heat. Add the onion and sauté about 5 minutes, stirring carefully, until translucent.
2. Add the eggplant and continue cooking 5 to 7 minutes.
3. Add the peppers and cook for 5 more minutes, stirring frequently.
4. Add the tomatoes, garlic, and basil and continue cooking 5 to 10 minutes more. Add the salt and pepper to taste. Set aside.
5. Place the potatoes on a baking sheet and bake for 35 to 45 minutes, depending on their size. They should be cooked through and slightly crispy.
6. Remove from the oven and let cool. Cut in half and scoop out the pulp, leaving a thin layer of potato in the skin. Brush the potato skins with olive oil, turn upside down, and return to the oven until crisp; 10 to 15 minutes.
7. Remove from oven, sprinkle the insides with Parmesan cheese, and fill with the vegetable mixture.
8. Sprinkle the tops with Parmesan cheese. Reduce the oven to 425°F and bake potatoes until heated through; 10 to 15 minutes. Serve immediately.

ADVANCE PREPARATION: The filling may be prepared up to 1 day ahead and refrigerated. Reheat before continuing.

NOTE: You will have extra filling, fortunately; it's delicious on pasta and chicken or as a filling for crêpes or omelettes.

Stuffed Baby Red Potatoes with Eggplant, Tomato, and Peppers

Baked Goat Cheese with Chutney Vinaigrette

SERVES 4

In this recipe, a sweet, slightly spicy vinaigrette offsets the warm, melting goat cheese surrounded by crisp bread crumbs. The salad greens refresh the palate and offer color.

RECOMMENDED WINE: Goat cheese requires a fairly substantial red wine to stand up to its intense flavor. Serve a Zinfandel, a Merlot, or a Cabernet Sauvignon.

- 2 tablespoons olive oil
- ¼ cup bread crumbs, made from French or whole wheat bread
- 8 ounces goat cheese, French or California
- 1 bunch spinach leaves, washed and dried
- 1 bunch romaine, hearts only, torn into 1-inch pieces

Chutney Vinaigrette
- ¼ teaspoon dry mustard
- ¼ cup red wine vinegar
- 2 tablespoons Peach-Jalapeño Chutney (see page 358) or Major Grey's Chutney
- ¼ teaspoon salt
  Pinch white pepper
- ¼ cup safflower oil
- ¼ cup olive oil

1. Preheat oven to 475°F. Spoon the olive oil into one bowl and the bread crumbs into another.
2. Cut the cheese into 4 wedges or cylinders. Dip them into the olive oil and then roll in the bread crumbs. Place in a shallow baking dish. Refrigerate for 15 minutes.
3. *To make the chutney vinaigrette:* Combine the mustard, vinegar, chutney, salt, and pepper in a small mixing bowl. Slowly

add both the oils and whisk until completely blended. Taste
for seasoning. Set aside.

4. Bake the goat cheese for 10 minutes or until golden brown
   on the outside.
5. While the cheese is baking, arrange some of the spinach
   leaves, pointed ends out, on salad plates. Toss the remaining
   leaves with the romaine lettuce and place in the center of
   each plate. Spoon a tablespoon of chutney vinaigrette over
   the greens. Place the warm goat cheese on top and spoon
   additional chutney vinaigrette over. Serve immediately.

ADVANCE PREPARATION: The vinaigrette may be made
up to 2 days in advance and refrigerated. The goat cheese may
be breaded up to 8 hours ahead and refrigerated.

Baked Goat Cheese with Chutney Vinaigrette

Soups

Golden Summer Soup

Suddenly everyone wants to eat yellow—*yellow pear and cherry toma-toes, yellow zucchini, yellow beets, yellow raspberries, and even yellow watermelon.*

In fact the yellows do taste terrific, and they're considerably less acidic than their red counterparts. This soup looks and tastes like pure summertime with its fresh just-picked corn, golden yellow sweet peppers, and yellow cherry tomatoes. If you can't find yellow tomatoes, use the red variety and sweet red peppers for an equally delicious variation. The Hot Pepper Oil gives it extra zing. Serve this as a first course for an outdoor luncheon in attractive pottery cups or small glass bowls. Follow with cold Rosemary Lemon Chicken and Marinated Lentil Salad. Finish with Hazelnut Plum Tart topped with Crème Fraîche.

    3 tablespoons olive oil
    6 scallions, white part only, finely chopped
    2 cups fresh corn kernels (about 4 medium ears)
    1 pint yellow cherry tomatoes, stemmed and coarsely
       chopped
    1 sweet yellow pepper, seeded and diced into ½-inch
       pieces
    6 cups chicken stock (see page 366)
    6 basil leaves
    ¼ cup whipping cream
    1 teaspoon salt
    ¼ teaspoon pepper
    1 teaspoon Hot Pepper Oil (see page 367)

Garnish
    ¼ cup sour cream
       Extra basil leaves, finely chopped just before serving
       to avoid darkening

1. Heat the olive oil in a large saucepan over medium heat. Add the scallions and sauté until slightly soft, about 3 minutes.

2. Reserve ¼ cup corn, ¼ cup tomatoes, and 2 tablespoons diced yellow pepper. Add the remaining tomatoes, yellow peppers, and corn to the pan and sauté for about 3 minutes.

3. Add the chicken stock and basil and bring to a boil. Reduce the heat and simmer slowly, uncovered, for about 10 minutes. Remove the basil leaves.

4. Place the soup in a blender or food processor fitted with a steel blade and process until puréed.

5. Pass through a food mill or strainer into a bowl, pushing down to get all of the essence. Return to the saucepan.

6. Add the cream, seasonings, and Hot Pepper Oil. Taste for seasoning. Chill for at least 3 hours.

7. Immerse the reserved corn and yellow pepper in boiling water for about 2 minutes. Drain, chill, and reserve.

8. *To serve:* Pour the soup into bowls and garnish with sour cream, tomatoes, yellow pepper, corn, and chopped basil.

ADVANCE PREPARATION: The soup and garnish may be prepared 1 day ahead through step 7 and refrigerated until serving.

Minted Chinese Pea Pod Soup

SERVES 4 TO 6

Mint and peas seem made for each other. I've added Chinese peas to sweeten and enliven the taste of the fresh peas. This versatile soup tastes just as good hot or cold. Served steaming hot on a cool evening, it's a wonderful opener for Eggplant Tomato Mushroom Tart. Chilled, it can precede Warm Grilled Chicken Salad with Lemon Mustard Dressing.

2 tablespoons safflower oil
6 scallions, white part only, finely chopped
1 large carrot, peeled and finely diced
1 head limestone lettuce
3 tablespoons coarsely chopped mint
1 quart chicken stock (see page 366)
1 cup Chinese or snow peas (½ pound), cleaned and trimmed
1 cup fresh shelled peas (about 1 pound unshelled) or 1 cup of frozen tiny peas, defrosted
2 tablespoons whipping cream or half-and-half
1½ teaspoons salt
¼ teaspoon white pepper
1 tablespoon fresh lemon juice

Garnish
1 tablespoon finely chopped scallion, green part only
¼ cup sour cream
1 tablespoon finely chopped mint

1. Heat the oil in a large saucepan over medium heat. Add the scallions and carrots and sauté, stirring occasionally, for 3 to 5 minutes.
2. Add the lettuce and sauté until wilted, about 5 minutes.
3. Add the mint, chicken stock, all but a small handful of snow peas, and the peas (if using defrosted frozen peas, add during the last five minutes). Cover and simmer 20 minutes.

4. Place the soup in a blender or food processor fitted with a steel blade and process until puréed. Return to the pan and add the cream, seasonings, and lemon juice. Simmer for about 5 minutes.

5. Slice the remaining snow peas in julienne and immerse in boiling water for about 1 minute. Remove from the water and let cool.

6. Refrigerate the soup until chilled, about 3 hours. Taste for seasoning right before serving.

7. *To serve:* Pour the soup into bowls and garnish with sour cream, chopped scallion, chopped mint, and the blanched, julienned snow peas.

ADVANCE PREPARATION: This may be prepared 8 hours in advance through step 6 and refrigerated until serving.

Curried Corn Soup

SERVES 6 TO 8

I never tire of fresh corn soups in the summertime. This version includes lemon slices and curry powder for a Far Eastern flavor. The lemon slices cook in the soup and then are puréed along with the rest of the ingredients to add a citrus tang. The amount of curry might seem overwhelming but, in fact, it's just right—so be fearless. Toasted Pita with Parmesan is perfect with the soup. Follow with Roasted Sea Bass with Herbs and Lemon Vegetable Rice.

2 tablespoons olive oil

2 medium leeks, white part only, cleaned and finely chopped

2 small red potatoes, about ½ pound, peeled and coarsely chopped

5 cups fresh corn kernels (about 6 large ears)

2 teaspoons curry powder

6 cups chicken stock (see page 366)

2 ¼-inch lemon slices

1 teaspoon salt

¼ teaspoon white pepper

Garnish

Thin lemon slices

½ cup sour cream

1. In a large saucepan heat the olive oil over medium heat. Add the leeks and sauté for about 5 minutes, turning frequently until softened.

2. Add the potatoes and all but ½ cup corn kernels and continue to cook about 2 more minutes. Add the curry powder and cook about 1 more minute.

3. Add the chicken stock and lemon slices and bring to a boil. Simmer, partially covered, until the potatoes are soft, about 20 minutes.

4. Place the soup in a blender or food processor fitted with a steel blade and process until puréed. Press through a food mill or fine strainer back into the saucepan.

5. Add the salt and pepper and taste for seasoning. Chill for at least 3 hours.

6. Immerse the remaining corn kernels in boiling water for about 1 minute. Drain and cool.

7. *To serve:* Pour the soup into bowls or mugs and garnish with lemon slices, a dollop of sour cream, and the corn kernels.

ADVANCE PREPARATION: This may be prepared 8 hours in advance through step 6 and refrigerated until ready to serve. This soup may also be served hot.

Yellow Squash Soup

SERVES 4 TO 6

This sunny yellow soup will brighten any table. And it cheers the cook too, since it can be put together in just a few minutes. Follow with Chicken Salad with Roasted Garlic Mayonnaise and String Bean–Golden Pepper Salad.

  1 tablespoon olive oil
1½ pounds yellow crookneck squash, shredded
  2 tablespoons finely chopped chives
3½ cups chicken stock (see page 366)
  1 tablespoon fresh lemon juice
  ½ cup sour cream
  ¼ teaspoon salt
  ¼ teaspoon white pepper

Garnish
  ¼ cup sour cream
  1 tablespoon finely chopped chives

1. Heat the olive oil in a medium saucepan over medium heat. Add the shredded squash and chives and sauté until just softened, about 3 minutes.
2. Add the chicken stock and simmer for about 5 minutes.
3. Place in a blender or food processor fitted with a steel blade and process until puréed. Refrigerate until cool.
4. Whisk in the lemon juice, sour cream, salt, and pepper until well combined. Taste for seasoning.
5. *To serve:* Ladle the soup into bowls and garnish with the sour cream and chives.

ADVANCE PREPARATION: This may be prepared one day in advance through step 4 and refrigerated until ready to serve.

Creamy Gazpacho

SERVES 6 TO 8

I first tasted this light and creamy soup at the Château San Martin in the hills of southern France, overlooking the Mediterranean. The setting was as memorable as the soup. The chef serves this gazpacho daily during the hot summer months. The anchovy paste and Crème Fraîche add an unanticipated complexity.

  2 teaspoons anchovy paste
2½ cups tomato juice
2½ pounds ripe tomatoes, peeled, seeded, and finely chopped
  2 cups beef broth
  ¼ cup extra virgin olive oil (optional)
  3 tablespoons red wine vinegar
  3 large garlic cloves, minced
  ½ teaspoon salt
  ¼ teaspoon black pepper
  2 medium cucumbers, peeled, seeded, and finely chopped
  1 small red onion, finely chopped
  ¼ cup finely chopped fresh basil
  1 small sweet red pepper, peeled, seeded, and very finely chopped
  1 small sweet yellow pepper, peeled, seeded, and very finely chopped
  ¼ cup sour cream or Crème Fraîche (see page 369)

Garnish
  ½ cup sour cream or Crème Fraîche (see page 369)
  2 tablespoons finely chopped basil

1. Stir the anchovy paste into the tomato juice until dissolved. Combine this mixture with the chopped tomatoes, beef broth, olive oil (if using), vinegar, garlic, salt, and pepper in a large mixing bowl. Whisk together until well blended.

2. Add the cucumbers, onion, and basil to the soup mixture. Reserve two tablespoons of the chopped red and yellow peppers for the garnish. Stir the remaining peppers into the soup. Refrigerate until chilled (at least 4 hours).

3. Just before serving, whisk the sour cream with a cup of the soup mixture in a small bowl until completely blended. Add to the remaining soup and whisk vigorously. Taste for seasoning.

4. *To serve:* Ladle the soup into bowls, garnish with the reserved chopped red and yellow pepper, sour cream or Crème Fraîche, and basil.

ADVANCE PREPARATION: This may be prepared 8 hours in advance through step 2 and refrigerated until serving.

Tomatillo Soup

SERVES 6

If you haven't used tomatillos before, you may be surprised to learn that this member of the gooseberry family comes packaged in a papery husk. Inside is a small ripe green tomato. This slightly sweet, slightly tart, green tomato is full of flavor and used frequently in Southwestern and Mexican cooking. Fresh tomatillos are available at Mexican markets and sometimes even turn up in supermarkets.

This lovely green soup is light and simple to prepare. Serve it with Tequila Lime Grilled Shrimp, Cuban Black Beans, and Tomato-Papaya Mint Salsa.

2 tablespoons safflower oil
1 large onion, finely chopped
2 pounds tomatillos, husked, washed, and quartered
2 medium garlic cloves, minced
4 cups chicken stock (see page 366)
2 tablespoons finely chopped cilantro
  Salt
  White pepper

Garnish

½ cup sour cream
½ cup ripe avocado (about half a medium avocado), cut
  into ¼-inch dice
Crisp Tortilla Chips (see page 281)

1. In a large saucepan heat the oil over medium heat. Add the
   onion and sauté until softened, about 3 minutes.
2. Add the tomatillos and stir until coated with onion. Add the
   garlic and chicken stock and bring to a boil. Lower the heat
   to simmer and cook, partially covered, until the tomatillos
   are tender; about 7 minutes.
3. Place the soup in a blender or food processor fitted with a
   steel blade and process until puréed. Press through a food
   mill or fine strainer into a bowl. Stir in the cilantro. Add the
   salt and pepper; taste for seasoning.
4. Chill for at least 4 hours.
5. *To serve:* Ladle the soup into soup bowls and garnish with
   the sour cream, diced avocado, and a few tortilla chips.

ADVANCE PREPARATION: This should be prepared through
step 4 no more than 8 hours in advance because it tends to
sour quickly. Keep refrigerated until ready to serve.

NOTE: This soup may also be served hot.

Avocado Soup with Tomato Cucumber Salsa

SERVES 4

The ideal summer soup doesn't require cooking. This cool, refreshing soup is amazingly simple—all you need is a food processor or blender. The crisp Tomato Cucumber Salsa spooned on top creates a striking color contrast. Serve it with Mexican Caesar Salad; together they make an easy, light meal that will keep you out of the kitchen on a hot summer day.

2 large ripe avocados
3 cups chicken stock (see page 366)
2 tablespoons fresh lemon juice
½ teaspoon chile powder
2 tablespoons finely chopped chives
1 teaspoon salt

Garnish
¼ cup sour cream
½ cup Tomato Cucumber Salsa (see page 350)

1. Peel the avocados and cut into large pieces. Place in a food processor fitted with a steel blade or in a blender and process until puréed.
2. Add the chicken stock, lemon juice, chile powder, chives, and salt, and process until smooth. Taste for seasoning. Chill for 4 hours.
3. *To serve:* Ladle the soup into bowls and garnish with a dollop each of sour cream and Tomato Cucumber Salsa.

ADVANCE PREPARATION: This may be prepared 8 hours in advance through step 2 and refrigerated until ready to serve.

DOG DAYS

Every summer has its dog days—those stifling hot days when there's no breeze anywhere and the only hope of comfort is to sit absolutely still. If you have company coming, the very thought of cooking is unbearable. Here are some suggestions for serving cool, delicious food with an absolute minimum of effort.

DRINKS

- Go light on alcoholic drinks—it's easy to drink too fast.
- Serve big bottles of icy cold sparkling mineral water with lime wedges.
- Serve fruit nectar and sparkling water combinations.

FIRST COURSES

- Chilled no-cook soup like Herbed Cucumber Soup with Walnuts or Iced Yogurt Peach Soup
- Smoked Trout with Roasted Garlic Mayonnaise
- Deviled eggs (see box, page 101)
- Crudités with Guacamole Salsa
- Goat Cheese and Pesto Torta with Hazelnuts
- Chilled cracked crab with Lemon-Chive Mayonnaise

LIGHT AND EASY MAIN COURSES

- A platter of sardines, sliced tomatoes, hard-cooked eggs, and olives
- A variety of sliced melons and Black Forest or Parma ham
- Halved hard-cooked eggs with Summer Vinaigrette, roasted peppers with balsamic vinegar, Niçoise olives, and really crusty French bread

- Salads that require a minimum of preparation, such as Mexican Caesar Salad

DESSERTS

- Honeydew Sorbet, Mixed Berries with Mint, your favorite ice cream, or a cheese and fruit platter with assorted tea breads or cookies.

Cold Beet Soup with Carrots, Cucumbers, and Sour Cream

SERVES 8 TO 10

This is a far cry from the bottled borscht I grew up on. Sweet, julienned carrots and refreshing cucumber added just before serving give it an extra crunch. I like to serve this in oversized glass balloon goblets for a dramatic presentation. Follow with Scallops Brochette with Spicy Caribbean Salsa and Lemon-Herb Roasted Potatoes.

     2 pounds beets, trimmed and scrubbed well, leaving the
       roots and ½ inch of the stems attached
     8 cups chicken stock (see page 366)
  1½ cups dry white wine
     1 tablespoon plus 1 teaspoon sugar
     2 medium carrots, peeled and julienned
     2 medium cucumbers, peeled, seeded, and julienned
     2 tablespoons finely chopped fresh dill
     2 tablespoons fresh lemon juice
     2 tablespoons red wine vinegar
       Salt
       Pepper

Garnish

     1 cup sour cream
     2 tablespoons finely chopped fresh dill

1. In a large nonaluminum soup pot, combine the beets, chicken
   stock, white wine, and sugar over medium-high heat and
   bring to a boil. Reduce the heat and simmer covered until
   beets are tender; 30 to 40 minutes.
2. Transfer the beets with a slotted spoon to a bowl and let
   cool. When cool enough to be handled, peel and cut into
   julienne strips. Chill in the refrigerator.
3. Strain the stock through a fine sieve lined with cheesecloth
   into a large bowl. Cover and refrigerate for at least 4 hours
   or overnight.
4. Blanch the carrots in a saucepan of boiling salted water for
   about 1 minute. Drain in a colander and run under cold
   water. Chill covered in the refrigerator.
5. Skim the fat from the surface of the chilled stock and add
   the beets, carrots, cucumbers, dill, lemon juice, vinegar, and
   salt and pepper to taste. Mix well. Taste for seasoning.
6. *To serve:* Ladle the soup into bowls and garnish with the
   sour cream and fresh dill.

ADVANCE PREPARATION: This may be prepared 1 day in
advance through step 5 and refrigerated until ready to serve.

Herbed Cucumber Soup with Walnuts

SERVES 6

This cool summer soup, made with cucumbers, herbs, yogurt, and buttermilk, is sometimes served with slivered almonds. Joan Lenoff, who tested many of the recipes in this book, offers this variation made with walnuts. Save this for a really hot day since no cooking is required. Serve with Chicken Salad with Roasted Garlic Mayonnaise and Cherry Tomato and Hearts of Palm Salad.

    1 European cucumber, peeled, seeded, and cut in half
  1½ cups lowfat yogurt
  1½ cups buttermilk
   ¼ cup finely chopped parsley
   1 medium garlic clove, minced
   2 tablespoons finely chopped chives
   2 tablespoons finely chopped fresh dill
   ½ cup walnuts, coarsely chopped
      Salt
      White Pepper

Garnish
   2 tablespoons walnuts, coarsely chopped

1. In a food processor fitted with a steel blade, purée half of the cucumber for about 20 seconds.
2. Combine the yogurt and buttermilk in a medium mixing bowl. Add the puréed cucumber, parsley, garlic, chives, dill, and walnuts. Mix until well combined.
3. In the food processor, chop the remaining cucumber into

⅛-inch pieces with the on/off pulse. Add to the soup mixture. Add the salt and pepper and taste for seasoning. Refrigerate until chilled.

4. *To serve:* Pour into individual soup bowls and garnish with the chopped walnuts.

ADVANCE PREPARATION: This may be prepared 8 hours in advance through step 3 and refrigerated until ready to serve.

Spiced Orange and Carrot Soup

SERVES 4 TO 6

This soup has accents of orange, cinnamon, and fresh ginger to enliven the sweet carrot taste. Let your guests ladle their soup into glass cups or mugs to enjoy while the rest of the dinner is cooking, or serve with a salad buffet of Couscous Salad with Spiced Fruit Vinaigrette; Thai Chicken Salad; Green Bean, Mushroom, and Walnut Salad; and Three Lettuce Salad with Tomato Tarragon Dressing.

   2 tablespoons unsalted butter
   1 tablespoon safflower oil
   2 medium leeks, white part only, thinly sliced
   1 pound carrots (about 6 medium), peeled and thinly sliced
   1 small red potato (about 8 ounces), peeled and coarsely diced
1¼ teaspoons minced fresh ginger
   4 cups chicken stock (see page 366)
 ¾ cup fresh orange juice
   2 teaspoons orange zest
 ¼ teaspoon cinnamon
 ½ teaspoon salt
 ¼ teaspoon ground white pepper

Garnish
  Sliced orange
  Grated carrot
  Fresh mint
  Herb blossoms (optional)

1. In a medium saucepan, melt the butter and oil over medium heat. Sauté the leeks for about 2 minutes. Add the carrots, potato, and ginger and sauté until the vegetables are just softened.
2. Add the chicken stock and bring to a simmer until vegetables are completely cooked; about 25 minutes. Place in a food processor fitted with a steel blade and process 15 seconds, leaving some texture.
3. Add the orange juice, orange zest, cinnamon, salt, and pepper and blend well. Taste for seasoning. Refrigerate until chilled; about 4 hours.
4. *To serve:* Ladle the soup into chilled glass serving bowls and garnish with a thin orange slice, grated carrot, and a sprig of fresh mint or herb blossoms.

ADVANCE PREPARATION: This may be prepared 1 day in advance through step 3 and refrigerated.

VARIATION: This soup is also excellent served hot, garnished with sour cream and fresh mint.

Iced Yogurt Peach Soup

SERVES 4

A fruit soup is especially welcome in the summer. Peach yogurt and fresh diced peaches give this soup an intense peach flavor. Most fruit soups are too sweet for my taste, but this one is sweetened just slightly with port and white wine, making it an ideal first course for a luncheon or a light ending to a late supper.

2 pounds ripe peaches
12 ounces peach yogurt
2 tablespoons Tawny Port
½ cup Johannesburg Reisling
¼ teaspoon ground ginger
¾ teaspoon Chinese Five Spice Powder

Garnish
Fresh mint leaves

1. In a large saucepan bring water to a boil. Immerse the peaches for about 20 seconds, then remove immediately.
2. Peel, cut in half, and remove the pit. Cut the peaches into small dice. Reserve ¼ cup for a garnish, cover, and refrigerate. Process the remaining peaches in a food processor fitted with a steel blade until puréed.
3. Pour the purée into a medium mixing bowl and blend in the yogurt, port, wine, and spices. Whisk until completely blended. Chill for at least 4 hours.
4. *To serve:* Ladle the soup into bowls and garnish with the reserved diced peaches and fresh mint sprigs.

ADVANCE PREPARATION: This soup may be prepared 8 hours in advance through step 3 and refrigerated.

Three Bean Soup

SERVES 6 TO 8

Bean soups are traditionally served during the cool months, but this lighter rendition is just as welcome in summer. It is delicious hot, cold, or at room temperature. If you take this soup on a picnic and want to serve it hot, heat your thermos with boiling water for a few minutes before pouring in the soup. If you plan to serve it ice cold, pour ice water into your thermos for a few moments to chill it properly before adding the soup. The soup is filling, so plan your menu accordingly.

1 cup dried pinto beans
1 cup dried kidney beans
1 cup dried white beans
2 tablespoons olive oil
2 medium onions, finely chopped
2 medium carrots, peeled and finely chopped
2 medium celery stalks, finely chopped
1 1-pound can tomatoes, seeded and diced
6 cups chicken stock (see page 366)
2 cups water
3 garlic cloves, minced
¼ cup finely chopped parsley leaves
1 bay leaf
 Salt
 Pepper

Garnish
½ cup sour cream
½ cup fresh Tomato Basil Sauce (see page 346)

1. Cover the beans with cold water and soak overnight. If you prefer to use the quick soak method, bring the beans and water to a boil for 2 minutes, cover, and let stand for 1 hour.
2. Drain, reserving 2 cups of the bean liquid, and set the soaked beans aside.
3. In a large soup pot heat the olive oil over medium-high heat. Add the onions and sauté about 3 minutes. Add the carrots and celery and continue to sauté for about 3 minutes.
4. Add the reserved bean liquid, beans, tomatoes, chicken stock, water, garlic, parsley, and bay leaf. Cover and bring to a boil. Reduce and simmer until the beans are tender; about 1 hour. Remove the bay leaf.
5. Place the soup in a blender or food processor fitted with a steel blade and process until puréed. Pour into a large

mixing bowl. Add the salt and pepper and taste for seasoning. Chill for at least 4 hours.

6. Serve the soup garnished with the sour cream and fresh Tomato Basil Sauce.

ADVANCE PREPARATION: This may be prepared 3 days in advance through step 5 and refrigerated until ready to serve. To serve at room temperature, remove it from the refrigerator 2 hours before.

Spinach and Watercress Vichyssoise with Lemon-Chive Cream

SERVES 6 TO 8

Fresh watercress and spinach brighten this classic summer soup. A finishing dollop of lemon-chive cream brings out its tangy flavor. This is a hearty dish, so serve small portions or consider it for a light main dish, accompanied by Herbed Garlic Cheese Bread.

  3 tablespoons safflower oil
  3 medium leeks, white part only, cleaned and coarsely
    chopped
1½ pounds white rose potatoes, peeled and coarsely
    chopped
  1 large bunch fresh spinach, cleaned and stemmed
  1 medium bunch watercress, cleaned and stemmed
  2 quarts chicken stock (see page 366)
 ½ teaspoon salt
 ½ teaspoon white pepper
  1 tablespoon fresh lemon juice

½ cup sour cream
2 tablespoons fresh lemon juice (optional)
1 tablespoon finely chopped chives

1. In a medium soup pot, heat the oil over medium heat. Add the leeks and sauté, stirring occasionally, until soft. Add the potatoes and continue sautéing until softened; about 5 minutes. Add the spinach and watercress and sauté until wilted; about 3 minutes.
2. Add the chicken stock and bring to a simmer. Partially cover and cook until the vegetables are tender; about 15 minutes.
3. Place the soup in a blender or food processor fitted with a steel blade and process until puréed. Pour into a large bowl and add the salt, pepper, and lemon juice. Taste for seasoning. Refrigerate for at least 4 hours or overnight.
4. *To make lemon-chive cream:* Combine all the ingredients in a small bowl and blend well.
5. *To serve:* Ladle the soup into serving bowls and garnish with a dollop of lemon-chive cream.

ADVANCE PREPARATION: The soup may be completely prepared 1 day in advance and refrigerated until ready to serve.

NOTE: This soup is also excellent served hot.

Spinach and Watercress Vichysoisse with Lemon-Chive Cream

Corn Chowder with Red Peppers

SERVES 6

Every summer includes a few chilly days when you crave something warm and substantial. I like to serve this soup on one of those cool summer days because it uses seasonal produce in a hearty way. Serve big bowls of this chowder with hot crusty French bread and Garden Salad with Goat Cheese Thyme Dressing. Mocha Mousse makes a spectacular finale.

¼ pound bacon, cut into ½-inch pieces
1 large onion, finely chopped
2 pounds white or red rose potatoes, peeled and cut into ½-inch pieces
1 large red pepper, seeded and finely diced
6 cups chicken stock (see page 366)
2 sprigs fresh thyme
4 cups corn kernels (about 8 medium ears of corn)
½ cup whipping cream
1 teaspoon salt
¼ teaspoon white pepper

1. Place the bacon pieces in a large nonaluminum soup pot over medium heat. Sauté until crisp and light brown; about 5 minutes. Remove from the pan and reserve.
2. Add the onion to the bacon drippings and sauté until softened but not browned; 3 to 5 minutes. Add the potatoes and sauté 3 more minutes. Add the red pepper and sauté another minute, stirring all the vegetables.
3. Add the chicken stock and thyme and bring to a boil. Reduce the heat and simmer, partially covered, until the potatoes are just tender; about 20 minutes. Discard the thyme leaves.
4. Pour about ¼ of the potato vegetable mixture into a food processor fitted with a steel blade and process until puréed. Return the purée to the soup.

5. Add the corn and cream and cook about 5 minutes longer. Stir in the salt and pepper and taste for seasoning. Serve immediately.

ADVANCE PREPARATION: This may be prepared 8 hours in advance and refrigerated. Gently reheat before serving.

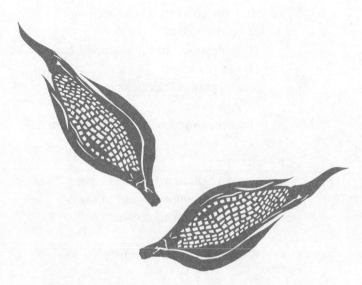

Corn Chowder with Red Peppers

Minestrone with Pesto Cream

This is my husband's favorite summer soup, a fine example of what he calls "real food." It can be served hot or cold, but I prefer to serve it at room temperature, which brings out the full flavor of the vegetables and herbs. Orzo, the tiny almond-shaped pasta, is added for its unusual shape and texture. But what makes this minestrone so special is the pesto cream, which is swirled in just before serving. This can be a simple, yet elegant first course when followed by Grilled Veal Chops with Fresh Corn and Tarragon Sauce and Crispy Grilled Potatoes.

  2 tablespoons olive oil
  2 medium onions, finely chopped
  4 medium carrots, peeled and cut into ¼-inch pieces
  ½ pound white or red rose potatoes, peeled and cut into ¼-inch pieces
  1 large zucchini, cut into ¼-inch pieces
  1 large yellow crookneck squash, cut into ¼-inch pieces
  1 Japanese eggplant or ½ small eggplant, cut into ¼-inch pieces
  ½ small cabbage, shredded
  1 cup fresh tomatoes, peeled, seeded, and puréed
  6 cups chicken stock (see page 366)
  2 garlic cloves
  1 tablespoon finely chopped basil
  1 teaspoon salt
  ½ teaspoon black pepper
  ¼ cup orzo
  1 cup canned white beans, drained

Pesto cream
  ½ cup Spinach Pesto (see page 351)
  1 tablespoon red wine vinegar
  ½ cup whipping cream
  ½ teaspoon salt
  ¼ teaspoon black pepper

1. In a large soup pot, heat the olive oil over medium heat. Add the onions and sauté for 3 to 5 minutes, stirring occasionally.
2. Add the carrots, potatoes, zucchini, summer squash, and eggplant and sauté about 3 more minutes. Add the cabbage and sauté just until softened.
3. Add the puréed tomatoes, chicken stock, garlic, basil, salt, and pepper and bring to a boil. Reduce the heat and simmer until the vegetables are tender; about 25 minutes. The soup will be slightly thickened.
4. In a separate medium-size pot, bring water to a boil. Add the orzo and cook just until done, about 10 minutes. Drain and add to the soup. Add the white beans, stir, and taste for seasoning. Cool to room temperature.
5. *To make the pesto cream:* Combine all the ingredients in a small mixing bowl and whisk until smooth. Taste for seasoning. Refrigerate.
6. *To serve:* Ladle the soup into bowls and swirl in a tablespoon of the pesto cream.

ADVANCE PREPARATION: The soup and sauce may be prepared 1 day in advance and refrigerated. Bring both to room temperature before serving.

Minestrone with Pesto Cream

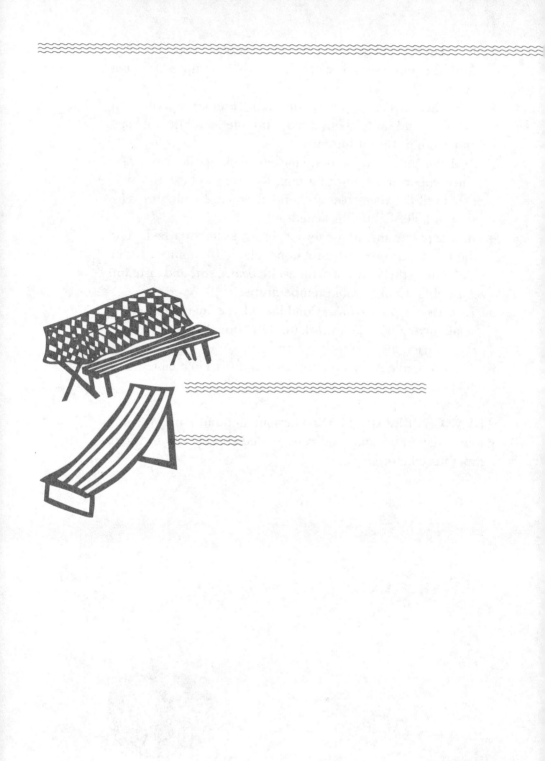

Light Entrees: Eggs and Pasta

EGGS

Summertime Frittata

SERVES 4 TO 6

The classic Italian frittata looks like a big, yellow pancake, though it's actually a flat round omelette cooked over low heat until firm. This version has sausages, zucchini, mushrooms, and plum tomatoes tucked inside, and it's decorated with dollops of sour cream and shredded basil. Frittatas can be eaten warm or at room temperature, and served for brunch, lunch, or supper. Start with Iced Peach Soup with Yogurt and serve the frittata with Lemon-Herb Roasted Potatoes. Finish with Raspberry Pound Cake and cool iced coffee.

RECOMMENDED WINE: Serve a snappy, young red: Gamay, Zinfandel, Bardolino, or Beaujolais.

2 sweet sausages (approximately ⅓ to ½ pound)

2 hot sausages (approximately ⅓ to ½ pound)

2 tablespoons unsalted butter

1 tablespoon olive oil

2 medium shallots, finely chopped

½ pound mushrooms, thinly sliced

2 small zucchini, thinly sliced

1 medium garlic clove, minced

¾ teaspoon salt

¼ teaspoon pepper

12 eggs

1½ cups shredded sharp Cheddar cheese (approximately 6 ounces)

4 medium plum (Roma) tomatoes, sliced

Garnish

¼ cup fresh basil, finely chopped

½ cup sour cream

1. In a medium skillet over medium heat, cook the sausage, turning frequently. Drain on paper towels and let cool. When cooled, slice it into ¼-inch pieces and set aside.
2. Heat the butter and olive oil in a 12-inch, nonstick skillet* with an ovenproof handle over medium-high heat. Add the shallots and sauté until soft but not brown, about 3 minutes. Add the mushrooms and sauté for 1 to 2 minutes. Add the zucchini and continue cooking for 2 minutes. Add the garlic and cook for 1 minute. Arrange the sausage slices around the vegetables and season with ¼ teaspoon salt and a pinch of pepper.
3. Preheat the oven to 425°F. In a medium bowl combine the eggs and the remaining salt and pepper, and whisk until well blended. Stir in 1¼ cups shredded cheese.
4. Pour the egg mixture over the sausages and vegetables in the skillet and cook over medium-low heat, stirring occasionally, until the bottom of the mixture is lightly browned,

about 5 minutes. Arrange the sliced tomatoes around the edge of the skillet. Sprinkle with the remaining cheese.

5. Transfer the skillet to the oven and bake until the frittata is puffed and brown, 10 to 15 minutes.

6. Remove from the oven and invert onto a plate. Invert again onto a serving platter, so the tomato border faces up. Place a large dollop of sour cream in the center and garnish with the fresh chopped basil.

ADVANCE PREPARATION: This may be prepared 2 hours in advance through step 2 and kept covered at room temperature. Although it will be completely different in texture and taste, the frittata may be made 1 day ahead, refrigerated, and served at room temperature.

* Use a non stick pan, if possible, for ease in inverting the frittata. The frittata may also be served right out of the pan.

Scrambled Eggs with Three Cheeses

SERVES 4 TO 6

On those lazy mornings when you want something absolutely delicious for breakfast, this luxurious scrambled egg dish with diced tomatoes is the thing to cook. The eggs and Parmesan cheese are cooked over low heat and stirred frequently for unbelievably creamy scrambled eggs. The other cheeses are barely melted into the eggs. The tomatoes are added off the heat to preserve their texture. Decorate the serving plates with crisp triangular croutons and sprigs of fresh herbs—rosemary, basil, or parsley. Serve with bacon and a large platter of mixed fruit.

3 square slices firm white bread, crusts trimmed
1½ tablespoons safflower oil
1 tablespoon unsalted butter

12 eggs
2 tablespoons freshly grated Parmesan cheese
½ teaspoon salt
¼ teaspoon pepper
¼ cup (½ stick) unsalted butter
½ cup shredded Cheddar cheese
½ cup shredded mozzarella cheese
2 firm medium tomatoes, peeled, seeded, and diced

1. *To make the croutons:* Cut each slice of bread into 2 triangles. Heat the oil and butter in a medium skillet over medium heat. Add the triangles in batches and brown on both sides. With a slotted spoon, transfer them to paper towels to drain.
2. Whisk the eggs with the Parmesan cheese, salt, and pepper.
3. Melt 2 tablespoons butter in a medium-size heavy saucepan. Add the egg mixture and cook over low heat, whisking constantly, until the mixture becomes thick but not dry. Remove from the heat and stir in the remaining butter, Cheddar cheese, and mozzarella. Gently stir in the diced tomatoes. Taste for seasoning.
4. Transfer the egg mixture to a serving bowl. Stick one corner of each crouton into the egg mixture at the edge of the bowl. Serve immediately.

Poached Eggs with Prosciutto and Tomato-Béarnaise Sauce

SERVES 2

A Franco-Italian adaptation of Eggs Benedict, this distinctive egg dish tastes like pure California. Ever since the Gold Rush days, Californians have been fanatic about sourdough bread. Proscuitto, the sweet, unsmoked, dry-cured ham, adds more taste than the conventional Canadian bacon and stands up to the bold Tomato-Béarnaise Sauce. Use the freshest eggs available so they will hold together while poaching. Follow with refreshing Frozen Peaches and Cream and Toasted Hazelnut Cookies.

RECOMMENDED WINE: An off-dry Reisling or Gewürztraminer should do the trick here, or try a Chardonnay or even a crisp White Zinfandel.

¾ cup Tomato-Béarnaise Sauce (see page 352)
4 fresh eggs
2 tablespoons white wine vinegar
4 thick slices sourdough bread
4 thin slices prosciutto (about 2 ounces)

Garnish
1 tablespoon chopped parsley

1. Prepare the Tomato-Béarnaise Sauce and pour into a small warmed thermos until serving.
2. *To poach the eggs:* Bring a saucepan full of water to a simmer and add the vinegar. Break the eggs into the water and swirl whites around the yolks with a spoon. Poach over low heat until the whites are set but the yolks are still soft, about 3 minutes. Transfer with a slotted spoon to paper towels. Using a knife or scissors, trim the whites into a neat shape.
3. Lightly toast the bread. Lay a slice of proscuitto on each slice of toast, top with an egg, and cover with the sauce. Garnish with the chopped parsley. Serve immediately.

ADVANCE PREPARATION: The eggs may be poached 1 day in advance and kept in a covered bowl of cold water in the refrigerator. Reheat the eggs by putting them in hot water for ½ minute; drain them on paper towels.

DEVILED EGGS

Deviled eggs, the beloved American classic, can be far from ordinary when sophisticated ingredients are added. The key to perfect deviled eggs is in the cooking: don't boil the eggs and don't cook them too long. These strategies will avoid tough eggs and those unappetizing gray circles around the yolks. Use extra large eggs, preferably at room temperature. Place them in a pan with cold water to cover and bring them just to a rolling boil. Turn off the heat and cover the pan for 12 minutes. Cool the eggs under cold running water. Crack, but don't peel them until right before preparing. A few excellent combinations to mix with the mashed yolks are:

- Chopped smoked salmon, chives, mayonnaise, and lemon juice
- Minced shallots, mayonnaise, and snipped dill, topped with caviar.
- Mayonnaise, mango chutney, and curry powder
- Pesto, mayonnaise, and chopped bay shrimp
- Yogurt, sour cream, chopped cucumber, and capers, garnished with watercress
- Saffron mayonnaise with chopped Italian parsley

Omelette with Zucchini, Tomato, and Basil

SERVES 6

This is my favorite summer omelette, perfect for an extremely informal, everyone-in-the-kitchen meal. I prepare the filling ahead of time and make the omelettes at the last minute—using two skillets. Serve chilled Champagne with framboise when your guests arrive. Accompany the omelettes with either Herbed New Potatoes with Vermouth or Lemon-Herb Roasted Potatoes. For dessert serve Poached Peaches in White Zinfandel with Fresh Raspberry Sauce and Almond Cookies with Lemon and Port.

Filling

    2 tablespoons unsalted butter
    1 shallot, minced
    ¼ pound mushrooms, thinly sliced
    1 medium zucchini, julienned
    1 medium tomato, peeled, seeded, and coarsely chopped
    ¼ teaspoon salt
    ⅛ teaspoon pepper
    2 tablespoons chopped basil
    6 tablespoons freshly grated Parmesan cheese

Omelettes

    12 to 18 eggs (2 to 3 per person)
       Pinch salt
       Pinch pepper
    1 tablespoon club soda
    6 tablespoons (¾ stick) unsalted butter

1. *To make the filling:* In a medium skillet, heat the butter over medium heat until melted. Add the shallot and sauté until soft; about 2 minutes. Add the mushrooms and sauté another 2 minutes. Add the zucchini and continue to sauté for 2 minutes.

2. Add the tomato and cook over high heat for 2 minutes to evaporate any excess liquid from the tomato. Add the salt, pepper, and basil and mix well. Taste for seasoning. Cover to keep warm.

3. *To prepare each omelette:* Whisk 2 to 3 eggs with a pinch of salt, a pinch of pepper, and ½ teaspoon club soda until smooth.

4. Melt 1 tablespoon butter in an 8-inch omelette pan or skillet over medium heat until it begins to sizzle.

5. Pour in the egg mixture and stir it in the center of the pan with the flat side of a fork. With the prongs of the fork, lift the edges of the omelette so any uncooked mixture runs to the edge of the pan. Vigorously slide the pan back and forth over the heat until the omelette begins to slip around freely.

6. When the omelette is lightly cooked but still creamy in the center, spoon about 2 tablespoons of the filling over the half of the omelette closer to the pan's handle. Sprinkle 1 tablespoon of the Parmesan cheese over the filling.

7. Quickly jerk the pan toward you with the handle so that the other half of the omelette flips over on top of the filling. Slide the folded omelette onto a serving dish. Serve immediately or keep warm in a low oven while preparing the remaining omelettes.

ADVANCE PREPARATION: The filling may be prepared 1 day in advance without the basil and refrigerated. Remove it from the refrigerator ½ hour before using, add the basil, and gently reheat.

Omelette with Zucchini, Tomato, and Basil

Cheese Soufflé with Spinach and Chicken

Cooler summer days call for heartier dishes. Soufflés are often too light for a main course, but this one is substantial without being heavy—it's elegant, airy, and fluffy. When you break into it with your fork, you release the seductive aroma of melting cheese, chicken, and spinach. Begin the meal with Green Salad with Grapefruit, Baby Beets, and Avocado, then serve the soufflé with Broiled Tomatoes with Mustard Herb Mayonnaise. Lattice Crust Pie with Rhubarb, Peaches, Strawberries and Plums, makes a satisfying ending.

RECOMMENDED WINE: A light Chardonnay or a crisp French Chablis is a good choice for this dish.

- 1½ cups chicken stock (see page 366), (optional)
- 1 whole chicken breast, skinned and boned
- 2 medium bunches spinach (about 1 pound)
- 1 teaspoon unsalted butter
- 1 cup plus 2 tablespoons grated Swiss, Parmesan, or Cheddar cheese
- ½ teaspoon salt
- 2 pinches white pepper
- 2½ tablespoons unsalted butter
- 3 tablespoons all-purpose flour
- 1 cup milk
- 4 egg yolks
  Pinch freshly grated nutmeg
- 5 egg whites
  Pinch salt
  Pinch cream of tartar
- 1 tablespoon breadcrumbs

1. In a medium skillet with high sides or a medium saucepan, bring the chicken stock with enough water to cover the chicken breast to a simmer. If using water only, add a pinch of salt. Immerse the chicken breast and simmer until just tender, 10 to 12 minutes.

2. Remove from the heat and cool the chicken in the liquid. Drain and cut into ½-inch pieces. Reserve.

3. Remove the spinach stems and rinse leaves thoroughly. Place in a 9-inch skillet and partially cover. Steam over moderately high heat for about 2 minutes. Remove from the heat and place in a strainer. Pour cold water over the spinach to stop the cooking. Drain and place the spinach in a dry dish towel. Wring out all the excess liquid. Chop the spinach coarsely with a knife or in a food processor fitted with a steel blade.

4. Prepare a 1½-quart soufflé dish by rubbing 1 teaspoon butter all over the inside and sprinkling with 1 tablespoon grated cheese.

5. Mix the chopped spinach with the chicken. Season with ¼ teaspoon salt and a pinch of white pepper. Spread the mixture evenly on the bottom of the soufflé dish and sprinkle with 1 tablespoon grated cheese.

6. Preheat the oven to 375°F. Melt the butter in a 2-quart saucepan over medium heat. Add the flour and mix with a wooden spoon for 1 minute. Let the flour and butter cook until bubbling but not browned.

7. Add the milk and whisk until thick and smooth. While whisking, bring the sauce to a boil. Remove from the heat and let cool for 10 minutes.

8. Add the egg yolks and whisk until smooth. Season with ¼ teaspoon salt, pinch of white pepper, and nutmeg.

9. In a large bowl with a large whisk or electric mixer, whip the egg whites with a pinch of salt and cream of tartar until stiff but not dry.

10. Gently fold half of the egg whites into the sauce. Add all but 1 tablespoon of the remaining grated cheese to the sauce and then fold in the rest of the egg whites. Pour into the soufflé dish. Sprinkle with the remaining tablespoon of cheese, then the bread crumbs.

11. Bake until brown, 30 to 35 minutes. Remove from the oven and serve immediately.

ADVANCE PREPARATION: This may be prepared 4 hours in advance through step 5 and kept covered at room temperature.

VARIATIONS: Use ½ pound cooked shrimp, crab, or lobster instead of chicken. Add another layer of ½ pound sliced, sautéed mushrooms between the spinach-chicken and the soufflé mixture.

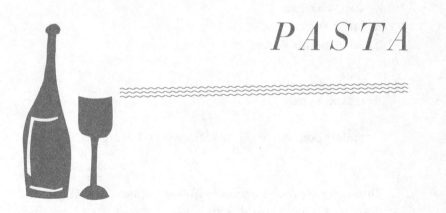

PASTA

Fresh Pasta

MAKES ¾ POUND
SERVES 2 TO 3 AS A MAIN COURSE;
4 TO 6 AS A FIRST COURSE

Although it's no longer impossible to find fresh pasta in most parts of the country, sometimes I still prefer to make my own. The combination of flours in this recipe give the pasta the necessary body without sacrificing its delicate texture. Remember that if the weather is humid this recipe needs less water, while in dry weather it requires more. Variations on color and flavor are given here to inspire you to create your own "special blend." Serving amounts will vary, depending on the cut of the pasta, which influences the volume. Angel hair, for instance, is thinly cut and will go a long way, while the wider cuts, such as linguine or tagliatelle, require more pasta per serving. If you don't want to fuss with fresh pasta, use the excellent dried durum wheat pasta imported from Italy, especially the De Cecco or Martelli brands.

1 cup bleached all-purpose flour
½ cup semolina
2 large eggs
2 tablespoons water

1 tablespoon olive oil
1 teaspoon salt

2 tablespoons olive oil or soft unsalted butter

1. *To prepare the dough by hand:* In a small bowl, combine the flour and semolina and pour onto a work surface, forming a mound. Make a well in the center with a knife or your fingers. Pour the eggs and water into the well. Using a fork, beat the eggs and water, gradually stirring in the flour. When the mixture becomes pasty, use your hands to work the remaining flour into the eggs by bringing flour from outside the well into the center. Form the mixture into a ball, flouring your hands and the work surface often.

2. Knead the dough for about 10 minutes by pushing and folding it with the heel of your hand. It should feel smooth and elastic without being tough. Divide the dough into 4 equal parts. Cover 3 of them with a damp cloth. Continue with step 4.

3. *To prepare the dough in a food processor:* Combine the flour, semolina, and eggs in a food processor fitted with a steel blade. Process until the dough begins to come together. Add water if necessary; the dough should be pliable enough to pat down for rolling but not so sticky that it will adhere to the rollers of the pasta machine. Divide the dough into 4 equal parts. Cover 3 of them with a damp cloth.

4. *To finish in a pasta machine:* Set the pasta machine rollers at the widest setting. Feed each of the 4 pieces of dough through the machine. Cover the pieces of dough that are not being kneaded with a damp cloth. Fold each piece in thirds and press down firmly to form a compact package. Knead each piece of dough in the machine 8 times. The

dough will begin to flatten out. Hang each piece on a chair or wooden laundry rack after it has been kneaded.

5. Readjust the pasta machine to the next thinnest setting and pass each of the 4 pieces of dough through it again. Repeat until the dough reaches the next to the thinnest setting. While feeding the dough through the rollers, dust it with flour if it becomes sticky.

6. Hang the pasta and let it dry for 10 to 15 minutes; do not let it become brittle.

7. Set the machine for the desired cut: fettucini (⅛-inch wide noodles); tagliatelle (¼-inch wide noodles); or tagliarini (1/16-inch wide noodles). Feed the dough through the cutters, holding your hand under the machine to catch the noodles. (This way, they will not stick to each other and will be easy to hang and dry.)

8. Hang the noodles for at least 10 to 15 minutes or up to 1 hour before cooking.

9. *To cook the pasta:* Add the olive oil and salt to a large pot of boiling water. Cook the fresh pasta over high heat from 20 to 30 seconds and then test for doneness by biting into a piece. It should be just slightly resistant to the teeth (al dente). Test it every 15 seconds thereafter.

10. Drain and place the pasta immediately into a medium bowl. Toss with the olive oil or soft butter to prevent the pasta from sticking together. Add the sauce of your choice and toss.

ADVANCE PREPARATION: Pasta may be prepared 2 days in advance and refrigerated in plastic bags. Cook it just before serving.

VARIATION: To vary the color and only slightly alter the taste, substitute 2 tablespoons red Swiss chard purée, or roasted sweet red or yellow pepper purée for the water.

NOTE: Some sauces may be finished in the pan with the pasta tossed right in. In this case, undercook the pasta slightly to compensate for additional cooking in the heated sauce.

Semolina Gnocchi with Pesto

SERVES 6

It's hard to improve on classic Italian recipes for gnocchi, that succulent dough cut into little morsels, sauced, cheesed, and grilled until bubbly. The secret ingredients here are mustard in the dough and pesto added to the topping, the inspiration of the noted food writer Laurie Burrows Grad. I like to serve this with Barbecued Leg of Lamb with a Mustard Sage Crust. Finish with Lemon Orange Sponge Pudding or Peach Brown Butter Tart.

> 4 cups whole milk
> 1 teaspoon salt
> 1 cup semolina or farina
> 6 tablespoons unsalted butter
> ⅔ cup freshly grated Parmesan cheese
> 2 teaspoons grainy mustard
> ½ teaspoon freshly ground white pepper
> ¼ cup Spinach Pesto (see page 351)

Garnish
> Sprinkling of freshly ground white pepper

1. Chill a jelly roll pan or large cookie sheet with a rim in the refrigerator. (This will help cool and set the gnocchi.)
2. In a large nonstick saucepan bring the milk to a boil over medium heat. Lower the heat, add the salt, and slowly pour the semolina into the simmering milk, stirring constantly to prevent lumping. Continue to cook over moderately high heat, stirring constantly, until the mixture is very thick and pulls away from the sides of the saucepan. This takes 20 to 30 minutes.
3. Remove the saucepan from the heat and add 4 tablespoons butter, ⅓ cup cheese, mustard, and pepper. Stir until smooth.
4. Remove the jelly roll pan from the refrigerator. Spread the mixture on the pan to form a ½-inch layer, cover with foil, and allow to cool. Chill for 1 hour.

5. When ready to bake, preheat the oven to 350°F. Lightly butter a large baking dish or au gratin casserole.

6. With a biscuit or cookie cutter, cut the chilled mixture into rounds, diamonds, crescents, or whatever shape you like and place in a single layer in the prepared dish.

7. Brush the top with Spinach Pesto, dot with the remaining 2 tablespoons of butter, diced, and sprinkle with the remaining ⅓ cup Parmesan cheese.

8. Bake until light golden brown, 25 to 30 minutes. (If not browned, place under the broiler for 1 to 2 minutes.)

9. Serve hot with a generous sprinkling of freshly ground white pepper.

ADVANCE PREPARATION: This may be prepared 8 hours in advance through step 6 (omitting step 5), covered with plastic wrap, and refrigerated. Remove from the refrigerator to bring to room temperature one half hour before baking.

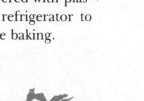

Pasta Shells with Peppers, Mushrooms, and Sausages

SERVES 6 TO 8

Pasta shells are pretty to look at and easy to eat. Sautéed vegetables simmered in port and stock reduce into a light sauce, while the grilled sausages add enough substance to make this a satisfying main dish pasta course. You can find sweet and hot sausages at most Italian grocery stores, where they often make their own blend. Begin this meal with Double Cheese Spread with Zesty Italian Salsa and crisp crackers. Serve the pasta with a simple mixed green salad with Summer Vinaigrette. Finish with Almond Zabaglione with Fresh Strawberries.

RECOMMENDED WINE: Serve a medium weight Zinfandel or a red from the Rhône Valley.

1 pound sweet Italian sausage
1 pound spicy hot Italian sausage

Sauce

3 tablespoons unsalted butter
2 tablespoons olive oil
1 large sweet red pepper, seeded and sliced into ¼-inch slices
1 large sweet yellow pepper, seeded and sliced into ¼-inch slices
4 medium shallots, finely chopped
1 pound mushrooms, sliced
½ cup Tawny Port
2 cups veal or chicken stock (see pages 364–66)
¾ cup whipping cream
1½ teaspoons salt
½ teaspoon finely ground white pepper
1 tablespoon finely chopped parsley

Pasta

1 tablespoon olive oil
1 teaspoon salt
1½ pounds pasta shells

Garnish

1 tablespoon finely chopped parsley
1 cup freshly grated Parmesan cheese

1. Prepare barbecue for medium-high-heat grilling. Grill the sausages for about 20 minutes, turning them until the fat runs clear. (You can also broil the sausages.) Remove to a platter and let cool.

2. In a large deep skillet, heat 1 tablespoon butter and 1 tablespoon olive oil over medium heat. When the butter has melted add the peppers and sauté for about 2 minutes. Remove to a side bowl.

3. Add the remaining butter and oil and then add the shallots and mushrooms to the skillet. Sauté, stirring occasionally, until cooked through; 3 to 5 minutes. Remove to the side bowl with the peppers.
4. Add the port, stock, and cream to the skillet and bring to a simmer. Cook until slightly thickened. Add the peppers, shallots, mushrooms, salt, pepper, and parsley. Taste for seasoning.
5. Cut the sausages diagonally into 1¼-inch-thick slices and add to the sauce.
6. Add the olive oil and salt to a large pot of boiling water. Add the pasta and cook over high heat until al dente; 7 to 10 minutes. Drain well.
7. Place in a large serving bowl. Pour the sauce over and mix well. Garnish with the parsley and a few tablespoons of the Parmesan cheese. Pass the remaining cheese separately. Serve immediately.

ADVANCE PREPARATION: This may be prepared 4 hours in advance through step 5.

Light Summer Pasta

SERVES 4 TO 6

One night a friend and I decided to come up with some no-cook pasta sauces. The friend happened to be Leslie Margolis, a cooking instructor who specializes in light cuisine. We got so carried away we made several sauces and invited other confirmed pasta lovers to choose the best one. This sauce was the winner. The only cooking required is for the pasta, which leaves you plenty of time to enjoy your company.

Sauce

    2 pounds ripe plum (Roma) tomatoes, peeled, seeded, and coarsely chopped

    1 bunch basil, coarsely chopped

    ½ cup finely chopped Italian parsley

    4 medium garlic cloves, minced

    ½ pound fresh mozzarella cheese, cut into ¼-inch dice

    4 tablespoons extra virgin olive oil

    ½ cup freshly grated Parmesan cheese

    ½ teaspoon salt

    ¼ teaspoon black pepper

Pasta

    1 tablespoon olive oil

    1 teaspoon salt

    1 pound spaghetti or linguini

Garnish

    Extra whole basil leaves

1. In a medium pasta serving bowl combine all the sauce ingredients except ¼ cup of the Parmesan cheese and mix well.
2. Add the olive oil and salt to a large pot of boiling water. Add the pasta and cook over high heat until al dente, about 8-10 minutes. Drain well. Place the pasta over the sauce.
3. Toss to combine. Garnish the bowl with fresh basil leaves and pass the remaining Parmesan cheese. Serve immediately.

ADVANCE PREPARATION: The sauce can be prepared 4 hours in advance, covered, and left at room temperature.

Spicy Capellini with Summer Vegetables

SERVES 4 TO 6

Capellini—that very thin, delicate pasta—goes nicely with this colorful variety of fresh summer vegetables. The crushed red pepper here adds a biting hotness to the sauce. If you've never tried aged California goat cheese as a variation on Parmesan cheese, you'll be pleasantly surprised. With the addition of a small amount of Summer Vinaigrette, the combination becomes pasta salad. Serve with a simple green salad and Herbed Garlic Cheese Bread for a light Sunday dinner.

Sauce
- 3 tablespoons olive oil
- 1 large carrot, peeled and julienned
- ½ pound mushrooms, julienned
- ½ pound snow peas, julienned
- 4 large tomatoes (about 2 pounds), peeled, seeded, and finely chopped
- ½ cup chicken stock (see page 366)
- 1 cup whipping cream
- 1 teaspoon tomato paste
- 2 tablespoons finely chopped basil
- 1 teaspoon salt
- ¼ teaspoon crushed red pepper flakes

Pasta
- 1 tablespoon olive oil
- 1 teaspoon salt
- 1 pound dried capellini

Garnish
- 1 cup freshly grated Parmesan or aged goat cheese

1. Heat 2 tablespoons olive oil in a large skillet over medium-high heat. Add the carrot, mushrooms, and snow peas and sauté, stirring continuously, for 3 to 4 minutes. The vegetables

should still be crisp. Remove to a colander set over the sink and drain the vegetables.

2. In the same skillet, heat the remaining tablespoon olive oil over medium heat. Add the tomatoes and sauté for 2 to 3 minutes or until softened. Add the chicken stock, cream, tomato paste, basil, salt, and pepper flakes. Bring to a simmer and let cook until slightly reduced and thickened.

3. Return the drained vegetables to the sauce and cook until just heated through.

4. Add oil and salt to a large pot of boiling water. Add the pasta and cook over high heat until al dente, 8 to 10 minutes. Drain well.

5. Place the drained pasta in a large pasta bowl and pour the vegetable sauce over it. Using pasta forks, toss the sauce with the vegetables until evenly distributed. Serve with Parmesan or aged goat cheese sprinkled on top.

ADVANCE PREPARATION: The sauce may be prepared 4 hours in advance through step 2 and kept at room temperature.

GRILLED CHEESE

Grilled cheese can be more than just the favorite American sandwich. Try wrapping chunks of melting cheese, such as provolone, Italian Fontina, or Monterey Jack, in rinsed preserved grape leaves, and then skewer them for the barbecue. Grill them until the cheese softens and serve immediately. You can also marinate the cheese in herbs and extra virgin olive oil before you wrap it in the grape leaves. Feta and fresh goat cheese are also delicious grilled but require careful attention, since they melt very quickly.

Vegetable Vermicelli with Tapenade Cream

SERVES 4 TO 6

When you add cream to rustic tapenade, made with Niçoise olives, garlic, capers, and anchovies, the resulting taste is both rich and earthy. This sauce blends with vermicelli and sautéed vegetables for a sensational first course. It's also excellent as a side dish to Grilled Halibut in Lemon-Mustard Tarragon Marinade or Grilled Chicken with Sun-Dried Tomato Paste.

Sauce
- 1 tablespoon olive oil
- 1 medium zucchini, julienned
- 1 medium yellow crookneck squash, julienned
- 1 large carrot, peeled and julienned
- ⅔ cup whipping cream
- 3 tablespoons Tapenade (see page 343)
- ½ teaspoon salt
- ¼ teaspoon black pepper

Pasta
- 1 tablespoon olive oil
- 1 teaspoon salt
- 12 ounces vermicelli

Garnish
- ¼ cup Parmesan cheese

1. Heat the olive oil in a medium skillet over medium heat. Add the zucchini, summer squash, and carrot and sauté until crisp-tender, 3 to 4 minutes. Reserve in a small bowl.
2. In the same skillet, over medium-high heat, bring the cream, Tapenade, salt, and pepper to a boil. Taste for seasoning.
3. Add the olive oil and the salt to a large pot of water and bring to a boil. Add the vermicelli and cook about 5 minutes. Drain thoroughly and place in a pasta serving bowl.

4. Add the vegetables to the sauce and cook a minute or two until heated through. Quickly bring the sauce to a boil and pour over the pasta. Toss until well combined. Serve immediately with Parmesan cheese on the side.

Ravioli Nudi

SERVES 6 TO 8

This recipe is perfect for those occasions when you want the taste of pasta without the bulk. Where's the pasta? Not in this dish. Poached fresh spinach ricotta balls are the "nude" ravioli, sauced with fresh red pepper and tomatoes. This recipe was inspired by one from Giuliano Bugialli, the noted Italian culinary historian and teacher. You can serve this as a first course or as a side dish with simple grilled foods. It also makes a light vegetarian luncheon dish when accompanied by the Garden Salad with Goat Cheese Thyme Dressing.

    2½ **pounds fresh spinach (4 bunches), cleaned**
      1 **pound ricotta cheese**
      4 **egg yolks**
    1½ **cups freshly grated Parmesan cheese**
     ¼ **teaspoon nutmeg, preferably freshly grated**
     ½ **teaspoon salt**
     ¼ **teaspoon black pepper**

      1 **teaspoon salt**
      1 **cup all-purpose flour**

      2 **cups Red Pepper Tomato Sauce, heated (see page 349)**

Garnish
     ½ **cup freshly grated Parmesan cheese**

1. Place the spinach in ½ inch of water in a large skillet over medium heat. Cover and steam 3 to 5 minutes. Drain and rinse the spinach in cold water. When cool, place the spinach in a dry dish towel and squeeze out all the excess liquid (this is very important because too much liquid will prevent the ravioli from holding together).
2. With a large, sharp knife, finely chop the spinach and place in a medium mixing bowl.
3. Add the ricotta, egg yolks, Parmesan cheese, nutmeg, salt, and pepper and mix together until completely blended.
4. Fill a large, deep sauté pan or dutch oven ¾ full of water. Add the teaspoon of salt and bring to a boil over high heat.
5. Sprinkle the flour on a cookie sheet and with your hands form the spinach mixture into balls the size of large walnuts. Roll the spinach balls in the flour until they are evenly coated.
6. To test the ravioli, drop a ball into the boiling water. It should come to the surface in about 2 minutes. Break it open to see if it is done in the center.
7. Continue cooking the ravioli about 6 at a time, depending on the size of your pan. Immediately remove them with a slotted spoon and place in individual, shallow pasta bowls. Spoon the sauce over the ravioli and serve immediately. Parmesan cheese separately.

ADVANCE PREPARATION: The ravioli may be prepared 4 hours in advance through step 3 and refrigerated.

Orzo with Goat Cheese

SERVES 4

Orzo is a tiny almond-shaped pasta that looks a lot like rice. This creamy dish should be made only moments before serving, so it's a good idea to make it for a small, informal dinner party. The goat cheese adds a dimension of pungent flavor beyond the more predictable Parmesan or Romano. Serve this as a first course or as a side dish to Grilled Chicken with Sun-Dried Tomato Paste.

> 3 tablespoons pine nuts
> 2 medium green zucchini, cut into ¼-inch dice
> 2 medium yellow zucchini or crookneck squash, cut into ¼-inch dice
> 2 tablespoons butter
> 1 tablespoon olive oil
> 1 large shallot, finely chopped
> ½ pound mushrooms, cut into ¼-inch dice
> 1 cup orzo
> 2 tablespoons whipping cream
> ¼ pound goat cheese
> ¼ cup Parmesan cheese
> 2 tablespoons finely chopped basil
> Cracked pepper
> Salt

1. Preheat the oven to 350°F. Toast the pine nuts until lightly browned, 5 to 7 minutes. Set aside.
2. Place the zucchini in a clean dish towel and squeeze out as much juice as possible.
3. Heat the butter and olive oil in a medium skillet over medium heat. Add the shallots and sauté until softened, about 3 minutes. Add the zucchini and continue to sauté for about 3 minutes. Add the mushrooms and sauté 2 to 3 more minutes.
4. Cook the orzo in boiling water for 8 to 10 minutes. Drain.
5. In a small saucepan combine the cream and goat cheese over low heat and stir until softened.

6. Combine the sautéed vegetables, orzo, warmed goat cheese, Parmesan cheese, and basil in a serving bowl. Carefully stir in the pine nuts. Add the salt and cracked pepper and taste for seasoning. Toss well and serve immediately.

ADVANCE PREPARATION: The vegetables may be prepared 4 hours in advance through step 3, covered, and kept at room temperature.

Parslied Couscous with Zucchini and Carrots

SERVES 4

Easy, attractive, delicious, and healthy—what more could you want? This dish is also perfect for last-minute entertaining because it takes just a short time to prepare and calls for ingredients that are usually kept on hand. Serve this as an accompaniment to Lamb Chops with Wine-Mint Marinade or Grilled Swordfish with Red Pepper Hollandaise Sauce. Entrées with spicy sauces are complemented nicely by this simple side dish.

    2 medium carrots, peeled and cut into ⅛-inch pieces
    2 medium zucchini, cut into ⅛-inch pieces
    2 tablespoons unsalted butter
    1 cup quick-cooking couscous
    2 tablespoons finely chopped parsley
    ½ teaspoon salt
    ⅛ teaspoon black pepper

1. Heat 1½ cups water in a medium saucepan over medium-high heat until simmering. Add the carrots, cover, and cook

for 2 minutes. Add the zucchini and cook another 2 minutes. Drain the vegetables in a colander and set aside.

2. Heat 1½ cups water and the butter in a medium saucepan over medium heat and bring to a boil. Add the couscous and cover. Remove from the heat and let stand for 5 minutes. Add the carrots, zucchini, parsley, salt, and pepper and toss to combine. Taste for seasoning.

3. *To serve:* Spoon into a serving dish and serve immediately.

ADVANCE PREPARATION: This may be prepared up to 2 hours in advance and kept at room temperature. Reheat it carefully in the top of a double boiler above hot water over medium heat for 10 minutes.

Orzo Vegetable Salad in Saffron Vinaigrette

SERVES 6 TO 8

Combining orzo with cooked green vegetables and the distinctive color and taste of saffron makes a highly unusual pasta salad. Try it with Scallops Brochette with Spicy Caribbean Salsa or Cold Poached Salmon or Grilled Whole Bluefish with Lemon Dill Butter.

Dressing
  ¼ cup red wine vinegar
  ½ teaspoon saffron threads
  2 tablespoons fresh lemon juice
  2 teaspoons Dijon mustard
  1 medium garlic clove, minced
  ½ cup olive oil
  ½ teaspoon salt
  ¼ teaspoon black pepper

  2 cups orzo (about 12 ounces)

1½ cups fresh peas (about 1½ pounds in the shell) or tiny
     frozen peas, defrosted
  ½ pound asparagus, peeled, with ends removed and cut
     into 1½-inch pieces
  2 medium zucchini, cut into 1½-inch pieces
  2 tablespoons freshly grated Parmesan cheese (optional)

Garnish
  2 tablespoons finely chopped parsley

1. *To make the dressing:* Pour the vinegar into a small saucepan.
   Add the saffron threads and bring to a simmer over medium heat. Immediately remove from the heat and cool,
   letting saffron infuse the vinegar.
2. In a medium mixing bowl combine the cooled vinegar and
   saffron, lemon juice, mustard, and garlic. Whisk in the olive
   oil and season with salt and pepper. Taste for seasoning.
3. Bring a large saucepan of salted water to a boil over high
   heat and add the orzo. Cook until the pasta is al dente, 8 to
   10 minutes. Drain and rinse with warm water. Drain well
   and place in a large mixing bowl.
4. Immerse the peas in a large pot of boiling water over high
   heat. Cook for 5 to 8 minutes, depending on their size and
   tenderness. (If using frozen defrosted peas, cook 2 minutes.) Drain and rinse with cold water. Drain well and add
   to the pasta.
5. Place the asparagus pieces in a skillet half filled with boiling

water over high heat. Simmer about 4 minutes, partially covered. Drain and rinse with cold water. Drain well and add to the pasta.

6. Immerse the zucchini in a pot of boiling water over high heat. Cook about 3 minutes. Drain and rinse with cold water. Drain well and add to the pasta.

7. Pour the dressing over the pasta and toss well with 2 large spoons. Add the Parmesan cheese and mix again. Taste for seasoning. Garnish with fresh parsley. Refrigerate until ready to serve.

ADVANCE PREPARATION: This may be prepared completely 8 hours in advance and refrigerated.

Lemon Pasta Salad with Clams and Mussels

SERVES 4 TO 6

This pasta salad has plenty of lemon to accent the shellfish. Instructions are given here for cleaning and poaching the clams and mussels, but if you don't have either the time or the inclination for this process, order shelled clams and mussels from your fish monger or market. Poach 3 to 4 minutes and then cool. Shellfish spoils quickly, so refrigerate it until serving. This is a great late-night supper dish. Minestrone with Pesto Cream is a pleasant beginning.

    3 pounds little neck clams
  1½ pounds medium mussels
    2 shallots, finely chopped
  1½ cups white wine
  1½ cups water

Dressing

    1 medium garlic clove, minced
   ¼ cup fresh lemon juice
   ½ teaspoon salt
   ⅛ teaspoon white pepper
   1 tablespoon whipping cream
   ½ cup olive oil
   ¼ cup finely chopped parsley

   1 tablespoon olive oil
  12 ounces dry linguine

1. Clean the mussels by soaking them in cold water for 15 minutes. Pull the beards away from the shells and brush the mussels vigorously under cold water to remove sand. Place in a bowl of cold water for 15 minutes. Repeat the process, making sure all the sand is washed off. Clean the clams by scrubbing them with a brush under cold water to remove any sand. Make sure that the mussels and clams are tightly closed. Discard any that are open.

2. In a large sauté pan combine the shallots, wine, and water and bring to a boil over medium-high heat. Add the clams and cover. Steam for 3 minutes and then add the mussels and cook another 3 minutes, covered. Both the mussels and clams should be open.

3. Remove the shellfish from the pan with a slotted spoon and let them cool on a large baking sheet. When cool, remove all but 6 of the clams and 6 of the mussels from their shells. (These will be used for a garnish.)

4. *To make the dressing:* Comine the garlic, lemon juice, salt, and pepper in a small mixing bowl. Slowly add the olive oil, whisking constantly, until blended. Add the cream and parsley and taste for seasoning.

5. Add the tablespoon olive oil to a large pot of boiling water. Add the pasta and cook over high heat until al dente, 8 to 10 minutes. Drain well and transfer to a serving bowl. Let

cool. Add the shelled clams and mussels, dressing, and parsley. Toss well. Garnish with the remaining clams and mussels in their shells and refrigerate for at least one hour. Serve chilled.

ADVANCE PREPARATION: This may be prepared 4 hours in advance and refrigerated.

Couscous Salad with Spiced Fruit Vinaigrette

SERVES 6 TO 8

Couscous, the tiny Middle Eastern pasta that is often mistaken for a grain, has come into fashion since the quick-cooking variety has become widely available—it takes only 5 minutes to prepare. Make sure you cut the vegetables into small dice for the most pleasant blend of textures. Lime juice, raspberry vinegar, ginger, and hot pepper add an invigorating zippiness. I like to serve this on a hot summer evening, accompanied by Grilled Turkey in Orange Honey Mustard Sauce. Finish with Fudgy Brownies and French vanilla ice cream.

- 2¼ cups boiling water
- 1 tablespoon olive oil
- 1½ cups quick-cooking couscous

Dressing

- 3 tablespoons raspberry vinegar
- 2 tablespoons fresh lime juice
- 1 teaspoon finely chopped lime zest
- 1 medium garlic clove, minced
- ¼ teaspoon ground ginger
- ¼ teaspoon salt
- ⅛ teaspoon cayenne pepper
- ½ cup plus 2 tablespoons olive oil

3 tablespoons pine nuts (about ½ pound in the shell)
½ cup fresh shelled peas, or frozen tiny peas, defrosted
1 medium yellow crookneck squash, cut into ⅛-inch dice
1 medium zucchini, cut into ⅛-inch dice
1 medium carrot, cut into ⅛-inch dice
1 tablespoon finely chopped Italian parsley

1. Bring the water and olive oil to a boil in a medium saucepan over medium-high heat. Pour the couscous into the pan, remove from the heat, and cover for 5 minutes.
2. The couscous should be plumped and cooked. Using 2 forks, fluff the couscous until no lumps remain. Do this from time to time until the couscous has cooled down. When cool, place in a large serving bowl.
3. *To make the dressing:* Combine the raspberry vinegar, lime juice, lime zest, garlic, ginger, salt, and cayenne pepper in a small mixing bowl. Whisk until well combined. Slowly add the olive oil, whisking constantly until incorporated. Taste for seasoning.
4. Preheat the oven to 350°F. Toast the pine nuts until lightly browned, about 5 minutes. Set aside.
5. Immerse the peas in a medium saucepan of boiling water over high heat. Cook for 5 to 8 minutes, depending on their size and tenderness. (If using defrosted frozen tiny peas, cook 2 minutes.) Drain and rinse with cold water. Drain well and add to the couscous.
6. Add the squash, zucchini, carrots, 1 tablespoon of Italian parsley, and 2 tablespoons of the pine nuts to the couscous. Toss well.
7. Add the dressing to the couscous and toss again thoroughly. Garnish with the remaining parsley and pine nuts.

ADVANCE PREPARATION: This may be prepared 8 hours in advance and refrigerated until ready to serve. Taste for seasoning just before serving.

Salads

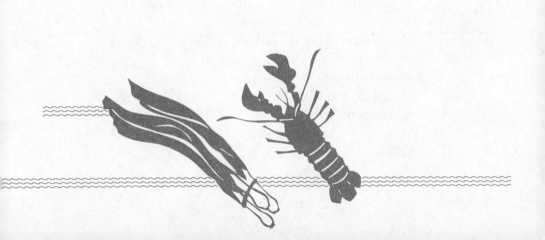

SMALL SALADS

Three Lettuce Salad with Tomato Tarragon Dressing

SERVES 4 TO 6

This first course salad is crisp, colorful, and simple enough to go with a number of entrées. Puréed tomatoes add extra body to the tarragon vinaigrette. For a complete meal serve this before a steaming bowl of Corn Chowder with Red Pepper and hot sourdough French rolls. For dessert, follow with Cherry Amaretti Crisp with Crème Fraîche on the side.

Dressing
- 1 medium shallot
- 1 medium garlic clove
- ½ pound red tomatoes, peeled, seeded, and chopped
- 2 teaspoons Dijon mustard
- 1 tablespoon finely chopped tarragon
- 3 tablespoons white wine vinegar
- ½ cup olive oil
- 1 tablespoon whipping cream
- ½ teaspoon salt
- ¼ teaspoon black pepper

Salad

    1 medium head butter lettuce, torn into bite-size pieces
    1 small head radicchio, torn into bite-size pieces
    4 medium heads Belgian endive
    3 medium carrots, peeled and julienned
    ½ European cucumber, julienned*

    1 medium avocado, peeled and sliced into ¼-inch slices

1. *To make the dressing:* Finely chop the shallot and garlic in a food processor fitted with a steel blade. With the motor running, add the tomatoes and purée. Add the mustard, tarragon, and vinegar and process until well blended.
2. Slowly add the olive oil, processing until completely blended. Add the cream, salt, and pepper. Taste for seasoning.
3. Arrange the butter lettuce and radicchio in a shallow salad bowl. Slice 2 endive stalks into ¼-inch slices and scatter on top of the lettuce. Separate the other endive leaves and arrange along the edge of the bowl.
4. Arrange the cucumber in the center, then surround it with the carrots, creating a colorful circular pattern.
5. When ready to serve, arrange the avocado slices around the outside edge. Pour the dressing over, toss, and serve.

ADVANCE PREPARATION: This can be prepared 4 hours in advance through step 4 and refrigerated until serving. The dressing may be prepared 2 days in advance and refrigerated.

*It is not necessary to peel the thin-skinned European cucumber.

Green Salad with Grapefruit, Baby Beets, and Avocado

SERVES 4 TO 6

This colorful salad, tinged with a rosy pink vinaigrette, is beautiful on a buffet table. It is also lovely served on individual plates for a more formal luncheon or dinner.

Salad

    2 bunches baby beets (about 18)
    1 large head red leaf lettuce, cleaned and torn into bite-size pieces
    2 medium pink grapefruit, peeled, seeds removed, and sectioned
    1 medium avocado, ripe

Dressing

    1 tablespoon fresh orange juice
    2 tablespoons fresh lemon juice
    1 tablespoon plus 1 teaspoon port
    1 tablespoon whipping cream
  ⅓ cup olive oil
  ¼ teaspoon salt
      Black pepper

1. In a medium saucepan bring water to a boil. Immerse the beets and cook until tender but slightly resistant, about 15 minutes. Drain and cool. Peel and reserve.
2. Place the lettuce in a large, shallow salad bowl. Position the baby beets around the outside edge, alternating with the grapefruit sections. In the center create a spokelike pattern with the remaining grapefruit sections.
3. Cut the avocado into ¼-inch slices and place between the grapefruit "spokes." Mound any remaining grapefruit in the center. Refrigerate until ready to serve.
4. *To make the dressing:* Combine the orange juice, lemon juice, port, and cream in a small mixing bowl. Whisk until well

blended. Slowly whisk in the olive oil until completely blended. Add the salt and pepper and taste for seasoning.

5. Pour the dressing over the salad and toss at the table. Serve immediately.

ADVANCE PREPARATION: The salad may be prepared 4 hours in advance through step 2 and refrigerated. The dressing may be made 1 day in advance and refrigerated until 1 hour before serving.

Garden Salad with Goat Cheese Thyme Dressing

SERVES 6 TO 8

The dressing is the unique element of this salad; the goat cheese and coddled eggs conjure up a cross between Roquefort and Caesar dressing. The bite of the fresh thyme leaves offsets the creamy richness of the goat cheese. Follow with Grilled Orange-Cured Salmon and Parslied Couscous with Zucchini and Carrots.

Dressing

  2 medium garlic cloves, minced
  6 tablespoons red wine vinegar
  1 cup plus 3 tablespoons olive oil
  2 large eggs, boiled for one minute
  2 ounces fresh goat cheese
1½ teaspoons finely chopped thyme leaves
 ½ teaspoon salt
 ¼ teaspoon black pepper

Salad

 2 medium heads butter lettuce, cleaned and torn into bite-size pieces
 ½ pound jicama, peeled and julienned or shredded
 2 medium carrots, peeled and julienned or shredded
 12 baby tomatoes, red or yellow or a combination, halved
 2 tablespoons crumbled goat cheese

Garnish
 Fresh thyme leaves (optional)

1. *To make the dressing:* Blend the garlic and vinegar in a blender or food processor fitted with a steel blade. With the motor running, slowly add the olive oil and coddled eggs. Add the goat cheese and process until creamy. Add the thyme, salt, and pepper. Taste for seasoning.
2. Place the butter lettuce on individual salad plates and arrange the vegetables on top in an attractive manner, distributing the cherry tomatoes around the edge. Sprinkle with the crumbled goat cheese.
3. *To serve:* Drizzle the dressing over, toss, and garnish with fresh thyme leaves, if you like.

ADVANCE PREPARATION: This may be prepared 4 hours in advance through step 2 and kept covered in the refrigerator.

NOTE: You may have extra dressing; cover and refrigerate to keep up to 4 days.

Mexican Caesar Salad

SERVES 4 TO 6

Invented in Tijuana, the Caesar Salad has as many variations as guacamole. Although this version relies heavily on its original heritage, I've substituted tortilla chips for garlic croutons. Jicama and diced tomatoes add sweetness. Enjoy this as a prelude to Grilled Mexican Chicken with Citrus Yogurt Sauce and a simple vegetable rice. For dessert I recommend Passion Fruit Caramel Custard.

½ cup safflower oil
1 medium garlic clove, crushed
36 corn tortilla triangles, cut from 6-inch tortillas

Dressing
3 medium garlic cloves, minced
¼ cup fresh lime juice
1 teaspoon anchovy paste
¼ teaspoon black pepper
1 egg
½ cup olive oil
½ cup freshly grated Parmesan cheese

Salad
2 heads romaine lettuce, dark leaves removed, and torn into bite-size pieces
½ pound jicama, peeled and cut into 2-inch julienne

Garnish
½ pound tomatoes, peeled, seeded, and finely chopped

1. In a large skillet, heat the oil over medium-high heat. Add the garlic clove and cook for about 1 minute. Remove the garlic clove and discard.
2. Add the tortilla triangles to the very hot oil and fry until crisp, about 2 minutes. Remove from the oil and drain on paper towels. (If you are making them in advance, place on a baking sheet lined with paper towels.) Reserve.
3. In a large salad bowl, place the garlic, lime juice, anchovy paste, and pepper. Whisk to combine.
4. Immerse the egg for exactly 1 minute in a small pan of boiling water. Remove and crack into the salad bowl. Whisk with the other ingredients until combined. Add the olive oil

in a steady stream, whisking until emulsified. Whisk in ¼ cup Parmesan cheese.

5. Toss with the lettuce, remaining cheese, and crisp tortilla chips (reserving 16 for the garnish). Place on individual plates and garnish the center of each salad with the chopped tomatoes and the remaining tortilla chips. Serve immediately.

ADVANCE PREPARATION: The chips may be prepared 2 hours in advance. After draining the chips, remove the paper towels from the baking sheet. Place the chips in a 225°F oven to keep warm until ready to serve.

VARIATION: Make Crisp Tortilla Chips (see page 281), which use less oil.

String Bean-Golden Pepper Salad

SERVES 4 TO 6

Full of crunchy, sweet vegetables, this salad is terrific for a barbecue menu. The high ratio of citrus to oil in the lemon-mustard dressing adds tang, making this a snappy side dish salad. Serve with Grilled Roast Beef with Sour Cream Herbed Sauce or with Grilled Marinated Chicken with Dijon Mustard, Tarragon, and Port.

Salad
- 1 pound string beans, ends removed
- 1 sweet yellow pepper, seeded and julienned
- ½ pound jicama, peeled and julienned

Dressing
- 1 teaspoon Dijon mustard
- ⅓ cup fresh lemon juice
- 1 teaspoon finely chopped chives
- ⅔ cup olive oil
- ½ teaspoon salt
- ¼ teaspoon black pepper

1. In a medium saucepan bring water to a boil. Immerse the string beans and cook for 7 to 10 minutes, depending on their size. The beans should be slightly crisp. Drain and place in ice water to stop the cooking. Drain well and place in a medium mixing bowl.
2. Add the peppers and jicama.
3. *To make the dressing:* In a small mixing bowl combine the mustard, lemon juice, and chives. Whisk to combine, slowly adding the olive oil until totally emulsified. Add the salt and pepper and taste for seasoning.
4. Combine the dressing with vegetables and thoroughly toss. Taste for seasoning. Refrigerate until ready to serve.

ADVANCE PREPARATION: This may be completely prepared 1 day in advance and refrigerated until serving.

Cherry Tomato and Hearts of Palm Salad

SERVES 6

Only in the summer does a tomato taste like a tomato should. Sweet, ripe tomatoes are combined here with the distinctive taste of hearts of palm, while basil enhances both flavors. I use cherry tomatoes because they're attractive and fit nicely on a fork when halved. A combination of yellow and red cherry or mini-pear tomatoes (if you can find them) make this salad especially colorful. Canned hearts of palm are available in the gourmet department of your supermarket.

> 2 pints cherry tomatoes, halved
> 2 14-ounce cans hearts of palm, drained, thoroughly rinsed, and thinly sliced
> 2 tablespoons finely chopped basil
> 2 tablespoons balsamic vinegar
> 2 tablespoons olive oil
>   Salt
>   White pepper

1. Combine the tomatoes and hearts of palm in a medium mixing bowl. Add the basil, vinegar, olive oil, salt, and pepper and gently combine. Taste for seasoning and refrigerate until ready to serve.

ADVANCE PREPARATION: This may be completely prepared 8 hours in advance and refrigerated. Do not add the chopped basil until just before serving.

Two-Color Coleslaw

SERVES 12 TO 14

You'll love this updated version of an old standard. Mound the green cabbage slaw into the center of the platter and then surround it with a border of the red cabbage slaw. Be sure to drain the cucumber well to avoid adding extra liquid to the salad. The flavor will be best if you prepare this a few hours ahead of serving or even the night before. Serve with Sweet and Hot Spare Ribs with Apricot-Plum Sauce and Baked Beans with Bourbon and Apple Cider.

Dressing

- 2 cups Basic Homemade Mayonnaise (see page 344)
- ¾ cup cider vinegar
- 2 tablespoons fresh lemon juice
- 6 tablespoons sugar
- ½ teaspoon salt
- ¼ teaspoon white pepper

Salad

- 1 medium green cabbage, finely shredded
- 4 medium carrots, peeled and finely shredded
- 1 medium bunch radishes, finely shredded
- 1 large European cucumber, shredded and well drained in a colander to remove excess liquid*
- 1 medium sweet red pepper, seeded and shredded
- 1 large Granny Smith apple, peeled, cored, and shredded

- ½ cup finely chopped parsley
- 1 medium red cabbage, finely shredded
- 2 tablespoons finely chopped fresh dill
- ¼ cup finely chopped red onion

Garnish

- 2 tablespoons finely chopped parsley

1. Combine all the dressing ingredients in small nonaluminum mixing bowl and whisk to blend. Set aside.

2. Combine the green cabbage, carrots, radishes, cucumber, red pepper, apple, and ¼ cup parsley in a large bowl.
3. Toss with enough dressing to moisten well. Taste for seasoning.
4. Combine the red cabbage, ¼ cup parsley, dill, and red onion and toss with enough dressing to moisten in a separate medium bowl.
5. Mound the green cabbage in the center of a large shallow serving bowl. Surround it with the red cabbage, mounded attractively. Sprinkle with the remaining parsley to garnish.

ADVANCE PREPARATION: This may be completely prepared 1 day in advance and refrigerated. Taste for seasoning before serving.

*It is not necessary to peel the thin-skinned European cucumber.

Green Bean, Mushroom, and Walnut Salad

SERVES 4 TO 6

This is excellent with cold chicken or beef—or as an extra side dish with Whole Poached Salmon with Pesto-Cucumber Sauce and Red Potato Salad with Celery Seed.

Salad
½ cup coarsely chopped walnuts
1 pound green beans, cut into 1½-inch pieces
1 tablespoon walnut oil
1 tablespoon olive oil
½ pound medium-size mushrooms, stemmed and cut into 1½-inch julienne

Dressing

    1 teaspoon Dijon mustard
    2 tablespoons red wine vinegar
    1 teaspoon whipping cream
   ¼ teaspoon salt
   ⅛ teaspoon white pepper
   ¼ cup walnut oil
    2 tablespoons olive oil

1. Preheat the oven to 350°F. Place the walnuts on a baking sheet and toast until lightly brown, 5 to 7 minutes. Cool.
2. In a medium saucepan bring water to a boil. Immerse the green beans and cook until crisp-tender, 5 to 7 minutes. Drain and place in cold water to stop the cooking. Drain well and transfer to a medium mixing bowl.
3. Heat the walnut oil and olive oil in a medium skillet over medium heat. Add the mushrooms and sauté about 3 minutes, stirring to cook evenly. Remove them with a slotted spoon and place in the bowl with the green beans.
4. *To make the dressing:* In a small mixing bowl, whisk together the mustard, vinegar, cream, salt, and pepper until well combined. Slowly add the oils, whisking constantly until emulsified. Taste for seasoning.
5. When ready to serve, add all but 1 tablespoon of the walnuts to the green beans and mushrooms. Pour the dressing over and toss to combine. Taste for seasoning. Place in a serving bowl and garnish with the remaining walnuts.

ADVANCE PREPARATION: This may be prepared 8 hours in advance through step 4. Refrigerate the beans and mushrooms.

NOTE: This salad may be served as a side dish or as a first course. Use red leaf lettuce to garnish the individual serving plates if serving as a first course.

Sugar Snap Pea and Carrot Salad with Tomato Mint Dressing

SERVES 4 TO 6

A quick and easy side dish salad with plenty of zest, this can be served with a simple grilled or roasted chicken dish. It's also perfect picnic food to accompany sandwiches.

Dressing

⅓ cup olive oil
1 medium shallot, finely chopped
3 tablespoons fresh lime juice
½ teaspoon salt
½ teaspoon black pepper
1 medium tomato, peeled, seeded, and finely chopped
2 tablespoons fresh mint, finely chopped

Salad

4 medium carrots, peeled and cut into 1½-inch long strips (the same size as the sugar snap peas)
1 pound sugar snap peas, cleaned and trimmed

Garnish

Fresh mint leaves

1. *To make the dressing:* In a medium skillet, heat the olive oil over medium heat. Sauté shallot until soft, about 2 minutes. Add the lime juice, salt, and black pepper. Reduce the heat and add the tomato and mint. Remove from the heat and set aside.
2. In a medium pan of boiling water, immerse the carrots and cook for about 3 minutes. Drain and place in cold water to stop the cooking. Drain well and set aside.
3. In a medium pan of boiling water, immerse the sugar snap peas and cook for about 3 minutes. Drain and place in cold water to stop the cooking. Drain again and set aside.
4. Place both the carrots and peas in a medium serving bowl.

Pour the vinaigrette over and toss until the dressing is well distributed. Taste for seasoning. Refrigerate until ready to serve.

ADVANCE PREPARATION: This may be prepared 8 hours in advance and refrigerated.

Red Potato Salad with Celery Seed

SERVES 6 TO 8

The red skins are left on the potatoes in this salad for extra color and texture. Celery seed and fresh celery add freshness and crispness, as well as a counterpoint for the tangy chives. This salad is perfect with cold roasted chicken.

3 pounds medium red-skinned potatoes

Dressing
¾ cup sour cream
¾ cup Basic Homemade Mayonnaise (see page 344)
2 celery stalks, finely diced
1 tablespoon celery seed
2 tablespoons chopped chives
1 teaspoon dried mustard
½ teaspoon salt
¼ teaspoon white pepper
¼ cup chopped parsley

Garnish
1 tablespoon chopped parsley
1 tablespoon finely chopped chives

1. In a large pot of boiling water, cook the potatoes until tender but slightly resistant when pierced with a fork, about

30 minutes. Drain and cool, but do not peel. When cool, cut into 1½-inch pieces and place in a medium bowl.

2. In a small bowl, combine the sour cream, mayonnaise, celery, celery seed, chives, mustard, salt, pepper, and parsley. Mix well.

3. Pour the mixture over the potatoes and toss gently until evenly coated. Taste for seasoning. Refrigerate 1 to 2 hours.

4. Transfer the salad to a serving bowl and garnish with parsley and chives. Serve cold.

ADVANCE PREPARATION: This may be prepared 1 day in advance through step 3 and refrigerated. Taste for seasoning before serving.

Potato Salad Niçoise

SERVES 6 TO 8

The creamy Italian tuna sauce called tonnato *is usually paired with veal, chicken, or turkey. In this variation,* tonnato *sauce, with a hint of anchovy, dresses the cold potato wedges and crisp tender green beans. This is a filling potato salad that can be served on a picnic with various cold meats and cheeses and sliced red tomatoes.*

    3 **pounds medium red-skinned potatoes**
    1 **pound green beans, cleaned and cut into 1-inch pieces**

Dressing
    1 **cup Basic Homemade Mayonnaise (see page 344)**
  ¼ **cup sour cream**
    1 **6½-ounce can white meat tuna, drained**
    3 **tablespoons fresh lemon juice**
    2 **teaspoons anchovy paste**
  ¼ **teaspoon white pepper**

Garnish
   Niçoise olives, well drained
   Capers, rinsed and well drained

1. In a large pot of boiling water, cook the potatoes until tender but slightly resistant when pierced with a fork, 20 to 30 minutes. Drain and cool. When cool, cut into 1½-inch pieces and place in a medium bowl.
2. In a medium saucepan of boiling water immerse the green beans and cook until crisp-tender, 5 to 7 minutes. Drain and place in cold water to stop the cooking. Drain well and place in the bowl with the potatoes.
3. Place all the ingredients for the dressing in a blender or food processor fitted with a steel blade, and process until creamy.
4. Pour the dressing over the potatoes and green beans and toss gently until they are evenly coated. Taste for seasoning. Refrigerate 1 to 2 hours.
5. Transfer the salad to a serving bowl or a deep dish and garnish with the olives and capers.

ADVANCE PREPARATION: This may be prepared 8 hours in advance through step 4 and refrigerated. Garnish it just before serving.

Wild Rice Salad with Carrots and Oranges

SERVES 4 TO 6

Wild rice is often thought of as a Thanksgiving or holiday-season side dish, but it's also great as a cold salad. Combining wild rice with long-grain white rice makes it light and fluffy. Serve this on a buffet table along with other cold salads or as an accompaniment to simple grilled chicken or duck.

Salad

    ½ cup wild rice
  2¾ cups water
    1 teaspoon salt
    ½ cup long-grain white rice
    3 medium Valencia oranges
    2 medium carrots, grated

Lime Juice Vinaigrette

    ¼ cup fresh lime juice
    1 teaspoon salt
    ¼ teaspoon black pepper
    1 teaspoon finely chopped chives
    1 tablespoon finely chopped parsley
    ½ cup safflower oil

1. Rinse the wild rice thoroughly with cold water in a strainer. Drain. Combine the wild rice, 1½ cups of the water, and salt in a medium saucepan. Cover and bring to a boil. Cook over low heat until the rice is tender, about 30 minutes. Cool completely.
2. Bring to a boil the white rice and 1¼ cups of water in a medium saucepan over medium-high heat. Cover, reduce the heat, and simmer 20 minutes. Cool completely.
3. Peel the 2 oranges, remove the white pith, and separate into sections. Cut them into ¾-inch pieces.
4. *To make the vinaigrette:* Combine the lime juice, salt, pepper, chives, and parsley in a small mixing bowl. Slowly add the oil, whisking until blended. Taste for seasoning.
5. Gently mix the wild rice and white rice with the carrots and orange sections. Add just enough vinaigrette to moisten. Taste for seasoning. Chill 1 to 2 hours to allow the flavors to blend.
6. Flute the peel of the remaining orange with a citrus stripper. Halve the orange lengthwise and cut each half into thin

crosswise slices. The orange slices will have a flower-like design.

7. Place the salad in a serving bowl or on a platter and surround with the orange slices to garnish. Serve chilled or at room temperature.

ADVANCE PREPARATION: This may be prepared 8 hours in advance through step 5 and refrigerated.

Cracked Wheat Vegetable Salad

SERVES 6

This is a variation on Tabouli, the Middle-Eastern cracked wheat salad made with lots of olive oil, lemon, mint, tomato, and parsley. In this version, cilantro replaces parsley and instead of tomatoes we have raw corn, chopped cucumber, and radishes. Summer corn is so sweet and tender that you don't need to cook it for this recipe. Be sure to buy medium *cracked wheat, also called bulgar. This makes an excellent presentation when served with Pork Tenderloin with Apricot-Bourbon Sauce. Place the Cracked Wheat Vegetable Salad in a mound in the middle of a platter, surround it with overlapping slices of Pork Tenderloin topped with Apricot-Bourbon Sauce.*

Salad

1½ cups medium cracked wheat
2½ cups boiling water
½ cup finely chopped red onion
½ cup finely diced European cucumber*
¾ cup finely diced radishes
¾ cup peeled and finely diced carrots
¾ cup fresh corn kernels (about 1 large ear)
2 tablespoons finely chopped parsley
2 tablespoons finely chopped chives
3 tablespoons finely chopped cilantro

Dressing

½ cup Summer Vinaigrette (see page 340)
2 tablespoons fresh lemon juice
1 teaspoon salt
¼ teaspoon coarse black pepper

Garnish

Whole cilantro leaves

1. Pour boiling water over the cracked wheat in a medium mixing bowl and let the wheat absorb the water. (This should take about 1 hour.)
2. Drain the wheat in a colander. Place in a dry tea towel and wring out any excess liquid. Place in a mixing bowl.
3. Add the red onion, cucumber, radishes, carrots, and corn. Mix with a two-pronged fork to keep the wheat fluffy. Add the chives, parsley, and cilantro.
4. *To make the dressing:* In a medium bowl, thoroughly whisk all the dressing ingredients together.
5. Pour the dressing over the wheat mixture and toss with two forks. Taste for seasoning. Place in a serving bowl and garnish with the cilantro leaves.

ADVANCE PREPARATION: This may be prepared 8 hours ahead and refrigerated.

*It is not necessary to peel the thin-skinned European cucumber.

Marinated Lentil Salad

SERVES 4 TO 6

I usually think of lentils when winter comes around and I want a thick bowl of comforting, hearty soup. But lentils make an excellent summertime dish as well. When simmered in chicken stock and combined with a variety of colorful, crunchy vegetables, lentils make a tasty salad with a refreshing bite. Good picnic fare—or serve before Grilled Chicken with Citrus Ginger Butter and Grilled Vegetable Brochettes.

1 cup dried lentils
2 cups chicken stock (see page 366)
4 tablespoons olive oil
1 medium red onion, finely chopped
1 medium celery stalk, finely cut into ¼-inch dice
1 medium carrot, peeled and finely cut into ¼-inch dice
½ small sweet red pepper, seeded and finely cut into ¼-inch dice
2 tablespoons red wine vinegar
1 tablespoon fresh lemon juice
1 tablespoon finely chopped chives
1 tablespoon finely chopped basil leaves
½ teaspoon salt
¼ teaspoon pepper
½ cup fresh mozzarella cheese, cut into ¼-inch dice

Garnish
1 head butter lettuce, cleaned and torn into small pieces

1. Soak the lentils overnight in cold water; or do a quick soak by bringing them to a boil in water to cover, boiling 2 minutes, covering, and letting them stand 1 hour.
2. Drain and put the soaked lentils into a medium saucepan. Add the chicken stock and bring to a boil. Let simmer 10 to 15 minutes, partially covered, until tender but not mushy. Drain and cool.
3. In a medium skillet heat 2 tablespoons olive oil over medium heat. Sauté the onion until soft, about 3 minutes. Add the

celery and carrots and continue cooking for about 5 minutes. Add the red pepper and cook for 2 more minutes.

4. Combine the lentils with the vegetables in a medium mixing bowl. Add the remaining olive oil, vinegar, lemon juice, chives, basil, salt, pepper, and cheese and mix well. Taste for seasoning.

5. Serve on a bed of lettuce arranged on a serving platter.

ADVANCE PREPARATION: This may be prepared 2 days in advance and refrigerated. You may need to add additional oil and vinegar or lemon juice to moisten the vegetables.

VARIATION: Other cheeses, such as goat cheese, sharp Cheddar, or Muenster, may be substituted for the mozzarella.

Salad of Peaches and Gorgonzola

SERVES 6

This salad is a particular favorite of mine. Gorgonzola, the bold, creamy Italian blue cheese, is a perfect foil for marinated peaches. The citrus and hazelnut oil dressing adds just the right touch to keep the peaches from being too sweet. Toasted hazelnuts add textural contrast. Enjoy this as a fruit and cheese course before dessert. It's terrific after Grilled Lamb Chops with Wine-Mint Marinade.

Dressing
>   Juice of 2 limes
>   Juice of 1 small orange
> ¼   cup hazelnut oil
> ½   teaspoon salt
> ⅛   teaspoon white pepper

Salad

> ¼ cup sliced or chopped hazelnuts
> 4 medium peaches
> 1 head red leaf lettuce, cleaned and separated into leaves
> 3 ounces Gorgonzola

1. *To make the dressing:* In a small bowl combine the lime and orange juices. Slowly whisk in the hazelnut oil until incorporated. Add the salt and pepper and taste for seasoning.
2. Preheat the oven to 350°F. Toast the hazelnuts until lightly browned, 3 to 5 minutes.
3. In a large saucepan bring water to a boil. Immerse the peaches for about 20 seconds and remove immediately. Peel and cut into ¼-inch slices.
4. In a medium mixing bowl combine the dressing and the peaches and marinate for about 10 minutes.
5. Distribute the lettuce leaves on individual salad or dessert plates. Arrange the peach slices in a spoke or flower design on the lettuce leaves. Drizzle the remaining dressing over. Sprinkle the peaches with crumbled Gorgonzola and then the toasted hazelnuts. Serve immediately.

ADVANCE PREPARATION: This may be prepared 8 hours in advance through step 2 and kept at room temperature.

MAIN DISH SALADS

Warm Spinach Salad with Pancetta

SERVES 4

Dark green spinach leaves, mahogany pancetta, and bright yellow egg yolks are composed into a dazzling salad. The sherry vinegar dressing adds a subtle finesse. I use only baby spinach leaves because they are tender and flavorful. Pancetta is an Italian bacon that is cured rather than smoked and has a spicier taste than regular bacon. Substitute regular bacon if pancetta is unavailable. If you cook the eggs in the manner described, the yolks will stay moist and bright yellow. Start with Curried Corn Soup and serve melon slices for dessert.

Salad

 2 medium bunches baby spinach leaves, cleaned,
   stemmed, well dried, and torn into bite-size pieces
 ½ pound pancetta, cut into 1-inch pieces
 4 large eggs

Dressing

 6 tablespoons olive oil
 2 medium shallots, finely chopped
 3 tablespoons sherry wine vinegar
 ⅛ teaspoon coarsely cracked black pepper

1. Place the spinach leaves in a large salad bowl and set aside.
2. Cook the pancetta over medium-low heat in a medium
   skillet until crisp and lightly browned. Remove and place on
   paper towels to drain. Leave 1 tablespoon of the pancetta
   drippings in the skillet.
3. Place the eggs in a medium saucepan and cover by 2 inches
   with cold water. Bring the eggs to a rolling boil over high
   heat. When they start to boil, immediately remove from the
   heat, cover, and let rest for 12 minutes. Cool the eggs under
   cold water.
4. In the same skillet add the olive oil to the pancetta drippings over medium heat. Add the shallots and sauté until
   just softened, about 2 minutes. Add the vinegar and pepper
   and boil for another minute. Taste for seasoning.
5. Pour the hot dressing over the spinach and toss to completely coat the leaves. Add ¾ of the pancetta and toss
   again.
6. Arrange the spinach and bacon mixture on serving plates.
   Peel and quarter the eggs lengthwise. Position the egg quarters along the edges of the plates. Garnish with the remaining pancetta. Serve immediately.

Cold Lobster Salad with Caviar-Dill Mayonnaise

SERVES 4

In this elegant salad, sweet lobster is dressed with a lemony mayonnaise and decorated with sprigs of dill and bright orange salmon caviar. This beautiful dish is the one to serve for a truly special occasion—it's not only extravagant but memorably delicious. Start with Golden Summer Soup and accompany the salad with Crispy Pita Triangles. For dessert serve Apricot Mousse, Frozen Peaches and Cream, or Poached Peaches in White Zinfandel with Fresh Raspberry Sauce.

RECOMMENDED WINE: Serve with Champagne.

   2 1½ pound lobsters, boiled or steamed, chilled

Dressing
  ⅔ cup mayonnaise
  ¼ cup fresh lemon juice
  3 tablespoons finely chopped dill
  ¼ teaspoon salt
  ¼ teaspoon white pepper
  ¼ cup salmon caviar

Garnish
  2 tablespoons salmon caviar
    Dill sprigs

1. Split the lobsters in half. With a small knife, carefully separate the meat from the shell. Try to keep the shell intact.
2. Cut the lobster meat into 1-inch pieces and place in a medium mixing bowl.
3. In a small mixing bowl combine the mayonnaise, lemon juice, dill, salt, and pepper and mix to combine. Gently stir in the caviar, being careful not to break the caviar. Taste for seasoning. Pour just enough dressing over the lobster to

moisten it well and toss. Cover the lobster and the dressing
and refrigerate until ready to serve.

4. Right before serving, mound one quarter of the lobster
   mixture in each lobster shell. Spoon a dollop of the remaining caviar mayonnaise on top and garnish with a large
   spoonful of salmon caviar and a dill sprig. Serve immediately.

ADVANCE PREPARATION: This may be prepared through
step 3 up to 2 hours ahead and refrigerated. Keep the lobster
tail shells well wrapped in the refrigerator until ready to assemble the dish.

VARIATION: The lobster salad may be placed on a bed of
mixed greens that have been lightly dressed with Summer
Vinaigrette (see page 340).

Cold Lobster Salad with Caviar-Dill Mayonnaise

HOW TO COOK A LOBSTER

If your lobster-cooking experience matches the lobster scene in *Annie Hall,* take heart; it's really not that difficult. Here are a few tips to make your lobsters extra-delicious.

- Choose the biggest, feistiest lobsters you can find— active lobsters are fresher and sweeter.
- If you have seawater at hand, use that instead of fresh water to cook the lobsters.

To cook live lobsters:

1. Fill a 16-quart pot ⅔ full of fresh or sea water. Add some lemon slices, lemon juice, and peppercorns and bring it to a rapid boil.

2. Place the live lobsters in the pot, cover it, and cook for about 10 minutes (for 2-pound lobsters).

3. Remove the lobsters and let them cool slightly. With poultry shears, cut the shells in half lengthwise and divide the lobsters in two. Remove the stomach sacs.

- Serve them hot with an herbed garlic butter or chilled with a chervil or dill vinaigrette.

Warm Grilled Chicken Salad with Lemon Mustard Dressing

SERVES 6 TO 8

Warm chicken salads are always greeted with enthusiasm. Here, marinated chicken is grilled, then placed on cooked green beans and a mixture of raw carrots, jicama, and mushrooms, all of which rests on a bed of lettuce. Toasted pine nuts are scattered on top. This is especially nice for an outdoor concert. Prepare the chicken just before leaving home and cover with foil; it will stay warm for up to an hour. Dress the salad just before serving. Start with Goat Cheese and Pesto Torta with Hazelnuts and Minted Chinese Pea Pod Soup. If it's a hot evening, try Creamy Gazpacho or Avocado Soup with Tomato Cucumber Salsa. For dessert enjoy freshly baked Blueberry Nectarine Buckle.

RECOMMENDED WINE: Serve a medium weight Chardonnay or a fresh, young Soave.

¼ cup pine nuts

Dressing
- ⅔ cup fresh lemon juice
- 2 tablespoons grainy mustard
- 2 tablespoons finely chopped chives
- 1⅓ cups olive oil
- Salt
- White pepper

- 4 medium whole chicken breasts, boned, halved, and skinned
- ½ pound green beans, cut into 1½-inch pieces
- 2 heads romaine lettuce, light green and white part only, torn into bite-size pieces
- 4 endive, cleaned and thinly sliced
- 3 medium carrots, peeled and shredded
- ½ pound jicama, peeled and julienned
- ¼ pound mushrooms, thinly sliced

1. Preheat the oven to 350°F. Toast the pine nuts until lightly brown, 5 to 7 minutes. Watch carefully.

2. *To make the dressing:* Mix the lemon juice, mustard, and chives together. Slowly whisk in the olive oil until blended. Add the salt and pepper and taste for seasoning.

3. Place the chicken breasts in a large, shallow, nonaluminum dish and pour half of the dressing over. Marinate for at least half an hour or up to 4 hours.

4. Cook the green beans in a large saucepan of boiling water 7 to 10 minutes, depending on their size. The beans should be crisp-tender. Drain and place in cold water to stop the cooking. Drain and chill until ready to prepare the salad.

5. Place the salad greens and endive in a large salad bowl. Arrange the green beans, carrots, jicama, and mushrooms on top.

6. Prepare the barbecue for medium-heat grilling. Grill the chicken breasts 6 to 8 minutes, depending on their thickness. Remove and carve them on the diagonal into ½-inch slices.

7. *To serve:* Arrange the warm strips of chicken on top of the salad. Scatter the pine nuts on top, pour enough dressing over to moisten, toss, and serve. Serve the remaining dressing on the side.

ADVANCE PREPARATION: This may be prepared 6 hours in advance through step 5 and refrigerated until ready to grill the chicken breasts.

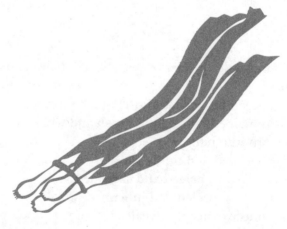

Chicken Salad with Roasted Garlic Mayonnaise

SERVES 4 TO 6

The Roasted Garlic Mayonnaise adds a sweet, mild pungency to this main course chicken salad. Toasted almonds and crisp broccoli give it extra texture. Begin with Golden Summer Soup and serve Toasted Pita with Parmesan with the salad. For dessert have Lemon Orange Sponge Pudding.

RECOMMENDED WINE: A big, oaky Chardonnay works well with this dish, or try a Pinot Noir or a slightly chilled Beaujolais.

½ cup thinly sliced almonds
3 cups chicken stock (optional) (see page 366)
2 pounds boned chicken breasts (about 2 large whole breasts)
1 pound broccoli, cut into flowerets, the top part of the stalk cut into 1½-inch pieces
2 tablespoons finely chopped scallions or chives
1 cup Roasted Garlic Mayonnaise (see page 345)
½ teaspoon salt
Pinch white pepper

Garnish
1 roasted sweet red pepper, thinly sliced (see page 362)

1. Preheat the oven to 350°F. Toast the almonds until lightly browned, about 5 minutes. Set aside.
2. In a medium skillet with high sides or a large saucepan, bring the chicken stock or enough of a combination of chicken stock and water to cover chicken to a simmer. If using water only, add ½ teaspoon salt.
3. Add the chicken breasts and simmer just until tender, 10 to 12 minutes. Cool the chicken in the liquid. Drain, remove

the skin, and cut into 1½-inch chunks. Place in a large mixing bowl.

4. Immerse the broccoli in boiling water and simmer until crisp-tender, 7 to 10 minutes. Remove from the heat and pour into a colander. Run cold water over the broccoli to stop the cooking. Drain and add to the chicken.

5. Combine the scallions and mayonnaise with the chicken and broccoli and toss.

6. Add the salt and pepper and taste for seasoning. Refrigerate for at least 2 hours.

7. Just before serving, carefully add all but 2 tablespoons of the toasted almonds, tossing until just mixed. Garnish with the red pepper slices and the remaining 2 tablespoons of almonds.

ADVANCE PREPARATION: This may be prepared 1 day in advance through step 6 and refrigerated until ready to serve. Taste for seasoning before serving.

Chicken Salad Niçoise

SERVES 6 TO 8

Classic salad Niçoise is made with tuna, but I prefer the lighter taste of chicken. A hearty combination of flavors, colors, and textures, this salad is an excellent main dish for lunch, dinner, or a late-night supper. Start with Goat Cheese and Pesto Torta with Hazelnuts and then serve Creamy Gazpacho. French or Italian country bread goes nicely with the salad, followed by Strawberry Shortcake with Raspberry Custard Sauce.

RECOMMENDED WINE: A big oaky Chardonnay or a slightly chilled Beaujolais goes well with this salad.

161

3 cups chicken stock (optional) (see page 366)
3 medium whole chicken breasts, boned
1 pound red-skinned potatoes
½ cup green beans, cleaned and cut into 1½-inch pieces
2 medium carrots, peeled and julienned
1 small sweet red pepper, seeded and julienned
½ cup Niçoise olives, drained and stemmed
1 small red onion, thinly sliced and cut into 1½-inch pieces
2 tablespoons capers, drained
2 tablespoons finely chopped chervil or basil
¼ teaspoon black pepper

Dressing
2 medium cloves garlic, minced
2 teaspoons Dijon mustard
2 tablespoons finely chopped chervil or basil
⅔ cup fresh lemon juice
1 cup extra virgin olive oil

½ teaspoon salt
¼ teaspoon pepper

Garnish
3 hard-cooked eggs, quartered
2 small tomatoes, sliced into sixths
Chervil sprigs or basil leaves and flowers

1. In a medium skillet with high sides or a large saucepan, bring enough chicken stock or a combination of chicken stock and water to cover the chicken to a simmer. If using water only, add ½ teaspoon salt.
2. Add the chicken breasts and simmer just until tender, 10 to 12 minutes.
3. Remove from the heat and cool the chicken in the liquid. Drain and remove the skin. Shred the chicken by tearing into long, thin pieces. Reserve in a large bowl.

4. In a large pot of boiling water, cook the potatoes until tender but slightly resistant when pierced with a fork, 20 to 30 minutes. Drain and cool. When cool, peel and cut into julienne slices. Place in the bowl with the chicken.

5. In a medium saucepan bring water to a boil. Immerse the green beans and cook until tender but slightly resistant, 5 to 7 minutes. Drain and place in ice water to stop the cooking. When cool, drain well and place in the bowl with the chicken and potatoes.

6. Add the carrots, red pepper, olives, red onion, capers, chervil or basil, and black pepper to the chicken and toss to combine.

7. *To make the dressing:* In a small bowl combine the garlic, mustard, chervil or basil, and lemon juice. Slowly whisk in the olive oil until thoroughly combined. Add the salt and pepper and taste for seasoning.

8. When ready to serve, use just enough dressing to moisten the salad. Toss carefully to combine, making sure not to break up the capers. Taste for seasoning.

9. Mound the salad high in a large, shallow bowl. Alternate the egg wedges and tomato wedges around the outside edge. Garnish with chervil sprigs or basil leaves and serve. Serve extra dressing on the side.

ADVANCE PREPARATION: This salad may be prepared through step 6 up to 6 hours ahead. Refrigerate the salad with the potatoes at the bottom of the bowl. The dressing may be left at room temperature. The salad may be made completely ahead, including the garnish, up to 2 hours before serving. Cover well and refrigerate.

VINAIGRETTES

These splendid salad dressings are not just for salads. You can also use them to dress grilled or steamed vegetables or grilled chicken, fish, or meat—a particularly appealing idea when you want a sauce but don't want to cook.

A successful vinaigrette depends upon excellent ingredients, the correct ratio of oil to vinegar, and the complete emulsification of the two. I prefer a ratio of three parts oil to one part vinegar. I use my food processor to make vinaigrette because it creates an emulsion that will last at least a few hours. If you don't have a food processor, put the ingredients in a small lidded jar and shake vigorously to emulsify. Vinaigrette will keep in the refrigerator for months. Just bring it to room temperature before using and re-emulsify.

There is an enormous variety of excellent oils and vinegars available that allow you to be really creative. Keep on hand extra virgin olive oil, safflower oil, aged sherry wine vinegar, tarragon vinegar, a quality red wine vinegar, and balsamic vinegar. Avocado oil, champagne vinegar, and raspberry vinegar make interesting alternatives. Hazelnut oil and walnut oil should be used sparingly because their flavors are very intense; I recommend using half nut oil and half olive oil. Almost all vinaigrettes should include a minced shallot and a garlic clove. Dijon mustard is another excellent flavor enhancer. Finally, I like to add just a touch of cream to smooth out the acid in the vinegar for a milder vinaigrette.

Here are some other combinations you might like to try:

- Red onion vinaigrette
- Tomato basil vinaigrette
- Chervil, dill, or burnet vinaigrette
- Tomato-mint vinaigrette
- Hazelnut or walnut vinaigrette
- Balsamic vinaigrette
- Sherry vinaigrette
- Chopped olive vinaigrette
- Roasted chile vinaigrette
- Red or green pepper vinaigrette

Thai Chicken Salad

I can never get enough of chicken salad and am always experimenting with different combinations. Here's an exotic one. A slightly sweet and hot dressing is added to the shredded chicken, vegetables, and rich, roasted peanuts. Fresh apricots are the secret ingredient that add just a touch of fruitiness. Since the season for fresh apricots is very short, you can either substitute dried diced apricots or just omit them—it's good even without the secret ingredient. Start with Curried Corn Soup. Warm French or pita bread makes a nice accompaniment.

RECOMMENDED WINE: Serve a big, oaky Chardonnay or a spicy, young Zinfandel, slightly chilled.

Dressing
- ¼ cup soy sauce
- ¼ cup rice wine vinegar
- 2 tablespoons fresh orange juice
- 2 tablespoons honey
- 2 tablespoons Hot Pepper Oil (see page 367)
- ¼ cup dark sesame oil

- 3 cups chicken stock (optional) (see page 366)
- 4 medium whole chicken breasts, boned
- 2 large carrots, peeled and thinly julienned
- 1 medium summer squash, thinly julienned
- 1 large zucchini, thinly julienned
- ½ cup roasted and salted peanuts
- ½ cup thinly sliced fresh apricots (about 4) or ½ cup diced dried apricots
- 3 scallions, thinly sliced (about ½ cup)

1. *To make the dressing:* Whisk together thoroughly all the dressing ingredients except the oils. Slowly whisk in the oils until combined. Set aside.
2. In a medium skillet with high sides or in a large saucepan, bring the chicken stock or enough of a combination of

chicken stock and water to cover the chicken to a simmer. If using water only, add ½ teaspoon salt.

3. Add the chicken breasts and simmer just until tender, 10 to 12 minutes.

4. Cool the chicken in liquid. Drain and remove the skin. Shred by tearing the meat into long, thin pieces (you may also shred it with a knife). Reserve in a medium serving bowl.

5. Add the carrots, summer squash, zucchini, all but 1 tablespoon of the peanuts, apricots, and scallions to the chicken.

6. Pour the dressing over and toss until all the ingredients are well coated. Garnish with the remaining peanuts.

ADVANCE PREPARATION: This may be prepared 4 hours in advance through step 4 and refrigerated until serving.

Thai Chicken Salad

Main Dishes

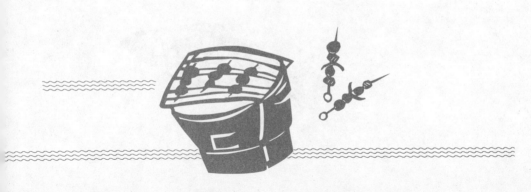

SEAFOOD

Grilled Sea Bass with California Salsa

SERVES 4

There are many varieties of sea bass. For this dish I recommend either Mexican sea bass or the richer Chilean sea bass. The mild salsa that tops this fish is an example of California simplicity at its best—fresh ingredients are quickly combined for an unbeatable natural taste. Vegetable Lemon Rice is an excellent accompaniment.

RECOMMENDED WINE: The salsa on this sea bass does well with a crisp, fruity Sauvignon Blanc or a dry Alsatian wine.

Sauce

   2 tablespoons olive oil
   2 medium shallots, finely chopped
  ¼ pound medium mushrooms, sliced
  ½ large sweet red pepper, seeded and cut into ½-inch dice
  ½ large sweet yellow pepper, seeded and cut into ½-inch dice
  4 ripe plum (Roma) tomatoes, peeled, seeded, and coarsely chopped
  ¼ cup white wine
  1 teaspoon freshly chopped fresh thyme leaves
  ¼ teaspoon salt
  ⅛ teaspoon white pepper

  2 pounds sea bass (preferably Chilean) fillets, whole or cut into four ½-pound pieces

Garnish

   Fresh parsley

1. In a medium skillet heat the olive oil over medium heat.
2. Add the shallots and sauté until softened, about 3 minutes.
3. Add the mushrooms and sauté 3 more minutes.
4. Add the diced peppers, tomatoes, wine, thyme, salt, and pepper. Turn up the heat to medium-high for about 5 minutes and let the sauce thicken. Taste for seasoning.
5. *To grill*: Prepare the barbecue for medium-heat grilling. Grill the fish about 3 inches from the flame 5 to 7 minutes on each side or until desired doneness.
6. *To serve*: Arrange the fish on individual plates. Spoon the sauce over the fish and garnish with the parsley. Serve immediately.

ADVANCE PREPARATION: The sauce may be prepared 6 hours in advance and refrigerated. Reheat the sauce gently.

Roasted Sea Bass with Herbs

SERVES 4

This simple dish is prepared at Antoine's, the elegant restaurant at the Meridien Hotel in Newport Beach, California. This is a lighter version, in which I've substituted olive oil for the melted butter. If you are lucky enough to have your own herb garden, use your favorite combination of just-picked herbs to mix into the bread crumb coating. Serve this with Ratatouille Gratinée and White Chocolate Terrine with Strawberries and Praline for dessert. If you serve the sea bass with a simple vegetable, accompany it with Tomato-Béarnaise Sauce.

RECOMMENDED WINE: A crisp, steely North Coast Sauvignon Blanc is ideal with this well-herbed dish.

> 4 ½-pound center pieces sea bass, about 1½-inches thick
> 2 tablespoons olive oil
> ½ cup bread crumbs
> ¼ cup minced parsley
> 2 tablespoons minced chives
> 1 tablespoon minced fresh thyme
> 2 tablespoons minced basil
> ¼ teaspoon salt
>   Pinch white pepper

1. Combine the bread crumbs, herbs, salt, and pepper; mix well.
2. Place the fish pieces on wax paper.
3. Preheat the oven to 350°F. With your hands, generously oil both sides of the fish. Sprinkle the herbs on the fish and pat them so that they adhere.
4. Place the fish on a cake rack and roast until flaky, 10 to 15 minutes. To crisp the top, turn the oven to broil and place the fish under the broiler for about 2 minutes. Serve immediately.

ADVANCE PREPARATION: This may be prepared 4 hours in advance through step 3 (except for preheating the oven) and refrigerated.

Although fresh herbs are plentiful in the summer months and are recommended for all my recipes, there may still be those times when you just don't have them on hand. The rule of thumb for substituting dried herbs for fresh is 1 part dried to 3 parts fresh. When using fresh herbs, always remove the leaves from the stems and chop only the leaves. Some leaves, like basil and tarragon, should be chopped—or torn—just before serving as they tend to darken quickly.

Grilled Swordfish with Red Pepper Hollandaise Sauce

SERVES 4

Swordfish steaks grill beautifully. These are marinated, grilled, and then finished with a red pepper hollandaise sauce. The fish is served garnished with strips of red pepper. Start with Garden Salad with Goat Cheese Thyme Dressing and accompany the swordfish with a simple vegetable rice.

RECOMMENDED WINE: Chardonnay is ideal with swordfish and the creamy hollandaise requires a wine with some substance, so look for one that's medium to full-bodied.

Grilled Swordfish with Red Pepper Hollandaise Sauce

4 swordfish steaks, ⅓ to ½ pound each, no more than 1-inch thick

Marinade
- 2 tablespoons olive oil
- 2 medium garlic cloves, minced
- 1 medium shallot, minced
- 2 tablespoons fresh lemon juice

Red Pepper Hollandaise Sauce
- 1 large sweet red pepper
- 3 egg yolks
- 2 tablespoons fresh lemon juice
- ½ teaspoon salt
- Pinch white pepper
- Pinch cayenne pepper
- ½ cup (1 stick) unsalted butter

Garnish
- 2 tablespoons unsalted butter
- 1 tablespoon olive oil
- 1 large red pepper, julienned
- 1 teaspoon fresh chopped parsley
- ¼ teaspoon salt
- Pinch pepper
- Sprigs of parsley

1. Place the swordfish steaks in a large nonaluminum dish.
2. Combine the marinade ingredients and pour over the fish. Marinate for 1 to 2 hours, turning once.
3. Pour boiling water into a wide-necked thermos jar to warm it.
4. *To make the sauce:* Roast and peel the pepper by placing it on a broiling pan and broiling approximately 6 inches from the heat until blackened on all sides. Use tongs to turn it.
5. Close the pepper tightly in a heavy paper bag. Let rest for 10 minutes.

6. Remove it from the bag, drain, and peel. Core and scrape out the seeds.

7. With a paper towel, blot out all the liquid from the pepper. Place in a food processor fitted with a steel blade and purée. Remove and set aside.

8. In the food processor or a blender, combine the egg yolks, lemon juice, salt, white pepper, and cayenne. Blend for 10 seconds.

9. Heat the butter in a small saucepan until sizzling hot but not browned. (This is important to enable the sauce to thicken properly.)

10. Slowly pour the hot butter in a thin stream into the blender or food processor while the motor is running. Add the red pepper purée and taste for seasoning.

11. Drain and dry the thermos jar and immediately pour the hot sauce into it. This will keep the sauce hot for up to half an hour.

12. Prepare the barbecue or grill for medium-heat grilling.

13. *To make the garnish:* In a medium skillet, heat the butter and oil over medium-high heat. Stir in the red pepper and sauté for 2 to 3 minutes, stirring constantly. The peppers should be crisp-tender. Add the chopped parsley, salt, and pepper and set aside.

14. Remove the fish from the marinade. Grill about 3 inches from the flame until done, about 4 to 5 minutes on a side.

15. Place a swordfish steak on each plate, spoon over some Red Pepper Hollandaise Sauce, and garnish with the sautéed red pepper and additional parsley. Serve immediately.

ADVANCE PREPARATION: The sauce may be prepared up to half an hour before serving. The fish may be marinated up to 2 hours before grilling.

Grilled Swordfish with Red Pepper Hollandaise Sauce

Spicy Citrus Grilled Swordfish

SERVES 4

Here's a simple method for serving swordfish—one that's light and easy to prepare. The predominant flavor in the marinade is fresh ginger. Serve with Vegetable Brochettes and Crispy Grilled Potatoes.

RECOMMENDED WINE: Chardonnay, Sauvignon Blanc, White Rhône, or Gavi from Italy will go well with this snappy dish.

Marinade
- 2 tablespoons fresh lime juice
- 3 tablespoons natural rice vinegar
- 1 tablespoon finely chopped ginger
- 1 tablespoon finely chopped scallions
- 3 tablespoons safflower oil
- 1 tablespoon light soy sauce
- ¼ teaspoon black pepper
  A few drops of Hot Pepper Oil (see page 367)

- 4 swordfish steaks, ⅓ to ½ pound no more than 1-inch thick

1. Whisk the marinade ingredients together in a medium bowl until blended.
2. In a large, shallow, nonaluminum dish, arrange the fish steaks and pour the marinade over. Marinate for ½ to 2 hours in the refrigerator.
3. Prepare the barbecue for medium-heat grilling. Remove the fish from the marinade and grill about 3 inches from the flame for 4 to 5 minutes on each side or until desired doneness. Serve immediately.

ADVANCE PREPARATION: May be prepared 2 hours in advance through step 2 and refrigerated.

Grilled Swordfish with Herbed Green Sauce

SERVES 6

The green sauce that accompanies this fish derives its earthy and piquant flavor from the capers and cornichons. Both of these specialty items can be found in the gourmet section of your grocery store. This sauce is also wonderful on other grilled fish or grilled chicken pieces. Served with Parslied Couscous with Zucchini and Carrots and Vegetable Brochettes.

RECOMMENDED WINE: A rich, oak-aged Sauvignon Blanc (Fumé Blanc is the same thing) works very well with this dish.

Marinade

- 2 medium garlic cloves, minced
- 2 medium shallots, finely chopped
- 6 tablespoons fresh lemon juice
- 1½ teaspoons minced lemon zest
- ¼ cup olive oil
- ¼ teaspoon salt
- ⅛ teaspoon black pepper
- 6 swordfish steaks, ⅓ to ½ pound each

Sauce

- ½ cup finely chopped parsley
- 1 medium shallot, finely chopped
- 1 medium garlic clove, minced
- 1 teaspoon finely chopped lemon zest
- 1 tablespoon drained capers, finely chopped
- 3 tablespoons finely chopped fresh cornichons (sour gherkins)
- 3 tablespoons fresh lemon juice
- ¼ teaspoon salt
- ⅛ teaspoon black pepper
- ½ cup extra virgin olive oil

1. Place the garlic, shallot, lemon juice, and lemon zest in a small mixing bowl and mix to combine. Add the olive oil and blend completely. Add the salt and pepper.

2. Arrange the swordfish steaks in a large, shallow, non-aluminum dish. Pour the marinade over, making sure the steaks are evenly coated. Cover and refrigerate for ½ to 2 hours.

3. *To prepare the sauce:* Whisk together all the sauce ingredients except the olive oil in a medium mixing bowl until well combined. Continue to whisk, pouring the olive oil in a steady stream into the mixture. You can also do this in a food processor fitted with a steel blade, using the pulse on/off motion. Be careful not to purée the mixture. Taste for seasoning.

4. Prepare the barbecue for medium-heat grilling. Remove the fish from the marinade, and grill about 3 inches from the flame for 4 to 5 minutes per side or until desired doneness.

5. Place the swordfish on a serving platter and spoon the herbed green sauce on top. Serve immediately.

ADVANCE PREPARATION: The sauce may be prepared 4 hours ahead, covered, and left at room temperature. The fish may be marinated and refrigerated 2 hours ahead.

Grilled Halibut in Lemon Mustard Tarragon Marinade

SERVES 6

Fresh tarragon is plentiful late in the spring and into the summer. It is so much more flavorful than its dry counterpart that I try to use it as much as possible while it's in season. Be sure you have real French

tarragon and not the tasteless grassy Russian tarragon. The citrus and
tarragon give this halibut a zesty flavor that belies its low calorie count.
If you want to cut calories even further, cut the olive oil in half or omit
it altogether. Serve with herbed rice and steamed zucchini and carrots
for a light summer dinner.

RECOMMENDED WINE: A spicy, crisp Sauvignon Blanc provides an excellent foil for this dish.

Marinade
- ½ cup fresh lemon juice
- 1 tablespoon minced lemon zest
- ¼ cup Dijon mustard
- 3 tablespoons finely chopped tarragon
- 2 tablespoons finely chopped chives or scallions
- ¼ cup olive oil
- ¼ teaspoon black pepper

- 6 ½ pound halibut steaks or fillets

Garnish
- Lemon slices
- Tarragon sprigs

1. Combine the lemon juice, lemon zest, Dijon mustard, tarragon, and chives in a small mixing bowl. Slowly whisk in the olive oil until well blended. Add the pepper and taste for seasoning.
2. Arrange the fish pieces in a large, shallow, nonaluminum dish. Pour the marinade over, coating all the pieces evenly. Marinate ½ to 2 hours.
3. Prepare the barbecue for medium-heat grilling. Grill about 3 inches from the flame for 5 to 7 minutes per side or until desired doneness. Garnish with the lemon slices and parsley and serve immediately.

ADVANCE PREPARATION: This may be prepared 2 hours in advance through step 2 and refrigerated.

Grilled Halibut in Lemon Mustard Tarragon Marinade

Sautéed Scallops with Zucchini and Mushrooms

SERVES 6

Sea or ocean scallops are larger than the tiny bay scallops. Either kind is excellent in this recipe; just cook the bay scallops for a shorter time so they stay moist. When choosing scallops, remember that they should smell mild and sweet. Beware if they are too opaque; it may mean they have been soaked in water. Crispy zucchini with soft scallops and mushrooms make a pleasant textural combination. This is one of those easy preparations that can be put together at the last minute. Serve with French bread and rice.

RECOMMENDED WINE: Sauvignon Blanc is good with this delicately flavored dish, but Chardonnay, Soave, Mâcon, or Portuguese Vinho Verde would also be fine.

> 2 pounds sea or bay scallops
> ¼ cup (4 tablespoons) unsalted butter
> 4 small zucchini, julienned
> 6 medium mushrooms, julienned
> 2 garlic cloves, minced
> ½ teaspoon salt
> ¼ teaspoon pepper
> 1½ tablespoons fresh lemon juice
> 1 tablespoon chopped parsley

1. If using sea scallops, remove the small muscle at the side of each one. Cut the scallops in half horizontally.
2. Heat 2 tablespoons butter in a large sauté pan. Add the zucchini and mushrooms and sauté over medium-high heat until both are just tender, about 3 minutes. Add the garlic, half the salt and pepper, and cook another minute.
3. Heat the remaining butter in another large sauté pan. Season the scallops with salt and pepper. Add to the pan in several batches and sauté over medium-high heat just until

tender, about 2 minutes on each side. Add the lemon juice and heat briefly.

4. To serve, spoon the zucchini and mushrooms onto a platter. Use a slotted spoon to set the scallops on top. Pour over the butter and lemon juice from the pan. Sprinkle with parsley and serve immediately.

Tomatillo Dressed Scallops in Cucumber Noodles

SERVES 4 AS A MAIN COURSE;
6 AS AN APPETIZER

The cucumbers are seeded, cut into thin, noodlelike strands, and fashioned into a nest in this spectacular-looking dish. The tiny bay scallops are gently poached in white wine, then tossed with a tomatillo sour cream sauce. Additional sauce may be served on the side. Serve as a first course followed by Grilled Veal Chops with Fresh Corn and Tarragon Sauce and simple steamed asparagus. You can also make larger portions to serve as a main course luncheon dish. Start with Spinach and Watercress Vichyssoise with Lemon-Chive Cream and hot French rolls. For dessert try Frozen Peaches and Cream.

RECOMMENDED WINE: A medium to light weight Chardonnay or a crisp, dry Riesling is just right with this dish.

1 cup white wine
2 cups water
1 pound bay scallops, cleaned

¾ cup Tomatillo Sauce (see page 348)
¼ cup sour cream

2 large European cucumbers, halved, seeded with a spoon, and refrigerated*

2 tablespoons Tomatillo Sauce (see page 348)
Red leaf lettuce or radicchio
Fresh cilantro leaves

1. In a medium saucepan bring the white wine and water to a simmer over medium heat. Poach the scallops in the liquid until just barely cooked through, about 2 minutes. Be careful not to overcook. Drain and cool.

2. Whisk the Tomatillo Sauce with the sour cream until well blended. Reserve 3 tablespoons and pour the rest over the scallops. Mix with a spoon until well coated. Refrigerate.

3. Just before serving, grate the cucumber with a mandoline or in a food processor fitted with a thin julienne blade. *Do not do this more than 1 hour before serving.* Put in a paper-towel-lined bowl and refrigerate.

4. *To serve:* Arrange the red leaf lettuce or radicchio on each plate. Remove the paper towel from the bowl and combine the remaining tomatillo cream with the cucumber. Mound the cucumber mixture in the center of the lettuce. Make an indentation in each mound and place the scallops in the center. Garnish with the Tomatillo Sauce and fresh cilantro leaves. Serve immediately.

ADVANCE PREPARATION: This may be prepared 6 hours in advance through step 2 and kept refrigerated.

*It is not necessary to peel the thin-skinned European cucumber.

Scallops Brochette with Spicy Caribbean Salsa

SERVES 6

Warm tropical breezes will come to mind every time you serve this intensely flavorful salsa with grilled scallops. The sweet taste of the scallops with the shallot salsa is great. Cook the scallops until golden brown on the outside and juicy tender on the inside. The salsa is a perfect companion to other grilled fish, such as halibut, sea bass, whitefish, or shrimp. Serve this with Grilled Japanese Eggplant and Cracked Wheat Vegetable Salad.

RECOMMENDED WINE: Serve an off-dry Gewürztraminer, a Sauvignon Blanc that is on the lemony side, or beer.

Salsa
- ¼ cup olive oil
- 5 large shallots, finely chopped
- 2 medium garlic cloves, minced
- 1 medium bunch chives, finely chopped
- 2 medium serrano chilies, seeded and finely chopped*
- ½ teaspoon salt
- ¼ cup fresh lime juice

Marinade
- 2 tablespoons finely chopped chives
- 1 medium garlic clove, minced
- 2 tablespoons fresh lime juice
- 1 tablespoon olive oil
- ¼ teaspoon salt
- ⅛ teaspoon black pepper

- 2 pounds sea scallops

1. *To make the salsa:* Heat 2 tablespoons olive oil in a medium skillet over medium heat and sauté the shallots for about 3 minutes. Remove from the heat and spoon into a medium

mixing bowl. Add the remaining ingredients and mix well. Taste for seasoning. Refrigerate until 1 hour before serving, then remove from the refrigerator to soften the salsa.

2. If using bamboo skewers, soak in cold water for at least 1 hour. This will prevent them from burning when grilled.

3. *To prepare the scallops:* Whisk the marinade ingredients together in a small bowl.

4. Thread the scallops onto the skewers and lay in a shallow, nonaluminum dish. Coat the scallops with the marinade and marinate for 30 minutes.

5. Prepare the barbecue for medium-high-heat grilling. Grill the scallops 3 inches from the flame for 3 to 4 minutes per side or until just done.

6. Place the brochettes on a serving platter and garnish with the salsa. Serve immediately.

ADVANCE PREPARATION: The salsa may be prepared 1 day in advance and refrigerated. Remove from the refrigerator 1 hour before serving.

*When working with chilies, always wear rubber gloves. Wash the cutting surface and knife immediately afterward.

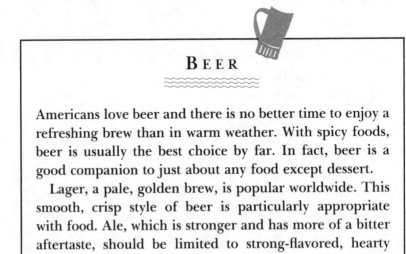

BEER

Americans love beer and there is no better time to enjoy a refreshing brew than in warm weather. With spicy foods, beer is usually the best choice by far. In fact, beer is a good companion to just about any food except dessert.

Lager, a pale, golden brew, is popular worldwide. This smooth, crisp style of beer is particularly appropriate with food. Ale, which is stronger and has more of a bitter aftertaste, should be limited to strong-flavored, hearty foods.

There are good beers produced in virtually every country in the world. Although there is really no difference between the ways they are made, beers of certain national origin seem to best complement food of their own ethnicity. Japanese beer seems made to go with sushi, and no beer is better with mole poblano than a Mexican beer.

Beer, like wine, can be overchilled. Any beverage that is too cold will stun the tastebuds and cut down on the enjoyment of not only the drink, but the food that goes with it. Keep the glasses chilled and the beer cool (50°F), not cold.

Grilled-Orange-Cured Salmon

SERVES 4

Curing cooks the fish without using heat; the marinade is the cooking agent. Usually, curing is a process complete unto itself, but in this recipe the salmon is half-cooked by curing and then finished on the grill. The flavor of the dry, aromatic orange marinade is sealed in by quick grilling. Plan to cure this 1 day before grilling. Start with Three Lettuce Salad with Tomato-Tarragon Dressing. Grilled vegetables and Herbed New Potatoes with Vermouth are good accompaniments. Almond Peach Clafouti with Amaretto Cream is a good choice for dessert.

RECOMMENDED WINE: A ripe, medium weight Chardonnay works very nicely with this dish.

2 1-pound salmon fillets or 4 ½-pound salmon fillets

Marinade
- 1 teaspoon coarse salt
- 6 white peppercorns
- 6 juniper berries
- 1 teaspoon finely chopped orange zest
- 1 teaspoon sugar

Orange Butter
- 6 tablespoons unsalted butter, softened
- 2 teaspoons finely chopped orange zest
- 2 tablespoons fresh orange juice
- ⅛ teaspoon salt
- Pinch white pepper

1. Place the salmon in a large, shallow, nonaluminum dish.
2. In a small bowl, combine the ingredients for the marinade. Spread evenly on the salmon and cover with wax paper. Weight with bricks or large cans and refrigerate. Turn every 6 to 8 hours. Marinate for one day.
3. Prepare the orange butter by combining all the ingredients in a medium bowl and whipping until well blended. Place on a sheet of wax paper and roll up into a cylinder. Refrigerate until ready to use, about 4 hours minimum. The butter should be very firm.
4. Remove the salmon from the marinade, clean it off, and pat it dry with a paper towel.
5. Prepare the barbecue for medium-heat grilling. Place the salmon on the grill, about 3 inches from the flame. Grill about 5 minutes on each side or until desired doneness.
6. *To serve:* Place the salmon on individual serving dishes. Slice the orange butter into equal pieces and arrange on top. Serve immediately.

ADVANCE PREPARATION: The orange butter may be prepared 2 days in advance and refrigerated.

NOTE: Freeze the remaining orange butter. It's delicious on grilled chicken.

Sweet and Spicy Grilled Salmon

SERVES 4

Brown sugar, cilantro, and ginger are added here for a sweet and spicy Asian-style sauce. Basting can lend as much flavor to fish as marinating if the fish is basted often, so remember to brush on the sauce every few minutes. Serve with Grilled Japanese Eggplant and simple steamed rice. Begin with Spiced Orange and Carrot Soup and finish with soothing Pink Honeydew Melon Sorbet.

RECOMMENDED WINE: Salmon is rich and oily and requires a fairly substantial wine to balance it. Rich, barrel-fermented Chardonnay is indicated here.

Sauce

  - 1 tablespoon unsalted butter
  - 2 medium shallots, finely chopped
  - ¼ cup fresh lemon juice
  - 1 tablespoon plus 1 teaspoon brown sugar
  - ⅛ teaspoon cayenne pepper
  - 1 tablespoon finely chopped ginger
  - ¼ cup red wine vinegar
  - 2 tablespoons soy sauce
  - 2 tablespoons finely chopped cilantro

  - 2 pounds salmon fillets, or 4½-pound pieces

Garnish

  Lemon slices
  Fresh parsley

1. In a small saucepan, melt the butter over medium heat. Add the shallots and sauté until softened, about 3 minutes.
2. Add the remaining ingredients except the cilantro and stir until well combined. Remove from the heat and add the cilantro.
3. Prepare the barbecue for medium-heat grilling.
4. Baste the salmon liberally with the sauce on both sides.
5. Grill the fillets about 3 inches from the flame for 7 to 10

minutes on each side, depending on their thickness and size. Baste frequently with the remaining marinade. Remove from the grill and serve immediately. Garnish with the lemon slices and parsley. Serve the remaining sauce separately.

ADVANCE PREPARATION: The sauce may be prepared 8 hours in advance and kept at room temperature. Reheat the sauce before basting the salmon.

Whole Poached Salmon with Pesto-Cucumber Sauce

SERVES 8

I can always tell summer's arrived because my phone starts ringing with questions about how I poach a whole salmon. Here's the answer: the key to poaching a salmon is to cook 10 minutes to the inch of thickness, then let the salmon cool in its stock for at least 6 hours or overnight. This method keeps the fish moist and extremely flavorful. Cold salmon is always a welcome summer offering and great to have on hand when people drop by unexpectedly. Sour cream, mayonnaise, and dill are traditional ingredients to sauce the salmon, but I like the addition of crunchy cucumber and the essence of fresh basil and pine nuts to the traditional sour cream mayonnaise. Serve this for a buffet dinner or luncheon, accompanied by Chilled Asparagus with Red Pepper Vinaigrette, Cherry Tomato and Hearts of Palm Salad, and Couscous Salad with Spiced Fruit Vinaigrette. Poach the salmon the day before serving.

RECOMMENDED WINE: A rich Chardonnay is needed here to balance the richness of the salmon and its creamy sauce.

Pesto-Cucumber Sour Cream Sauce

¾ cup sour cream

½ cup Basic Homemade Mayonnaise (see page 344)

¼ cup Spinach Pesto without cheese (see page 351)

½ cup coarsely chopped European cucumber

¼ teaspoon salt

¼ teaspoon white pepper

1 whole or half salmon, head removed

2 quarts fish stock (see page 368)

Garnish

Cucumber slices

Watercress sprigs

Cherry tomatoes

1. For the sauce, combine all the ingredients and blend well. Taste for seasoning. Refrigerate until ready to serve.

2. It is best to use a fish poacher for this recipe. If you do not have one you can use a large deep roasting pan with a round metal cooling rack (one that you would use for cooling cakes and cookies) placed in the middle. Wrap the salmon in a triple thickness of cheesecloth, leaving extra cheesecloth to tie at both ends. Use string or plastic twist-ties to secure the ends of the salmon.

3. Pour the fish stock into the poacher or roasting pan. Place the rack in the pan and then lay the salmon on top. Add enough water to cover.

4. Place the poacher on two burners over medium heat. Bring the liquid to a rapid simmer and then reduce to a very slow simmer. (If it is too high the salmon will fall apart.) Cook for 20 to 30 minutes, depending on the thickness of the fish (10 minutes per inch measured at the thickest part). When done remove the salmon from the heat and let cool in the liquid for at least 6 hours or overnight.

5. Using 2 spatulas remove the salmon from the broth. Remove the cheesecloth. Place the salmon on a platter and let drain for 30 minutes.

6. Remove the skin by pulling it off; it should peel off easily. Use a sharp knife to remove any gray flesh. The salmon should be completely pink.

7. Remove any visible bones with a small pair of pliers.

8. When ready to serve, decorate the salmon with the sliced cucumbers, fresh watercress leaves, and cherry tomatoes. Serve the Pesto-Cucumber Sauce on the side.

ADVANCE PREPARATION: The salmon and the sauce may be prepared 1 day in advance and refrigerated.

NOTE: You may also have the salmon cut in half lengthwise so that you can poach the halves in separate pieces of cheesecloth. In this way you will have 2 separate platters, which works out well for a buffet.

Tequila Lime Grilled Shrimp

SERVES 4 TO 6

This is a great party dish when accompanied by Cuban Black Beans, Tomato Papaya Mint Salsa, and Vegetable Lemon Rice. Begin with frosty margaritas and Guacamole Salsa with Crisp Tortilla Chips.

RECOMMENDED WINE: Crisp Sauvignon Blanc or French Chablis would be fine here.

2 pounds large shrimp, unpeeled

Marinade
- ¼ cup fresh lime juice
- ¼ cup tequila
- 2 medium garlic cloves, minced
- 2 medium shallots, finely chopped
- 2 teaspoons cumin
- 1 teaspoon salt
- ½ teaspoon pepper
- ½ cup olive oil

Garnish
- Lime slices
- 1 bunch watercress

1. If using bamboo skewers, soak them in cold water for at least 1 hour. This will prevent them from burning when grilled.
2. Thread the shrimp on the skewers (3 to 4 to each skewer). Lay in a shallow, nonaluminum dish, large enough to hold the skewered shrimp.
3. *To prepare the marinade:* Whisk together the lime juice, tequila, garlic, shallots, cumin, salt, and pepper. Slowly add the olive oil, whisking until combined. Taste for seasoning.
4. Pour over the shrimp and marinate for at least ½ and up to 4 hours.
5. Prepare the barbecue for medium-heat grilling.
6. Grill the shrimp on each side for about 4 minutes or to desired doneness. Remove from the grill and take the shrimp off the skewers. Garnish with the fresh watercress and lime slices. Serve immediately.

ADVANCE PREPARATION: This may be prepared 4 hours in advance through step 4 and refrigerated.

Softshell Crab with Lemon Butter

SERVES 2 AS A MAIN COURSE;
4 AS A FIRST COURSE

What is a softshell crab? It's an ordinary blue crab that has shed its hard outer shell during the normal process of seasonal growth. The crabs have an entirely different taste when they are in this state, and the delicate soft shells add a nice crunch. The peak of the softshell crab season is in July and August. This delicacy is most delicious when sautéed quickly. Save yourself extra fuss by having the crabs cleaned at the fish market. Two-Color Cole Slaw and tiny roast potatoes round out this meal.

RECOMMENDED WINE: A crisp and snappy white—Soave, dry Riesling, medium to light weight Chardonnay or Australian Semillon—provides just the right balance here.

Coating
- ¼ cup all-purpose flour
- ⅛ teaspoon black pepper
- ⅛ teaspoon salt
- ⅛ teaspoon ground red pepper
- ⅛ teaspoon paprika

Crabs
- 4 tablespoons butter
- 1 tablespoon safflower oil
- 1 medium shallot, finely chopped
- 8 softshell crabs
- ¼ cup fresh lemon juice
- 2 medium garlic cloves, minced
- 2 tablespoons finely chopped parsley
- ¼ teaspoon salt
- Pinch pepper

Garnish
- 1 lemon, sliced
- Parsley sprigs

1. Remove the feelers underneath the crab shells on both sides. Wash the crabs and dry carefully.
2. Combine the flour, pepper, salt, red pepper, and paprika in a shallow medium dish and mix well.
3. Heat the butter and oil in a large skillet over medium heat. Sauté the shallot for about 1 minute.
4. Roll the crabs in the flour mixture. Place them in the skillet and sauté about 3 minutes per side, turning once. When they have finished cooking and are pink in color, add the lemon juice, garlic, parsley, salt, and pepper and cook another minute or two. Make sure the garlic is cooked but *not* browned. Taste for seasoning. Arrange on serving plates and garnish with lemon and parsley. Serve immediately.

Herbed Crab Cakes with Lime Butter Sauce

SERVES 4 (8 CRAB CAKES)

These crab cakes cook best when the mixture is briefly chilled before placing on the griddle. Alaskan Snow Crab may be used, but my personal preference is Alaskan King Crab because of its sweeter and richer flavor. The lime butter sauce is an adaptation of the classic white wine butter sauce known as beurre blanc. *Fresh lime juice is used instead of white wine, which accents the crab cakes beautifully. The trick to making a perfect butter sauce is to slowly whisk in the butter just as it's beginning to melt so that it emulsifies into the sauce. If you decide to strain it, serve it immediately or it will start to separate. This sauce also goes well with grilled or poached scallops, shrimp, or lobster. Serve these crab cakes with a simple arugula salad dressed with Summer Vinaigrette.*

RECOMMENDED WINE: Medium weight Chardonnay is delicious with this richly flavored dish.

Crab Cakes

1 egg yolk
1 large egg
2 tablespoons whipping cream
1 teaspoon Dijon mustard
¼ teaspoon salt
  Pinch cayenne pepper
1 teaspoon finely chopped chives
1 tablespoon finely chopped parsley
1 pound fresh crabmeat
½ cup fresh bread crumbs
½ cup dried bread crumbs

4 tablespoons butter
2 tablespoons safflower oil

Lime Butter Sauce

¼ cup fresh lime juice
2 tablespoons white wine vinegar
3 shallots, minced
½ teaspoon salt
¼ teaspoon white pepper
¾ cup (or 1½ sticks) cold butter, cut in cubes

Garnish

2 limes, quartered

1. Beat the egg yolk and egg in a medium mixing bowl. Stir in the cream, mustard, salt, pepper, chives, and parsley. Add the crabmeat and the fresh bread crumbs, mixing well.
2. Spread the dried bread crumbs on a cookie sheet.
3. Divide the crab mixture into 8 cakes and shape into patties about 3 inches in diameter.
4. Roll the crab cakes in the dried bread crumbs. Place on a large plate, cover with plastic wrap, and refrigerate for at least 1 hour.
5. While the crab cakes are chilling prepare the lime butter sauce: In a heavy saucepan boil the lime juice, vinegar, and

shallots until about 2 tablespoons liquid remain. Add the salt and white pepper.

6. Over low heat, gradually add the cubes of butter to the shallot mixture, whisking constantly; add 1 or 2 at a time and wait until they are absorbed before adding more. If the pan begins to get too hot, remove it from the heat and add some of the butter cubes off the heat to cool the sauce slightly. Remove from the heat as soon as the last butter cube is added.

7. Strain the sauce if a smoother consistency is desired. Taste for seasoning. Keep warm in a double boiler or heated thermos and serve as soon as possible.

8. For each batch of crab cakes, heat 2 tablespoons butter and 1 tablespoon oil in a medium skillet or on the griddle on medium-high heat. Cook 4 crab cakes at a time, 3 to 4 minutes per side or until golden brown on both sides. Turn them carefully so they don't break up. Place the first batch on a baking sheet in a 300°F oven to keep warm.

9. Sauté the remaining crab cakes. Place on individual serving plates and spoon some lime sauce on top. Garnish with the lime wedges and serve immediately.

ADVANCE PREPARATION: This may be prepared 4 hours ahead through step 4 and refrigerated.

GRILLED SHELLFISH

If you're in the mood for something light and delicious to take the edge off your appetite, grilled shellfish is the answer. Clean clams, mussels, and oysters carefully. Prepare the barbecue for medium-high-heat grilling. Place the shellfish on the grill and cover the barbecue for 3 to 5 minutes or until the shellfish begin to open. Serve them in a deep bowl with wedges of lime. These are great with just a splash of lime juice or accompanied by Tomatillo Sauce or Tomato Basil Sauce.

Herbed Crab Cakes with Lime Butter Sauce

Grilled Whole Bluefish with Lemon Dill Butter

SERVES 4

Eastern bluefish, with its meaty richness, is especially delicious when grilled with an herb butter. If the fish is large, it's helpful to make a cut every 2 inches without cutting through the bone so that after cooking, it can be easily divided with a spatula into serving sizes. A wire grilling basket is very useful when grilling whole fish. Start with Bruschetta with Tomato, Basil, and Mozzarella Relish and serve Orzo with Goat Cheese. Cherry Amaretti Crisp with French vanilla ice cream is a perfect ending.

RECOMMENDED WINE: Bluefish is rich and oily and needs a big, oaky Chardonnay for balance. Another suggestion is a crisp Sauvignon Blanc to provide contrast.

Lemon Dill Butter
- ½ cup (1 stick) unsalted butter, at room temperature
- 1 medium shallot, finely chopped
- 2 tablespoons finely chopped dill
- 1 medium garlic clove, minced
- 2 tablespoons fresh lemon juice
- 1 teaspoon minced lemon zest
- ¼ teaspoon salt
- Pinch cayenne pepper
- 1 whole bluefish, 3 to 4 pounds, cleaned and head removed
- ½ teaspoon salt
- ¼ teaspoon black pepper

Garnish
- 1 bunch dill
- 2 lemons, thinly sliced

1. *To make lemon dill butter:* In a small mixing bowl cream the butter until soft. Add the dill, lemon juice, lemon zest, salt, and cayenne pepper and mix well. Taste for seasoning.

2. Season the bluefish with salt and pepper. Spoon approximately half the butter into the cavity of the bluefish. Arrange the dill and lemon slices over the butter in the cavity. Spread more butter over the outer surfaces.

3. Prepare the barbecue for medium-heat grilling. Place the fish in a large grilling basket, if available. If not, be sure to place the fish on the grill carefully. Grill, covered, about 3 inches from the flame for about 8 to 10 minutes on each side or just until tender when pierced with a skewer. Serve immediately with the remaining lemon dill butter.

ADVANCE PREPARATION: The lemon dill butter may be prepared 3 days in advance and refrigerated.

POULTRY

Sautéed Chicken with Balsamic Vinegar and Sun-Dried Tomatoes

SERVES 4 TO 6

Certain dishes literally sing of summertime. Fresh basil, marinated sun-dried tomatoes, and poached garlic create the perfect backdrop for a simple sautéed chicken. This dish may be prepared ahead of time and gently reheated just before serving. Serve with Gratin of Summer Squash, Leeks, and Rice for a sensational combination of flavors.

RECOMMENDED WINE: This hearty dish does very nicely paired with a big, oaky Chardonnay. Lightly chilled Chianti, Valpolicella, or Zinfandel are also good choices.

- ½ cup dry-packed sun-dried tomatoes, julienned
- ¼ plus ⅓ cup balsamic vinegar
- 3 tablespoons olive oil
- 2 tablespoons unsalted butter
- 3 large whole chicken breasts, skinned, boned, halved, and flattened
- 2 large shallots, finely chopped
- 1 medium head garlic (about 15 cloves)
- 2 cups veal stock or chicken stock (see pages 364-66)
- 1 medium bunch basil leaves, finely shredded
- ½ teaspoon salt
- ¼ teaspoon black pepper
- 2 tablespoons unsalted butter, cut into small pieces

Basil leaves

1. Place the sun-dried tomatoes in a small bowl. Pour boiling water over them and let soften for 15 to 30 minutes. Drain and combine with ¼ cup balsamic vinegar in a small bowl to marinate.
2. In a large sauté pan, melt 2 tablespoons olive oil and 1 tablespoon butter over medium-high heat. Dry the chicken pieces carefully and sauté until nicely browned, 5 to 7 minutes per side. Remove to a side platter and cover with aluminum foil to keep warm.
3. Add the remaining butter and oil and sauté the shallots over medium heat until soft, 2 to 3 minutes. Using a heavy cleaver, break up the garlic cloves. (You do not need to peel them since they will be strained.) Add the garlic cloves and sauté about 2 more minutes.
4. Pour in the remaining ⅓ cup balsamic vinegar and deglaze the pan, scraping up the brown bits stuck to the bottom. Add the veal or chicken stock and simmer partially covered until the garlic cloves are soft when pierced with a knife, about 20 minutes.
5. Purée the sauce in a food processor fitted with a steel blade. Pour through a fine-meshed strainer and then return to the pan.
6. Bring the sauce to a simmer and add all but 2 tablespoons of the basil, salt, pepper, and drained sun-dried tomatoes. (After tasting the sauce, you may want to add some of the balsamic vinegar that the tomatoes marinated in.)
7. Add the butter piece by piece, whisking constantly. This will give a slight shine to the sauce. Taste for seasoning.
8. Add the chicken and the chicken juices and reheat gently. Arrange the chicken breasts on a platter and pour the sauce over. Sprinkle with the remaining basil and serve immediately.

ADVANCE PREPARATION: This may be prepared 8 hours in advance through step 6 and refrigerated. Return to room temperature before reheating.

Sautéed Chicken with Balsamic Vinegar and Sun-Dried Tomatoes

Sautéed Chicken with Tomato-Leek Sauce

SERVES 4

I like to serve this dish at small dinner parties because I can make it in the morning when it's cool and reheat it while I'm entertaining my guests. The tomato-leek sauce, with its thyme and crushed red pepper, is a bold addition to the chicken. Sautéed Zucchini and Arugula make an appropriate accompaniment.

RECOMMENDED WINE: This dish works well with a big, full-bodied Chardonnay or a velvety, young Cabernet Sauvignon.

- 2 tablespoons unsalted butter
- 2 tablespoons olive oil
- ¼ pound pancetta or bacon, cut into ¼-inch dice
- 2 large whole chicken breasts, boned, skinned, halved and flattened
- 2 medium leeks, white part only, cleaned and finely chopped
- 2 medium tomatoes, skinned, seeded, and finely chopped
- ½ cup chicken stock (see page 366)
- ¼ cup whipping cream
- 1 teaspoon tomato paste
- 2 teaspoons finely chopped fresh thyme
  Pinch crushed red pepper flakes
- ¾ teaspoon salt

Garnish

Sprigs of thyme

1. In a medium skillet, melt 1 tablespoon butter and 1 tablespoon olive oil over medium-high heat and brown the pancetta or bacon for 3 to 5 minutes. (If using bacon, immerse in boiling water for 30 seconds to rid it of its smoky flavor before browning.) Remove the pancetta and reserve. Dry the chicken pieces carefully.

2. Add the remaining butter and olive oil to the pan and sauté the chicken until nicely browned, 5 to 7 minutes per side. Remove to a side platter and cover with aluminum foil to keep warm. Discard all but 2 tablespoons of fat from the sauté pan.

3. Add the leeks and sauté 3 to 5 minutes.

4. Add the tomatoes and lower the heat to medium. Cook 3 to 5 minutes.

5. Add the chicken stock, cream, and tomato paste and increase the heat to medium-high. Reduce by ¼. Stir in the thyme, crushed red pepper, and salt.

6. Return the chicken breasts and pancetta to the sauce and heat for about 5 minutes. Taste for seasoning. Garnish each chicken breast with thyme sprigs and serve immediately.

ADVANCE PREPARATION: This may be prepared 8 hours in advance through step 5 and refrigerated. Return to room temperature before reheating.

Chicken in Tomatillo Sauce

SERVES 4 TO 6

This dish can be as mild or hot as you like. For the mild version use the gentle Anaheim chile; for the hot version use the spicier poblano. They must both be roasted, peeled, and seeded before they are added to the sauce. Ground cumin seed gives an exotic taste that marries well with the Mexican tomatillo. If you are unable to find fresh chilies, the canned variety will do. For a Mexican-style dinner start with Guacamole Salsa with toasted tortilla chips. Follow with Mexican Caesar Salad. Serve the chicken with Crispy Grilled Potatoes. Dessert can be either Passion Fruit Cream Caramel or Crushed Strawberry Ice Cream with Toasted Hazelnut Cookies.

RECOMMENDED WINE: Serve a crisp, fruity Sauvignon Blanc with this dish. The wine's herbal character matches the peppers nicely.

3 medium Anaheim or poblano chilies*
¼ cup safflower oil
1 medium chicken fryer, cut up
2 whole medium chicken breasts, halved and skinned
1 large onion, finely chopped
2 cups chicken stock (see page 366)
6 medium garlic cloves, minced
1½ pound tomatillos, husked and quartered
3 tablespoons finely chopped cilantro
½ teaspoon cumin
2 tablespoons fresh lime juice
   Salt
   Pepper

Garnish
   Fresh cilantro

1. To peel the chilies, place on a broiler pan and broil approximately 6 inches from the heat until blackened on all sides. Use tongs to turn.
2. Close tightly in a brown paper bag. Let rest for 10 minutes.
3. Remove the chilies from the bag, drain, and peel. Make a slit in each chile and open it up. Core, cut off the stem, and scrape out the seeds and ribs. Chop the chilies into ¼-inch pieces.
4. In a large sauté pan heat half of the oil over medium-high heat. Dry the chicken pieces carefully. Sauté until lightly browned, 3 to 5 minutes per side. You may have to do this in batches, adding the remaining oil as needed. Remove to a side platter.
5. Add the onion and sauté over medium heat until soft but not brown, 3 to 5 minutes.
6. Add the chicken stock and deglaze the pan by turning up the heat and scraping the brown bits off the bottom.
7. Add the garlic, chilies, tomatillos, cilantro, and cumin. Bring

to a boil, then reduce to a simmer. Add the browned chicken pieces and simmer on low, covered, turning the chicken once to cook evenly. Simmer until the chicken pieces are just done, about 20 minutes. (Remove the smaller pieces first.)

8. Remove the chicken onto a serving platter and cover with aluminum foil to keep warm.

9. Add the lime juice to the pan and then reduce the sauce until slightly thickened. Add the salt and pepper. Taste for seasoning. Pour over the chicken pieces and garnish with the fresh cilantro leaves.

ADVANCE PREPARATION: This may be prepared 2 days in advance and refrigerated. Return to room temperature before reheating.

VARIATION: The sauce is also delicious served on grilled or poached chicken.

*When working with chilies always wear rubber gloves. Wash the cutting surface and knife immediately afterward.

Grilled Chicken with Citrus Ginger Butter

SERVES 4 TO 6

Citrus and ginger give a wonderful flavor to this California-style chicken. The marinade is used to flavor both the chicken and the compound butter that is placed on top of the crispy, caramelized chicken. Chill the citrus-ginger butter in the freezer if you are running short of time. Start with Yellow Squash Soup and serve the chicken with Tri-Color Vegetable Terrine. For dessert try Almond Zabaglione with Strawberries.

RECOMMENDED WINE: A fruity, off-dry Johannesberg Riesling is excellent here, or you might even try a crisp White Zinfandel.

Marinade

½ cup fresh lime juice

2 tablespoons lime or orange marmalade

2 teaspoons minced fresh ginger

1 garlic clove, minced

¼ cup white wine

¼ cup safflower oil

¼ teaspoon salt

⅛ teaspoon pepper

3 tablespoons unsalted butter, softened

3 medium whole chicken breasts, boned and halved

Garnish

2 limes, cut into quarters or halves

1. Thoroughly combine the marinade ingredients in a small bowl and taste for seasoning. Reserve 1 tablespoon.

2. Arrange the chicken pieces in a large, shallow, nonaluminum dish and pour the marinade over. Marinate in the refrigerator for at least 1 hour and up to 6 hours, turning occasionally.

3. To make the lime or orange ginger butter, in a small bowl combine the tablespoon reserved marinade and butter, and beat together with a wooden spoon until smooth. Place on a sheet of wax paper and roll up into a cylinder. Refrigerate until ready to use. It should become very firm.

4. Prepare the barbecue for medium-heat grilling. Remove the chicken from the marinade and grill 3 inches from the flame for 7 to 10 minutes on each side.

5. Place the chicken on individual serving plates. Cut the lime-ginger butter into ¼-inch slices and arrange on top. Garnish with the lime wedges and serve immediately.

ADVANCE PREPARATION: This may be prepared 6 hours in advance through step 3 and refrigerated.

Grilled Mexican Chicken with Citrus Yogurt Sauce

SERVES 6 TO 8

Marinating overnight is the secret to locking in the flavor and producing tender, succulent chicken. Reserve a cup of the marinade to serve on the side. I like to serve this for informal outdoor dinners with family and friends. Start with Mexican Caesar Salad and serve the chicken with Cracked Wheat Vegetable Salad. Dessert calls for Hazelnut Plum Tart with a bowl of Crème Fraîche on the side.

RECOMMENDED WINE: Try a big, fruity Chardonnay or a spicy Gewürztraminer.

Marinade

- 2 cups plain lowfat yogurt
- 2 medium shallots, finely chopped
- 3 medium garlic cloves, minced
- ¼ cup fresh orange juice
- 2 tablespoons fresh lime juice
- 2 tablespoons finely chopped cilantro
- ½ teaspoon ground cumin
- ¼ teaspoon white pepper
- ½ teaspoon salt

- 3 medium whole chicken breasts, halved
- 1 fryer (about 3½ pounds) cut into pieces

Garnish

- 2 oranges, sliced
- 2 lemons, sliced
- 1 bunch parsley

1. Thoroughly combine the marinade ingredients in a bowl large enough to hold the chicken. Taste for seasoning.
2. Reserve 1 cup of the marinade for the sauce. Refrigerate.
3. Place the chicken pieces in the bowl and, using your hands,

evenly coat all the pieces with the marinade. Cover and refrigerate overnight and up to 24 hours for the best flavor, turning occasionally.

4. Prepare barbecue for medium-heat grilling. Remove the chicken from the marinade and grill 3 inches from the flame for 7 to 12 minutes on each side, depending on size.

5. Place on serving platter, garnished with orange and lemon slices and fresh parsley. Serve immediately with the reserved sauce.

ADVANCE PREPARATION: This may be prepared 1 day in advance through step 4, if serving cold.

Grilled Marinated Chicken with Dijon Mustard, Tarragon, and Port

SERVES 4 TO 6

This winning combination of savory mustard, sweet wine, and aromatic tarragon with grilled chicken is light and easy to prepare for last-minute cooking. Serve with Grilled Japanese Eggplant. Start with Green Salad with Grapefruit, Baby Beets, and Avocado.

RECOMMENDED WINE: The rich port and pepper flavors need a hearty red wine such as a ripe Zinfandel or a spicy Rhône.

Marinade
- ½ cup Dijon mustard
- ½ cup port
- 2 tablespoons finely chopped tarragon
- ¼ teaspoon black pepper

- 3 large whole chicken breasts, boned and halved

1. Combine marinade ingredients in a small bowl. Mix well.
2. Place the chicken pieces in a large, shallow, nonaluminum dish and pour the marinade over, turning the pieces to coat well. Marinate for ½ to 4 hours in the refrigerator.
3. Prepare the barbecue for medium-heat grilling. Remove the chicken from the marinade and grill 3 inches from the flame for 7 to 10 minutes on each side.
4. Place the chicken on individual serving plates and garnish with the tarragon leaves.

ADVANCE PREPARATION: This may be prepared 4 hours in advance through step 2 and refrigerated.

Grilled Chicken with Sun-Dried Tomato Paste

SERVES 4 TO 6

Basil, olive oil, mustard, and sun-dried tomatoes combine to make a barbecue paste that forms a crisp mahogany crust on the grilled chicken. I prefer to use dry-packed sun-dried tomatoes, since they are about a quarter the price of the imported Italian oil-packed variety. Soften the tomatoes in boiling water for at least 15 minutes before using them. Serve this to your friends who like a little extra spice. Accompany with Sautéed Zucchini and Arugula.

RECOMMENDED WINE: This full-flavored dish does nicely with fruity reds such as Beaujolais or Gamay.

¾ cup dry-packed sun-dried tomatoes

4 medium garlic cloves

1 teaspoon extra virgin olive oil

1 teaspoon crushed red pepper

2 tablespoons Dijon mustard

2 tablespoons balsamic vinegar

¼ teaspoon salt

⅛ teaspoon black pepper

3 large whole chicken breasts, boned, halved, and flattened

4 tablespoons unsalted butter, at room temperature

1. Pour boiling water over the sun-dried tomatoes in a small bowl. Let soften for 15 to 30 minutes. Drain well.
2. Mince the garlic in a food processor fitted with a steel blade. Add the drained tomatoes and the rest of the ingredients for the paste and process until puréed and the consistency of a thick paste. Reserve 2 tablespoons.
3. Place the chicken breasts in large, shallow, nonaluminum dish and coat evenly with the paste. Make sure to put some marinade *under* the skin. Refrigerate 2 to 8 hours, turning several times to make sure the marinade is adhering to the chicken. (The longer it marinates, the spicier it will be.)
4. In a food processor fitted with a steel blade process the butter with the reserved tomato paste until well blended. Place it on a sheet of wax paper and roll up into a cylinder. Refrigerate it for at least 4 hours or until ready to use. It should become very firm.
5. Prepare the barbecue for medium-heat grilling. Grill the chicken 3 inches from the flame for 7 to 10 minutes per side, basting with a slice of the butter mixture on each side.
6. *To serve:* Arrange the chicken on individual plates and top each piece with a thin slice of the butter.

ADVANCE PREPARATION: This may be prepared 8 hours in advance through step 4 and refrigerated.

Crispy Roast Chicken with Spinach Pesto Cream

SERVES 6 TO 8

Guests always rave about this dish—it's a great entrée for large parties. Roast the chicken while your guests are enjoying their drinks and first course. The smell of the roasting, pesto-marinated chickens sweetens the air. I've suggested garnishing the platter with red and green basil leaves and flowers; if you have access to society garlic flowers, they make a spectacular addition.

Layering flavors is a cooking technique that infuses the food with a particular flavor in successive steps. This chicken is first marinated with a pesto base and then stuffed with pesto-flavored bread crumbs. Finally cream and pesto are blended together for a smooth sauce that is poured over the hot, crispy chicken. A triple taste of pesto may sound excessive but in fact it is an ideal balance.

For a large dinner party, start with Corn-Leek Cakes with Caviar, Smoked Salmon, and Crème Fraîche. If you serve this for a buffet, accompany it with large platters of Chilled Asparagus with Red Pepper Vinaigrette, Cracked Wheat Vegetable Salad, and Garden Salad with Goat Cheese Thyme Dressing. Serve loaves of country French bread and crocks of sweet butter. Prepare a dessert sideboard of Poached Peaches in White Zinfandel with Fresh Raspberry Sauce, Lattice Crust Pie with Rhubarb, Peaches, Strawberries, and Plums, and Chocolate Pecan Torte with Espresso Crème Anglaise.

RECOMMENDED WINE: The complex flavors of this dish are nicely highlighted by a well-balanced and fairly young Cabernet Sauvignon or Merlot.

Sauce
- ½ cup Spinach Pesto (see page 351)
- 1 tablespoon red wine vinegar
- ½ cup whipping cream
- ½ teaspoon salt
- ¼ teaspoon black pepper

Marinade

¼ cup dry white wine

¼ cup Spinach Pesto (see page 351)

¼ teaspoon salt

¼ teaspoon black pepper

Stuffing

1 cup bread crumbs

3 tablespoons freshly grated Parmesan cheese

2 tablespoons Spinach Pesto (see page 351)

Pinch salt

¼ teaspoon black pepper

4 large whole chicken breasts, boned and halved

Garnish

Red and green basil leaves and flowers

1. *To make the sauce:* Combine all the sauce ingredients in a small mixing bowl and whisk until smooth. Tastes for seasoning and refrigerate.
2. *To make the marinade:* In a small mixing bowl combine all the marinade ingredients and mix well.
3. Arrange the chicken breasts in a large, shallow, nonaluminum dish. Pour the marinade over the chicken until generously covered. Marinate for ½ to 4 hours in the refrigerator.
4. *To make the stuffing:* Combine all the stuffing ingredients in a medium mixing bowl. Mix together until the pesto has been absorbed.
5. Remove the chicken breasts from the marinade and place in a large roasting pan, skin side up.
6. Preheat the oven to 425°F. Place a heaping tablespoon of stuffing underneath the skin by carefully lifting up the skin, being careful not to tear it, and evenly spreading the stuffing mixture. Place the skin back down and pat it to help distribute the stuffing.
7. Place the chicken breasts in the oven and roast for 20 to 25 minutes. They should be golden brown and crisp. If not, remove them from the oven and preheat the oven to broil.

Broil the chicken breasts until crisp, 3 to 5 minutes. Remove and drain off any excess oil.

8. Arrange the chicken breasts on a serving platter and spoon 1 tablespoon of sauce on each breast. Garnish with basil sprigs and flowers and serve immediately.

ADVANCE PREPARATION: The sauce may be prepared 1 day in advance and refrigerated. Remove from the refrigerator half an hour before serving. The marinade may also be prepared 1 day in advance and refrigerated. Remove from the refrigerator 1 hour before using.

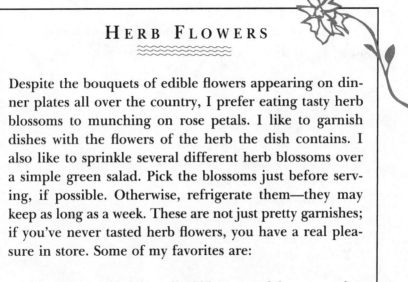

HERB FLOWERS

Despite the bouquets of edible flowers appearing on dinner plates all over the country, I prefer eating tasty herb blossoms to munching on rose petals. I like to garnish dishes with the flowers of the herb the dish contains. I also like to sprinkle several different herb blossoms over a simple green salad. Pick the blossoms just before serving, if possible. Otherwise, refrigerate them—they may keep as long as a week. These are not just pretty garnishes; if you've never tasted herb flowers, you have a real pleasure in store. Some of my favorites are:

- Green or red basil—spiked blossoms of the same color
- Borage—blue-purple pink flowers
- Garlic chive—white flowers
- Society garlic—purple flowers
- Thyme—tiny purple flowers
- Lavender—purple wands
- Pineapple sage—scarlet flowers
- Oregano—tiny mauve and white flowers
- Arugula or roquette—creamy white flowers with a dash of black and red near the center
- Rosemary—tiny bright sky-blue flowers

Crispy Roast Chicken with Spinach Pesto Cream

Roasted Cornish Hens with Raspberry Tarragon Marinade

SERVES 2

Tarragon has a surprisingly sweet taste when combined with raspberries. This simple marinade perfumes the hens as they roast. Although a full 24 hours is required for marinating the hens, the cooking time is short, so your kitchen will stay cool. Serve with Orzo with Goat Cheese. For dessert, Frozen Praline Mousse with Bittersweet Hot Fudge Sauce would be a good choice.

RECOMMENDED WINE: The raspberry flavors found in good young Zinfandel blend perfectly with this dish.

Marinade
    6 ounces raspberries (¾ cup)
    3 tablespoons olive oil
    2 tablespoons raspberry vinegar
    1 tablespoon finely chopped fresh tarragon
    1 medium shallot, minced
    ⅛ teaspoon salt
      Pinch white pepper

    2 Cornish hens

Garnish
      Extra raspberries
      Tarragon leaves

1. In a food processor fitted with a steel blade, process the raspberries until puréed. Press through a fine sieve over a nonaluminum mixing bowl large enough to hold the hens.
2. Add the olive oil, vinegar, tarragon, shallot, salt, and pepper and whisk to combine. Taste for seasoning.
3. Moisten your fingers with the marinade and separate the skin from the meat at the neck ends of the hens, leaving the tail ends intact. (Use rubber gloves if you have long nails.)

Being careful not to rip the skin, carefully slip your moistened fingers under the skin of the breast portion and massage with the marinade until well coated.

4. Place the hens in the marinade, turning to coat evenly. Cover and refrigerate. Marinate for 1 day, turning occasionally.
5. Preheat the oven to 425°F. Remove the hens from the marinade and pat dry with paper towels.
6. Split the hens so they will cook evenly. They should be almost flat.
7. Place the halves, legs up, on a roasting rack in a roasting pan. Roast until done, 30 to 35 minutes. Test for doneness (the legs should wiggle easily in the socket). Garnish with fresh raspberries and tarragon leaves.

ADVANCE PREPARATION: This may be prepared 1 day in advance through step 4.

Roasted Rosemary-Lemon Chicken

SERVES 4

Perfectly cooked, fragrant chicken can be served at any temperature and for any occasion. In this rendition the chicken is split and flattened for even cooking. Rosemary is tucked underneath the skin to infuse the bird with its unmistakable aroma. Serve this with Wild Rice Salad with Carrots and Oranges and Green Bean, Mushroom, and Walnut Salad.

RECOMMENDED WINE: Rosemary and chicken work very well with big, oaky Chardonnays.

    1 3½-pound fryer, split
    1 bunch of rosemary

2 teaspoons finely chopped fresh rosemary
3 medium garlic cloves, minced
¼ cup fresh lemon juice
¼ cup olive oil
1 teaspoon soy sauce
¼ teaspoon salt
¼ teaspoon cayenne pepper

1. With the side of a heavy cleaver, flatten the chicken halves by pounding very hard a few times.
2. In a large mixing bowl thoroughly whisk the marinade ingredients together. Taste for seasoning.
3. Separate the skin from the chicken by placing your fingers under the skin and gently loosening it. Tuck as many rosemary leaves as you like under the skin.
4. Place the chicken in a bowl with the marinade and rotate until completely coated. Marinate for 2 to 4 hours in the refrigerator.
5. Preheat the oven to 425°F. Remove the chicken from the marinade and place on a roasting rack in a roasting pan. Pour in 1 cup water to keep the pan from burning. Roast the chicken 45 to 50 minutes, basting a few times with the remaining marinade mixture. You may need to add more water to the bottom of the pan if it begins to burn. Remove the chicken from the oven when golden brown. Serve hot, bring to room temperature and serve, or serve chilled.

ADVANCE PREPARATION: This may be completely prepared 2 days in advance. It is excellent served at room temperature or slightly chilled.

Chicken Chili

SERVES 10 TO 12

Marlene Sorosky, the noted cookbook author, introduced me to the idea of using chicken in chili. I prefer it now, since it's lighter than the heartier beef versions and more pleasing during the hot summer months. I like to serve this on cool evenings to a large crowd when I want a substantial and informal main course. Serve with Grilled Green Chile and Corn Pudding or with corn bread and a green salad. Put out big bowls of Guacamole Salsa to start and serve your favorite Mexican beer.

RECOMMENDED WINE: This spicy dish would blend well with Gewürztraminer, but beer may be the best accompaniment.

- 6 medium whole chicken breasts, boned
- 5 tablespoons safflower oil
- 3 large onions, finely chopped
- 1 jalapeño chile, seeded and finely chopped*
- 8 medium garlic cloves, finely minced
- 4 teaspoons ground oregano
- 3 tablespoons ground cumin
- 2 teaspoons ground coriander
- 1 teaspoon cinnamon
- ½ cup chili powder
- 2 12-ounce cans of beer
- 2½ cups chicken stock (see page 366)
- 1 28-ounce can crushed tomatoes
- 2 sweet red peppers, seeded and cut into ½-inch dice
- 1 sweet yellow pepper, seeded and cut into ½-inch dice
- 1 approximately 15-ounce can kidney beans, drained
- 1 16-ounce can pinto beans, drained
- 1 square unsweetened chocolate, grated
- 2 to 3 teaspoons salt, or to taste

*When working with chilies, always wear rubber gloves. Wash the cutting surface and knife immediately afterward.

Sour cream
Tomato salsa or jalapeño salsa
Grated, sharp Cheddar cheese
Chopped green or red onion

1. Fill a large, deep pan ¾ of the way up the sides with water and bring to a boil. Place the chicken breasts in the boiling water and turn off the heat. Cover and let sit for 25 minutes. Remove the chicken, cool, skin, and cube into 1-inch pieces. Cover and refrigerate. Remove from refrigerator ½ hour before adding to the chili.

2. In a large 6-quart pot, heat 3 tablespoons oil over medium heat. Add the onions and sauté until soft, 3 to 5 minutes. Add the jalapeño chile and sauté another minute. Add the garlic, oregano, cumin, coriander, cinnamon, and chili powder and stir until well combined.

3. Add the beer, chicken stock, and tomatoes and bring to a low simmer. Simmer partially covered for 1 hour, stirring occasionally.

4. Meanwhile, heat the remaining 2 tablespoons oil over medium heat in a medium skillet. Add the diced red and yellow peppers and sauté until slightly cooked but still crisp, 3 to 5 minutes. Set aside.

5. Add the kidney and pinto beans to the chili mixture and continue simmering for 30 more minutes, uncovered. The sauce should be slightly thickened.

6. Add the chicken, sautéed peppers, grated chocolate, and salt, and stir until the chocolate is melted. Taste for seasoning. Serve in large chili or pottery bowls, surrounded by small bowls of sour cream, salsa, grated Cheddar cheese, and chopped onions.

ADVANCE PREPARATION: May be prepared 3 days in advance through step 5 and kept in the refrigerator. Cover the chicken and the peppers separately and refrigerate. Remove from the refrigerator 1 hour before beginning to complete the dish.

Grilled Chicken Sandwich with Watercress and Tapenade Mayonnaise

SERVES 4

Sometimes all you want to eat is a sandwich. This elegant version of the venerable chicken sandwich is superb eaten hot off the grill or served cold. The peppers and mayonnaise can be prepared ahead of time. Accompany with Cherry Tomato and Hearts of Palm Salad and Two-Color Coleslaw for a great combination. For dessert serve Fudgy Brownies.

1 medium sweet red pepper

Sauce

2 tablespoons Tapenade (see page 343)
½ cup Basic Homemade Mayonnaise (see page 344)

Chicken

2 medium whole chicken breasts, skinned, boned, and halved
1 tablespoon fresh lemon juice
1 tablespoon Dijon mustard

4 sourdough French rolls
1 medium bunch watercress, leaves only

1. To peel the pepper, place on a broiler pan and broil approximately 6 inches from the heat until blackened on all sides. Use tongs to turn.
2. Close it tightly in a brown paper bag. Let rest for 10 minutes.
3. Remove from the bag, drain, and peel. Make a slit in pepper and open it up. Core, cut off the stem, and scrape out the seeds and ribs. Slice thinly and set aside.
4. Blend the tapenade and mayonnaise in a small mixing bowl.
5. For the marinade, combine the lemon juice and mustard in a small mixing bowl. Spoon over the chicken breasts in a

shallow, nonaluminum dish. Marinate for at least 15 minutes and up to 4 hours.

6. *To serve:* Prepare the barbecue for medium-heat grilling. Grill the chicken breasts for 5 to 7 minutes on each side. Cool about 5 minutes. Slice diagonally into ¼-inch-thick slices.

7. Cut the sourdough rolls in half and spread ¾ tablespoon of the tapenade mayonnaise on each half. Arrange the watercress on top of one half, followed by the chicken breast slices, slightly overlapping. Place a dollop of the mayonnaise on top and garnish with the red pepper strips. Cover with the other half of the roll and serve.

ADVANCE PREPARATION: This may be prepared 4 hours ahead through step 3 and refrigerated.

PAN BAGNAT

One of my favorite summer sandwiches is the French one called pan bagnat, the provençal salad sandwich. These are made with French bread baguettes or sourdough sandwich rolls that have been sliced with ⅔ of the bread for the bottom and ⅓ for the top. Most of the bread is then scooped out, leaving a thick crust with a thin layer of bread. An herbed vinaigrette, such as Summer Vinaigrette, is brushed on the bread. It is then topped with any combination of the ingredients below. Layer the vegetables on the bottom, then spinkle them with a little more vinaigrette. Put the top on and cover tightly. These are great for picnics because the flavors improve if they are left to mingle for a few hours—but keep them in a cooler. They can also be placed in a grill basket and quickly grilled if they include cheese. Grilling will melt the cheese and give the bread a lovely crisp crust.

Sliced, roasted red, green, or golden peppers
Sliced tomatoes
Pitted Niçoise olives
Marinated artichoke hearts
Anchovies
Imported ham
Roast chicken slices
Watercress leaves, arugula, or basil leaves
Goat cheese, mozzarella, or provolone
Celery slices
Cucumber slices
Capers

SANDWICH COMBINATIONS

These sandwiches are based on simple combinations; their chief requirements are excellent fresh bread or rolls and the best ingredients at hand.

- Grilled sharp Cheddar cheese, bacon, and tomato, spread with Basil Shallot Mayonnaise, open faced on whole wheat or pumpernickel
- Cold, marinated, sliced flank steak and arugula leaves on sourdough rolls spread with Ancho Chili Mayonnaise
- Prosciutto, tomatoes, and roasted peppers, spread with Roasted Garlic Mayonnaise on sesame seed bread
- Chopped smoked salmon and egg salad on rye bread
- Smoked turkey slices, sliced tomatoes, red onion slices, basil, chervil or burnet leaves, spread with Lemon-Chive Mayonnaise on whole wheat bread
- Cold grilled chicken slices, sliced avocado, and Tomato Cucumber Salsa, stuffed in a warm sesame pita bread
- Fresh crumbled goat cheese, marinated sun-dried tomatoes, and roasted red and yellow peppers on a sourdough roll spread with Roasted Garlic Mayonnaise

Grilled Turkey Breast in Orange Honey Mustard Sauce

SERVES 4 TO 6

Thin slices of turkey breast resembling veal scallopine are now available nationally and can be cooked in a number of different ways. I've found that marinating and fast grilling the slices is a good technique for keeping them moist and flavorful. In this recipe, the spirited marinade flavors the turkey with a blend of ginger, honey, and citrus. The remaining marinade is reduced with just a touch of cream to ensure a smooth sauce. Serve with Parslied Couscous with Zucchini and Carrots and grilled seasonal vegetables.

RECOMMENDED WINE: A spicy, fresh Gewürztraminer is delightful with this dish, but Beaujolais would also do the job.

Marinade
- 1 medium orange, juiced
- Grated orange zest
- 1 medium lemon, juiced
- 2 tablespoons soy sauce
- 1 tablespoon finely chopped ginger
- 2 medium garlic cloves, minced
- 2 medium shallots, finely chopped
- 1 tablespoon honey
- 2 teaspoons Dijon mustard
- ¼ cup olive oil

1½ pounds turkey breast, cut into ½-inch slices

Sauce
- ½ cup chicken stock (see page 366)
- 2 tablespoons whipping cream
- ¼ teaspoon black pepper
- 1 tablespoon finely chopped parsley

1. *To prepare the marinade:* Whisk together all the marinade ingredients in a small mixing bowl.
2. Place the turkey slices in a large, shallow, nonaluminum dish. Pour the marinade over, cover, and refrigerate for 2 to 4 hours.
3. Prepare the barbecue for medium-high-heat grilling. Remove the turkey slices from the marinade and shake off the excess marinade. Grill about 3 minutes per side. Remove from the heat and place on a platter.
4. Pour the remaining marinade into a small saucepan and add the chicken stock. Bring to a boil over high heat. Add the cream, pepper, and parsley. Taste for seasoning. Pour over the turkey slices and serve immediately.

ADVANCE PREPARATION: The marinade may be prepared 1 day in advance and refrigerated. Remove from the refrigerator half an hour before using.

A FEW WORDS ABOUT WINE TEMPERATURE

Most Americans drink white wines too cold and red wines too warm. In the summer it is quite acceptable to chill Chardonnays and other whites, but too much cold will shut down their flavor. Keep them at around 55°F, no less. Half an hour in the refrigerator is time enough to cool your wine; more than that will take the edge off the flavor. As for reds, it is perfectly okay to pop them into the refrigerator for fifteen minutes or so, especially on hot summer days. Beaujolais and Zinfandel are particularly good when turned down to 60°F or 65°F. A slight chill can add a refreshing dimension to other reds too, but don't get carried away.

Grilled Turkey Breast in Orange Honey Mustard Sauce

MEATS

Grilled Roast Beef with
Sour Cream Herbed Sauce

SERVES 4 TO 6

Grilling large pieces of roast beef can sometimes be unwieldy. That's why I prefer to use the triangle tip roast—sometimes called the bottom sirloin cut. The tri tip, named for its triangular shape, is just the right size and is nicely marbled with fat—ideal for cooking on the grill. The roast beef is delicious hot or chilled; either way, cook it medium rare, about 135° to 140°F. Use an instant meat thermometer to get an accurate reading. The herbed sour cream sauce is a refreshing accompaniment. Serve this cold with a simple coleslaw or right off the grill with Sautéed Zucchini and Arugula or Tri-Color Vegetable Terrine.

RECOMMENDED WINE: Cabernet Sauvignon is the answer here. Look for a lush, velvety version with some of that characteristic Rutherford mintiness.

Herb Paste
- 2 garlic cloves, minced
- ½ teaspoon turmeric
- ½ teaspoon ground cumin
- ½ teaspoon pepper
- 1 teaspoon salt
- 1 teaspoon fresh finely chopped oregano, or ½ teaspoon dried
- 2 tablespoons finely chopped mint leaves
- 2 tablespoons safflower oil
- ¼ teaspoon Hot Pepper Oil (see page 367)
- 1 2-pound triangle tip roast

Sour Cream Sauce
- 1 cup sour cream
- ½ cup finely chopped European cucumber*
- 1 tablespoon fresh lemon juice
- 1 teaspoon finely chopped chives
- 1 tablespoon finely chopped fresh mint
- 1 teaspoon finely chopped fresh dill
- ½ teaspoon Hot Pepper Oil or to taste (see page 367)
- ⅛ teaspoon ground cumin
- 2 teaspoons mint jelly
- ½ teaspoon salt
- ¼ teaspoon white pepper

1. Combine all the ingredients for the herb paste in a small mixing bowl and mix until the consistency is pastelike. Place the beef in a shallow, nonaluminum dish and coat evenly with the paste.
2. Refrigerate for 4 hours; turn the meat several times to make sure the paste adheres to it.
3. *To make the sour cream sauce:* Whisk together all the sauce ingredients in a small bowl until well blended. Cover and refrigerate until serving.
4. Prepare the barbecue for medium-high-heat grilling. Remove beef from the marinade and grill about 3 inches from the fire. Sear each side for about 3 minutes. Turn down the barbecue to medium heat. Cover and grill each side about

10 more minutes. Use an instant meat thermometer to get an exact reading (135°F rare, 140°F medium rare).

5. If serving hot, slice on the diagonal and pour a little sauce over the sliced beef. If you prefer to serve it chilled, let the beef come to room temperature before you refrigerate it. Carve the beef into about ¼-inch-thick slices and overlap on a platter. Garnish the platter with fresh herbs used in the sauce and serve the sauce on the side.

ADVANCE PREPARATION: This can be prepared 1 day in advance if serving chilled. If serving hot, the sauce may be prepared 1 day in advance and the meat may be marinated up to 1 day in advance; both should be refrigerated.

NOTE: It's not necessary to peel the thin-skinned European cucumber.

Barbecued Brisket of Beef

SERVES 6 TO 8

Brisket needs a long, slow cooking time to become tender—here it is roasted and then sliced before it goes near the grill. It's wonderful for a celebration like Memorial Day or the Fourth of July because you can roast it a few days before your party. After slicing the meat, place it on heavy-duty aluminum foil and spoon on the barbecue sauce. Seal the packet by double-folding the edges. When ready to eat, simply warm the brisket in the packets on the grill. The lemon barbecue sauce uses beer, chili powder, and hot red pepper so it's tangy rather than sweet. This barbecue sauce is also great on sandwiches. Baked Beans with Bourbon and Cider and Two-Color Coleslaw make perfect side dishes. Start with Vegetable Platter with Grilled Red Pepper and Garlic Sauce or other sauces of your choice. For dessert have Strawberry Shortcake with Raspberry Custard Sauce.

RECOMMENDED WINE: A fine, complex Cabernet Sauvignon, Merlot, Barbaresco, or Zinfandel is the right choice for this hearty dish.

1 4 to 5 pound brisket
   Salt
   Pepper
2 cups veal or chicken stock (see pages 364-66)

Sauce

2 tablespoons safflower oil
1 medium onion, sliced
2 garlic cloves, minced
2 cups crushed tomatoes
1 12-ounce can beer
½ cup dark brown sugar, firmly packed
1 tablespoon Hungarian paprika
1 tablespoon Dijon mustard
1 tablespoon chili powder
¼ teaspoon dried chili flakes or red pepper flakes
1 small lemon, thinly sliced
½ teaspoon salt

Optional

8 French rolls, sliced in half

1. Preheat the oven to 325°F. Season the brisket with salt and pepper evenly on both sides. Place in a roasting pan, add the stock, and cover. Roast for 3 to 4 hours, depending on the size of the meat, until tender when pierced with a fork. Remove from oven. Cover with foil and let the meat cool.
2. Slice the brisket into ¼-inch slices against the grain and place in heavy-duty aluminum foil, sealing tightly, until ready to finish cooking.
3. While the brisket is cooking prepare the sauce. In a large saucepan add the oil and bring to medium heat. Add the onion and sauté until just softened, about 3 minutes. Add the garlic and sauté about another minute.
4. Add the remaining ingredients and bring to a boil. Turn

down the heat and simmer for 45 minutes, partially covered. Remove from the heat and let cool. Remove the lemon slices and purée the sauce in a blender. Taste for seasoning. Add the juices from the roasted brisket and stir.

5. When ready to finish cooking, prepare the barbecue for medium-heat grilling. Open the foil packet and generously brush the brisket slices with some of the barbecue sauce. Close the foil tightly, making sure there are no holes or openings.

6. Place the brisket package on the grill and cover. Grill until the sauce is bubbling and the meat is heated through, 15 to 20 minutes. (You may need to open the dampers to control the fire if it gets too hot.)

7. Remove the brisket slices from the foil and arrange on a platter. Serve with extra barbecue sauce.

8. If making sandwiches, toast the halved French rolls on the grill just until hot. Arrange the brisket slices on half of a roll, spoon on some sauce, and cover with the other half. Serve immediately.

ADVANCE PREPARATION: The brisket may be prepared 2 days in advance, sliced, covered, and refrigerated. The sauce may be prepared 2 days in advance and refrigerated.

Grilled Marinated Flank Steak

SERVES 4 TO 6

Flank steaks need to be tenderized by pounding, slow cooking, or marinating. Here, red wine, citrus, and curry make a tasty marinade. Grill the steak until just medium rare; further cooking will toughen the meat. This is great to have on hand for weekend sandwiches. When making sandwiches spread French rolls with Ancho Chile Mayonnaise. Layer the rolls with slices of flank steak, very ripe sliced tomatoes, and arugula leaves.

RECOMMENDED WINE: Hearty reds such as Zinfandel, Côtes du Rhône, Petite Sirah, or Charbono are just right here.

Marinade

- ¾ cup red wine
- 2 medium garlic cloves, minced
- 2 tablespoons olive oil
- 1 tablespoon fresh lemon juice
- 2 tablespoons fresh orange juice
- 1 teaspoon orange zest
- 1 teaspoon lemon zest
- 1 teapoon soy sauce
- ¼ teaspon salt
- ¼ teaspoon black pepper
- ½ teaspoon curry powder

- 1 2-pound flank steak

1. Combine all the marinade ingredients in a medium mixing bowl and whisk until well combined. Taste for seasoning.
2. Flatten out the flank steak in a large, shallow, nonaluminum dish. Pour the marinade over and marinate 2 to 4 hours in the refrigerator.
3. Prepare the barbecue for medium-heat grilling. Remove the steak from the marinade and grill 3 inches from the flame, 5 to 7 minutes per side for medium rare.
4. Place on a carving platter and slice thinly against the grain. Serve immediately.

ADVANCE PREPARATION: This may be prepared up to 4 hours in advance through step 2 and refrigerated. May be completely prepared 1 day in advance and refrigerated, if serving cold.

Grilled Marinated Flank Steak

Grilled Steaks, California Style

_When I was a child, teriyaki-marinated steaks were a staple summer
dinner. This simple marinade is an updated version, still using soy
sauce, but adding balsamic vinegar for its musty, sweet flavor. Serve
with Quick Cabbage Sauté or Broiled Tomatoes Glazed with Mustard
Herb Mayonnaise for a speedy but delicious dinner. A good ending is
Mocha Mousse._

RECOMMENDED WINE: Drink your best Cabernet Sauvignon
or Merlot with this beefy dish.

Marinade
- 2 medium garlic cloves, finely chopped
- 2 medium shallots, finely chopped
- 2 tablespoons soy sauce
- 4 tablespoons balsamic vinegar
- 2 tablespoons olive oil
- ¼ teaspoon black pepper

- 4 steaks, Spencer, sirloin, or New York (½ to ¾ pound each)

1. _To make the marinade:_ Thoroughly whisk the marinade ingredients together in a small bowl.
2. Arrange the steaks in a medium, nonaluminum, shallow dish. Pour the marinade over and marinate for 2 to 4 hours in the refrigerator.
3. Prepare the barbecue for medium-high-heat grilling. Preheat the broiler if necessary. Grill or broil the steaks about 3 inches from the heat until browned but still rare, about 4 minutes on each side. Serve immediately.

ADVANCE PREPARATION: This may be prepared 4 hours
in advance through step 2 and refrigerated.

Barbecued Lamb with Orange Tahini Peanut Sauce

SERVES 6

Definitely out of the ordinary, this lamb sirloin is highly appealing because of its tangy and fragrant flavor. First it is marinated in a savory mixture of orange juice, herbs, and curry powder and then grilled. Tahini paste (ground sesame seeds) is added to the dark, creamy peanut sauce for an exotic touch. The sirloin portion is from the top part of the leg of lamb. Although it is smaller than the rest of the leg, it is the tenderest part. Use this cut when you are cooking for a small group since there will be little waste. This is very good with Vegetable Lemon Rice and Grilled Japanese Eggplant. For dessert enjoy White Chocolate Terrine with Strawberries and Praline. This is also excellent served cold accompanied by Cracked Wheat Vegetable Salad and a side bowl of the Orange Tahini Peanut Sauce.

RECOMMENDED WINE: Cabernet Sauvignon and lamb are one of those wine and food marriages that are near-perfect. Look for a fairly rich and assertive wine to go with this flavorful dish.

Marinade

- 1 medium garlic clove, minced
- 1 medium shallot, finely chopped
- ¼ cup soy sauce
- 1 tablespoon Dijon mustard
- ¼ cup white wine
- 1 medium orange, juice and zest
- 1 teaspoon chopped fresh thyme, or ½ teaspoon dried
- 1 teaspoon curry powder
- ¼ teaspoon pepper
- 2 teaspoons light brown sugar

- 1 3-pound lamb sirloin, butterflied

Orange Tahini Peanut Sauce

¼ cup crunchy peanut butter

3 tablespoons dark soy sauce

¼ cup tahini paste

2 tablespoons dark sesame oil

1 tablespoon rice wine vinegar

3 tablespoons fresh orange juice

½ teaspoon orange zest, finely chopped

2 medium garlic cloves, minced

1 tablespoon Hot Pepper Oil (see page 367)

2 tablespoons chicken stock (see page 366)

2 tablespoons orange-flavored honey

1. Combine all the marinade ingredients in a medium bowl and whisk. Place the lamb sirloin in a shallow, nonaluminum dish and pour the marinade over.
2. Refrigerate at least 4 hours and up to 24 hours ahead; turn the meat several times to marinate evenly.
3. *To make the orange tahini peanut sauce:* Whisk together all the sauce ingredients in a small bowl. The oils should be well emulsified.
4. Prepare the barbecue for medium-high-heat grilling. Remove the lamb from the marinade and grill 3 inches from the flame, searing each side for about 3 minutes. Turn down the barbecue to medium heat. Cover the barbecue and grill each side of the sirloin for about 15 minutes for medium rare. Use an instant meat thermometer to get an exact reading (140°F medium rare, 150°F medium).
5. Remove the meat to a wooden cutting board; let rest for 10 minutes, and then slice on the diagonal. Serve with the sauce. You may need to whisk the sauce together right before serving if it has separated.

ADVANCE PREPARATION: The lamb may be marinated 1 day in advance and refrigerated. The sauce may also be prepared 1 day in advance and refrigerated. Whisk the sauce right before serving.

NOTE: Rack of lamb or the whole leg of lamb may also be used.

Barbecued Leg of Lamb with a Mustard Sage Crust

SERVES 8 TO 10

If you have an herb garden, you know the delight of experimenting with a variety of fresh herbs in your cooking. Pineapple sage is one of my loves. Rich with a fragrant musty taste and the fruitiness of ripe pineapple, this herb was my inspiration for the following recipe. If you don't have pineapple sage, however, any sage will do. Here the whole leg of lamb is boned and butterflied, then pounded into a uniform thickness so that it will cook more evenly. It's marinated overnight in red wine and olive oil with plenty of fresh sage. Before cooking, it is coated with a savory mustard and sage paste that becomes a delectable crust when grilled. Finally, a sauce of veal stock and sage is spooned over the medium rare lamb slices. This is ideal for a dinner party of 8 to 10. Begin with Stuffed Baby Red Potatoes with Eggplant, Tomato, and Peppers as an appetizer, followed by Garden Salad with Goat Cheese Thyme Dressing. Serve the lamb with Semolina Gnocchi with Pesto. For dessert serve Chocolate Pecan Torte with Espresso Crème Anglaise.

RECOMMENDED WINE: Use a good quality Cabernet in cooking (it may not seem so, but it is easy to tell when a poor or mediocre wine is used in preparing a dish) and serve the same wine with dinner.

Marinade
- 3 large shallots, finely chopped
- 2 medium garlic cloves, minced
- 1 cup Cabernet Sauvignon or other full-bodied red wine
- ½ cup olive oil
- ¼ cup finely chopped fresh sage (preferably pineapple sage)

or

- 2 tablespoons dried sage
- 1 teaspoon salt
- ¼ teaspoon pepper

1　9 to 10 pound leg of lamb with sirloin attached, boned and butterflied (5 to 6 pounds boned)

Crust

1　4-ounce jar grainy mustard
3　tablespoons finely chopped fresh sage

or

1　tablespoon dried sage
¼　teaspoon cracked black pepper
3　tablespoons olive oil

Sauce

1　cup remaining marinade
2　cups veal stock (see page 364)
1　tablespoon finely chopped fresh sage leaves

or

½　tablespoon dried sage
2　tablespoons unsalted butter, slightly softened

Garnish

Fresh sprigs of sage (optional)

1. Combine the marinade ingredients in a small, nonaluminum bowl and blend well. Place the leg of lamb in a large, shallow, nonaluminum pan and pour the marinade over, making sure it is evenly distributed. Refrigerate, covering with plastic wrap and occasionally turning it to marinate evenly. Marinate 1 day in advance, if possible.
2. When ready to grill, prepare the mustard coating. In a small mixing bowl combine the mustard, sage, and pepper and mix. Whisking, slowly add the olive oil.
3. Remove the lamb from the marinade and pat dry. Reserve the marinade. Place the lamb on a large platter and, using your hands, coat both sides with the mustard coating. Prepare the barbecue for medium-high-heat grilling. Place the

lamb on the grill 3 inches from the flame and sear each side for about 3 minutes. Turn down the barbecue to medium heat. Cover and grill each side about 20 to 25 more minutes. You may need to cut a piece off before the rest is finished if the lamb is much thicker in certain places. The meat should be very pink inside. Use an instant meat thermometer to get an exact reading (140°F medium rare, 150°F medium).

4. Pour the remaining marinade into a small saucepan and boil until reduced to ½ cup. In a separate small saucepan bring the veal stock to a boil and reduce to ½ cup. The stock should be somewhat thickened. Combine the stock and the marinade and bring to a simmer. Just before serving add the sage and then the butter, whisking it in slowly so that the sauce is slightly shiny. Taste for seasoning.

5. Place the lamb on a wooden carving platter and let rest for about 10 minutes. Slice against the grain and serve with a little sauce poured over each portion. Garnish with fresh sage if available.

ADVANCE PREPARATION: This may be prepared 1 day in advance through step 1 and refrigerated.

Grilled Lamb Chops with Wine-Mint Marinade

SERVES 4

French rib lamb chops with their elegant long bones make a pretty presentation when crossed on the plate. Mint and lamb are wonderful together; for this summer dish, fresh mint and mint jelly are used in the marinade instead of the standard mint jelly served on the side. Use any variety mint you prefer for this light, quick dish. (English mint, Mint the Best, applemint, or pineapple mint work nicely.) And garnish the plate with a sprig of fresh mint. Serve with Grilled Japanese Eggplant and Crispy Grilled Potatoes; follow with Salad of Peaches and Gorgonzola.

RECOMMENDED WINE: A soft, lush, and relatively young Cabernet Sauvignon would be ideal here. Use the same wine in the marinade.

Marinade
- 1 medium garlic clove
- 1 medium shallot
- 1 tablespoon finely chopped mint
- 3 tablespoons red wine
- 1 teaspoon mint jelly
- ¼ cup olive oil

8 thick French rib lamb chops (up to ¾-inch thick)

Garnish
Fresh mint leaves

1. In a food processor fitted with a steel blade, finely chop the garlic and shallot. Add the mint, red wine, mint jelly, and olive oil and process until well blended. Taste for seasoning.
2. Arrange the lamb chops in a large, shallow, nonaluminum dish. Pour the marinade over, making sure both sides of the

lamb chops are evenly covered. Marinate for 2 to 4 hours in the refrigerator.

3. Prepare the barbecue for medium-high-heat grilling. Remove the lamb chops from the marinade and grill 3 inches from the flame for 5 to 7 minutes per side, depending on their thickness. Place on serving plates and garnish with fresh mint leaves. Serve immediately.

ADVANCE PREPARATION: This may be prepared 4 hours in advance through step 2 and refrigerated.

GRILLING AHEAD

Although grilled and barbecued food is traditionally served hot off the fire, it tastes every bit as good—and maybe even better on a very hot day—several hours later. Bypassing all the drama of whether the fire will light and the split-second timing required to prepare hot grilled food, this method gives you all of the pleasures and none of the aggravation of cooking in front of your guests. Almost all of the grilled main courses and vegetables in this book may be served at room temperature or just slightly chilled. Vegetables, fish, and poultry are as well suited to being served this way as red meats.

Grilled Lamb Chops with Wine-Mint Marinade

Grilled Veal Chops with Fresh Corn and Tarragon Sauce

SERVES 4

When Jan Weimer, the food editor at Bon Appetit *magazine, suggested that I create a corn and tarragon sauce for veal chops, I was skeptical. Wouldn't the corn be too grainy as a sauce? Was tarragon really a complementary flavor to corn? While it's important to think about how combinations work best, this was one time when I had nothing to worry about. This dish was simply sublime. The euphoria that it caused reminded me that sometimes instinct wins out over logic. Serve these juicy veal chops with Tri-Color Vegetable Terrine or Spicy Potatoes Gratinée. Serve Frozen Peaches and Cream for dessert.*

RECOMMENDED WINE: This saucy dish needs a frisky red such as fresh Zinfandel, Beaujolais, or Syrah.

Sauce

  2 cups fresh corn kernels (about 4 medium ears)
  3 tablespoons unsalted butter
  2 medium shallots, finely chopped
  1 cup reduced veal stock (see page 364)
  2 tablespoons whipping cream
  2 tablespoons finely chopped tarragon
    Salt
    Pepper

Veal

  4 6 to 8 ounce veal loin chops
  2 tablespoons virgin olive oil
    Salt
    Finely ground pepper

1. Immerse ½ cup corn kernels in boiling water for about 1 minute. Drain and reserve for garnish.
2. Heat the butter in a medium skillet over medium heat and add the shallots. Sauté until just softened, about 2 minutes.

Add the remaining corn kernels and sauté about 2 more minutes.

3. Add the veal stock, increase the heat to high, and cook until slightly reduced, 5 minutes.

4. Process in a food processor fitted with a steel blade until puréed and then press through a food mill or a very fine strainer. Pour into a clean saucepan.

5. Add the cream and tarragon and cook about 2 minutes. The sauce should coat a spoon. Add the salt and pepper. Taste for seasoning.

6. Prepare the barbecue for medium-heat grilling. Generously brush both sides of the veal chops with olive oil. Grill about 3 inches from the flame for 5 to 7 minutes on each side, depending on their thickness. The veal should be very pink inside. Sprinkle with salt and pepper and spoon some sauce over them. Garnish with the reserved corn kernels and serve immediately.

ADVANCE PREPARATION: The sauce may be prepared 4 hours in advance, covered, and left at room temperature. Gently reheat just before serving.

Grilled Veal Chops with Fresh Corn and Tarragon Sauce

Grilled Veal Chops with Peach-Jalapeño Chutney

SERVES 4

Chutneys are usually thought of as condiments to use on the side like relish. This peachy, spicy chutney, however, is blended right into the peach nectar marinade and then spooned on top of the grilled veal chops. Use mesquite hardwood or presoaked mesquite wood chips to impart an undeniably Southwestern flavor to the dish. Serve with grilled summer vegetables or Gratin of Summer Squash, Leeks, and Rice.

RECOMMENDED WINE: A richly flavored dish such as this calls for an assertive red that adds some acidity to the match-up. Moderately rich Zinfandel, medium weight Pinot Noir, or zesty Côtes dû Rhone will do nicely.

Marinade
- ½ cup white wine
- ¼ cup peach nectar
- Good pinch cayenne red pepper
- ⅛ teaspoon salt
- 1 teaspoon finely chopped chives
- 1 medium garlic clove, minced
- 2 tablespoons Peach-Jalapeño Chutney (see page 358)
- ¼ cup olive oil

- 4 veal rib chops, 1-inch thick
- Salt
- Pepper

Garnish
- 1 cup Peach-Jalapeño Chutney (see page 358)

1. Whisk together the marinade ingredients in a small bowl until well blended.
2. Place the veal chops in a large, shallow, nonaluminum pan

and pour the marinade over. Marinate for 2 to 4 hours, turning at least once.

3. Prepare the barbecue for medium-heat grilling. Grill the veal chops about 3 inches from the flame for 5 to 7 minutes on each side. The veal should be very pink inside. Remove from the grill and sprinkle with salt and pepper on each side.
4. Place the remaining marinade in a small saucepan and bring to a boil. Reduce until it is slightly thickened.
5. Arrange the veal chops on a serving plate, spoon on the hot marinade, and place a dollop of Peach-Jalapeño Chutney on top. Serve immediately.

ADVANCE PREPARATION: This may be prepared 4 hours in advance through step 2 and refrigerated.

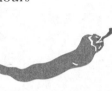

Sweet and Hot Spare Ribs with Apricot-Plum Sauce

SERVES 4

Barbecued ribs are an American institution. I use the individually cut Chinese-style baby back ribs rather than slab ribs because of their lean meatiness. The sweet and hot sauce is made by simmering fruit with garlic, ginger, and crushed red pepper flakes. The result is a spicy, chutney-like flavor. Grill the pork loin ribs on a hot fire flavored with mesquite. The sweetness of the glaze intermingled with the aromatic mesquite brings a unique taste to these all-time favorite ribs. Serve extra Apricot-Plum Sauce on the side. This is a particularly good choice for a Fourth of July celebration. Two-Color Coleslaw, Baked Beans with Bourbon and Apple Cider, and Grilled Corn on the Cob with Ancho Chile Butter complete this meal.

RECOMMENDED WINE: Gewürztraminer is fine with this dish but, if you want to be a bit daring, serve a spicy Zinfandel.

½ cup dry white wine
½ cup Apricot-Plum Sauce (See page 422)
4 pounds pork loin ribs cut Chinese style

1. Combine the white wine and Apricot-Plum Sauce in a large nonaluminum bowl and blend well.
2. Add the ribs to the sauce and marinate in the refrigerator for 2 to 8 hours, turning occasionally.
3. Prepare the barbecue for medium-heat grilling. Grill the ribs about 3 inches from the flame for 10 to 12 minutes on each side or until they reach the desired doneness. Baste with the remaining marinade. Serve immediately with extra Apricot-Plum Sauce, if desired.

ADVANCE PREPARATION: This may be prepared 8 hours ahead through step 2.

After you've served grilled chicken, spare ribs, or corn on the cob, everyone's hands will, of course, be a mess. To remedy the situation put out individual fingerbowls—any small china or glass bowls filled with warm water will do. Try one of the following suggestions to take this little ritual out of the realm of washing-up and give it a special touch:

- Add a few drops of orange flower water to each fingerbowl and float a thin slice of orange or lemon on top.
- Add a few drops of rose water to the bowl and float rose petals on top.
- Place a sprig of fresh rosemary in the bowl, then pour warm water over the rosemary to release its powerful fragrance. The rosemary will float to the top.
- Accompany the fingerbowl with a small napkin, rolled with a fresh herb sprig tucked inside, for your guests to dry their hands.

Pork Tenderloin with Apricot-Bourbon Sauce

SERVES 4 TO 6

Double-flavoring meat by marinating and then creating a sauce with the reserved marinade intensifies the taste substantially. This marinade calls for a full pound of golden ripe apricots, their flavor accentuated by combining them with bourbon and ginger. The sauce is a reduction of the marinade, with a touch of cream to smooth it out. Serve Cracked Wheat Vegetable Salad mounded high in the center of a platter, surrounded by overlapping pork slices. Drizzle the golden apricot sauce on the pork slices.

RECOMMENDED WINE: Try Chianti, Valpolicella, or a young, fruity Zinfandel with this richly flavored dish.

Marinade
> 1 pound fresh apricots, pitted and cut into quarters
> 2 large shallots, minced
> 2 tablespoons bourbon
> 1 tablespoon fresh lemon juice
> 2 medium garlic cloves, minced
> 1 tablespoon ginger, finely chopped
> 1 teaspoon finely chopped thyme
> ¼ teaspoon salt
> ⅛ teaspoon white pepper

> 3 ¾-pound pork tenderloins

Sauce
> 1 tablespoon bourbon
> ½ cup chicken stock (see page 366)
> 2 tablespoons whipping cream
> 1 teaspoon finely chopped thyme
> ¼ teaspoon salt
> Pinch white pepper

Garnish
> Watercress

1. Process the apricots in a food processor fitted with a steel blade until puréed. Add the remaining marinade ingredients and process until finely puréed. Taste for seasoning.
2. Arrange the pork tenderloins in a large, shallow, non-aluminum dish and pour the marinade over, making sure the tenderloins are evenly coated. Marinate for 2 to 4 hours in the refrigerator.
3. Prepare the barbecue for medium-heat grilling. Remove the tenderloins from the marinade and sear on each side for

about 2 minutes. Cover the grill, making sure the vents are open, and grill for 15 minutes, basting occasionally. Turn the meat over and grill until the internal temperature is 160°F, about another 10 minutes. Remove from grill and let stand for 10 minutes.

4. Place the remaining marinade in a small saucepan and add the bourbon, chicken stock, cream, and thyme. Bring to a boil and simmer until the sauce lightly coats a spoon, about 5 minutes. Add the salt and pepper and taste for seasoning.

5. Slice into ¼-inch slices and arrange on a platter garnished with the watercress. Drizzle some sauce over the pork and serve the remaining sauce separately.

ADVANCE PREPARATION: This may be prepared 4 hours in advance through step 2 and refrigerated.

Pork Tenderloin with Apricot-Bourbon Sauce

Vegetables and Other Side Dishes

Quick Cabbage Sauté

SERVES 4 TO 6

Although cabbage is often thought of as a winter vegetable, it is primarily grown in the summer months and kept in cold storage for year-round availability. Cabbage is good cooked or raw, but the secret to success with this recipe is quick cooking. Chile paste and soy sauce give this sautéed cabbage an Asian flavor. Toasted pine nuts are sprinkled on top to add their delicate note. Serve with Spicy Citrus Grilled Swordfish or Grilled Chicken with Citrus-Ginger Butter.

> 2 tablespoons pine nuts
> 3 tablespoons peanut or safflower oil
> 1 leek, white part only, finely chopped
> 2 carrots, peeled and julienned
> ½ sweet red pepper, seeded and julienned
> 1 medium cabbage, cored and finely shredded
> 1 teaspoon chile paste with garlic
> 2 tablespoons soy sauce
> ¼ cup dry sherry
> Salt
> Pepper

1. In a large skillet toast the pine nuts over medium heat for 3 to 5 minutes. Shake the pan constantly to avoid burning them. Remove and set aside.

2. In the same skillet heat the oil over medium-high heat. Sauté the leeks until slightly softened, about two minutes. Add the carrots and red pepper and sauté for about 3 more minutes. Add the cabbage and sauté until just wilted, about 3 minutes more.

3. Add the chile paste, soy sauce, sherry, and salt and pepper to taste. Stir to combine, bring to a boil and cook for another minute. Taste for seasoning and add the pine nuts. Serve immediately.

ADVANCE PREPARATION: The vegetables may be prepared up to 4 hours in advance and refrigerated. Prepare the recipe just before serving.

Ratatouille Gratinée

SERVES 6 TO 8

Ratatouille, that wonderful jumble of cooked vegetables, is usually sautéed and simmered, then served as a side dish. It is a very popular item in French delicatessens or charcuteries; however, it's definitely not visually appetizing. In this gratinée version, rounds of zucchini sprinkled with herbs and Parmesan cheese are layered with a tomato, sweet pepper, and eggplant stew. This rustic dish looks beautiful on the table. This is especially good served with Roasted Sea Bass with Herbs, Grilled Steaks, California Style, or any simple grilled poultry.

¾ cup olive oil
2 large onions, thinly sliced
2 sweet red peppers, seeded and finely sliced
1 green pepper, seeded and finely sliced
8 Japanese eggplant, sliced into ¼-inch rounds
1 pound mushrooms, thinly sliced
3 medium garlic cloves, minced
2½ cups canned crushed tomatoes
1 teaspoon salt
½ teaspoon pepper
6 medium zucchini, cut into ⅛-inch slices
¼ cup finely chopped parsley
1 tablespoon finely chopped fresh thyme
¼ cup finely chopped basil leaves
½ cup freshly grated Parmesan cheese
  Salt
  Pepper

1. In a large skillet heat ¼ cup olive oil over medium heat. Add the onions and sauté until softened, about 4 minutes. Add the peppers and cook until slightly wilted, about 3 minutes more. Remove to a side bowl.

2. Add ¼ cup more olive oil and sauté the eggplant slices in batches for about 2 minutes on each side. Remove to the side bowl. Add 2 more tablespoons olive oil and sauté the mushrooms and 1 clove of minced garlic for about 3 min-

utes. Return the vegetables to the skillet, add the crushed tomatoes, and simmer, covered, over medium-low heat for 10 to 12 minutes. Remove the lid and bring to a boil for 5 to 10 minutes to remove the excess liquid. The mixture should not be watery. Add the salt and pepper and taste for seasoning.

3. Preheat the oven to 400°F. Brush a 10 × 3-inch gratin dish with olive oil. Spoon half the tomato-vegetable mixture on the bottom of the dish. Arrange a layer of the zucchini slices slightly overlapping one another on top. Brush with the remaining olive oil and sprinkle with salt and pepper.

4. Spoon the remaining tomato-vegetable mixture over the zucchini and then repeat the process with the remaining zucchini slices.

5. In a small bowl combine the remaining garlic, parsley, thyme, and basil. Sprinkle on top of the zucchini. Sprinkle Parmesan cheese evenly over the top.

6. Place the gratin dish on a baking sheet. Bake until all vegetables are soft but not mushy, 30 to 35 minutes. Check after 20 minutes; if the gratin is becoming too brown, cover with aluminum foil and continue baking. After removing from the oven you may need to use a bulb baster to remove the excess liquid that has accumulated. Let rest 10 minutes before serving.

ADVANCE PREPARATION: This may be prepared completely 8 hours in advance through step 5, covered, and refrigerated. Remove from refrigerator and bring to room temperature before baking.

NOTE: The thin slicing blade for the food processor may be used to slice the eggplant. The regular slicing blade may be used for the zucchini.

Gratin of Summer Squash, Leeks, and Rice

SERVES 6

Subtle, sautéed green and white leeks interlaced with colorful shredded summer squash and creamy rice contrast deliciously with sharp Parmesan cheese. This "all in one" vegetable dish may be served as a first course or on the side. Try Gratin of Summer Squash with Sautéed Chicken with Balsamic Vinegar and Sun-Dried Tomatoes.

2½ pounds yellow and green zucchini, mixed
1 teaspoon salt
½ cup long grain white rice
4 tablespoons (¼ cup) olive oil
3 medium leeks, cleaned white and light green parts only, finely chopped (about 3 cups chopped)
2 medium garlic cloves, minced
2 tablespoons Italian parsley, finely chopped
2 tablespoons all-purpose flour
2 cups half-and-half
¾ cup grated Parmesan cheese
½ teaspoon salt
¼ teaspoon pepper

1. Shred the yellow and green zucchini with the shredder blade of a food processor. Place in a colander and add the salt, mixing until it is evenly distributed. Place the colander over a bowl and let sit for 15 to 30 minutes to collect the juices.
2. Wring the zucchini in a clean dish towel over the bowl to collect the juices. Set the juices aside and dry the squash carefully.
3. In a medium saucepan bring 1½ cups water to a boil and add the rice. Simmer for 5 minutes. Drain and reserve.
4. In an 11-inch ovenproof pan or skillet, heat 3 teaspoons

olive oil over medium-high heat. Sauté the leeks until slightly soft, about 5 minutes.

5. Add the remaining tablespoon of olive oil and sauté the zucchini. Sauté until almost tender, about 3 minutes. Add the garlic and parsley and sauté for another minute.

6. Sprinkle in the flour and stir over medium heat (a pasta fork works well for this) for 2 minutes. Remove from the heat and add the half-and-half and squash liquid. Continue to cook, stirring constantly until slightly thickened, about 3 minutes.

7. Add the rice and all but 2 tablespoons of the Parmesan cheese and mix well. Add the salt and pepper and taste for seasoning.

8. Preheat the oven to 425°F. Sprinkle the remaining cheese on top of the dish. Bake until browned and bubbling and the rice has absorbed the liquid, about 25 minutes.

ADVANCE PREPARATION: This may be prepared in the morning through step 7 and refrigerated. Bring to room temperature before baking.

Sautéed Zucchini and Arugula

SERVES 4 TO 6

This simple but unusual vegetable sauté has the bite of zesty, slightly bitter arugula. Serve it as an accompaniment to Sautéed Chicken with Tomato-Leek Sauce or Grilled Swordfish with Herbed Green Sauce.

 4 zucchini (about 1 pound), coarsely shredded
 2 tablespoons unsalted butter
 2 medium bunches arugula, thinly shredded
 1 medium garlic clove, minced
 1 teaspoon grated lemon zest
 1 tablespoon fresh lemon juice
 ¼ teaspoon salt
  Pinch pepper

1. Place the zucchini in a dry dish towel and wring out all the excess moisture. Dry the squash carefully with a dry dish towel.
2. In a medium sauté pan melt the butter over medium heat.
3. Add the zucchini and stir for 2 minutes. Add the arugula and continue stirring another minute or two. Add the garlic, lemon zest, lemon juice, salt, and pepper. Stir until combined and serve immediately.

Sautéed Tomatoes with Basil Cream

SERVES 4

This dish is ideal for the home gardener who has the tomatoes and basil within easy reach. Cook the whole cherry tomatoes quickly; otherwise they may burst. The tomatoes are glazed with a touch of cream and accented with chopped basil. This dish goes well with Roasted Sea Bass with Herbs, Grilled Marinated Chicken with Dijon Mustard, Tarragon, and Port, or Grilled Steaks, California Style.

   2 tablespoons unsalted butter
   1 pint cherry tomatoes, stemmed
   2 tablespoons whipping cream
   2 tablespoons basil
  ¼ teaspoon salt
  ¼ teaspoon pepper

1. Melt the butter in a medium skillet over medium heat. Sauté the cherry tomatoes for about 2 minutes, rolling them around continuously.
2. Add the cream and turn up the heat to create a glaze. This should take about a minute. (Don't let the tomato skins burst.)
3. Add the basil, salt, and pepper. Continue rolling the tomatoes around until evenly coated. Serve immediately.

Broiled Tomatoes Glazed with Mustard Herb Mayonnaise

SERVES 6

Beautiful, ripe tomato halves or slices are brushed with a tangy mustard-mayonnaise topping, baked and then broiled right before serving. These bubbly, golden brown tomatoes are excellent with Sautéed Scallops with Zucchini and Mushrooms, Roasted Rosemary Lemon Chicken, or Grilled Marinated Flank Steak.

- 3 medium tomatoes
- 3 tablespoons mayonnaise
- 1 teaspoon Dijon mustard
- 2 tablespoons finely chopped parsley
- 2 teaspoons finely chopped chives
- ¼ teaspoon salt
-    Pinch black pepper
- 3 tablespoons freshly grated Parmesan cheese

1. Preheat the oven to 400°F.
2. Cut the tomatoes in half or into 1½-inch-thick slices. Place cut side up in medium ovenproof baking dish.
3. In a small mixing bowl, combine the mayonnaise, mustard, 1 tablespoon parsley, chives, salt, pepper, and 2 tablespoons Parmesan cheese.
4. Spoon a heaping teaspoon of the mayonnaise mixture on top of each tomato, spreading to cover the top. Sprinkle tomatoes with the remaining tablespoon of Parmesan cheese.
5. Bake 10 to 12 minutes, depending on the size of the tomato slices, or until hot. Turn the oven to broil and switch tomatoes to the broiler and brown until glazed and bubbling. Remove from oven and sprinkle with remaining parsley to garnish. Serve immediately.

ADVANCE PREPARATION: This may be prepared up to 4 hours in advance through step 4 and refrigerated. Remove from the refrigerator ½ hour before baking.

Grilled Japanese Eggplant

SERVES 6

Almost every vegetable cooks beautifully on the barbecue, but Japanese eggplant with its elongated pear shape is particularly well suited for grilling. Cook individual slices or leave the stem on and slice the eggplant lengthwise to create a fan pattern. This is great either hot off the grill or at room temperature. Serve with Scallops Brochette with Spicy Caribbean Salsa or Grilled Lamb Chops with Wine-Mint Marinade.

12 Japanese eggplant
 3 tablespoons olive oil or avocado oil
 2 tablespoons fresh lemon juice
 1 tablespoon finely chopped parsley
½ teaspoon salt
¼ teaspoon black pepper

1. Slice the eggplant lengthwise into ¼-inch-thick pieces. Brush with oil and place on a platter.
2. Prepare the barbecue for medium-heat grilling. Grill the eggplant slices 3 inches from the flame for 3 to 4 minutes per side, depending on their thickness. They should have grill marks on them but not be burnt.
3. Place on a serving platter, sprinkle with lemon juice, herbs, salt, and pepper. Serve immediately.

ADVANCE PREPARATION: May be prepared completely up to 8 hours in advance and refrigerated. Remove from the refrigerator 1 hour before serving to reach room temperature.

Vine-ripened tomatoes are an essential element of summer's romance. Biting into a sun-warmed perfectly ripe tomato is a definite reward of the season. While we are used to enjoying the classic red tomato, we now have the option of eating yellow and orange and even white ones too. The varieties most available include:

- Plum, Roma, or Italian Style: These are small, pear-shaped tomatoes, 2 to 3 inches long. They are firm-fleshed and are excellent for sauces and ratatouille because they have more flesh than juice. They are also good for salads and are the tomato of choice for sun-drying.
- Cherry Tomatoes: These sweet little gems come in round and pear shapes and can be red, orange, or yellow. The yellow and orange varieties tend to be less acidic. Toss them in a salad halved or whole when tiny.
- Beefsteak Tomatoes: This is the king of tomatoes in both size and flavor. Beefsteaks are now also available in green and yellow as well as the usual red.

TO PEEL OR NOT TO PEEL

There is always a great controversy about whether or not to peel tomatoes. I enjoy their skin when I am eating them raw, but I prefer to peel and seed them before cooking them in a sauce. The best way to peel tomatoes is to immerse them for 10 seconds in a large pan of boiling water and then remove them immediately. Run cold water over the tomatoes to cool them, and then peel them. To seed the tomatoes, cut them in half and then carefully squeeze out the seeds and some of the juice. Or peel, seed, and purée them all at once by running them through the food processor and straining the purée.

A FEW QUICK WAYS TO ENJOY TOMATOES:

- Mix red and yellow cherry or pear tomatoes with oil and vinegar and shredded basil; then mound the mixture on a dark-colored plate for a striking contrast.
- Layer tomatoes with fresh, sliced mozzarella. Sprinkle olive oil and balsamic vinegar on top and garnish with strips of sun-dried tomatoes and basil.
- Glaze tomatoes with Roasted Garlic Mayonnaise under the broiler just before serving.
- Make the ultimate B-L-T by spreading basil-flavored mayonnaise on toasted French bread and layering it with crisp bacon, sliced tomatoes, and young butter lettuce.
- Halve and scoop out the pulp of cherry tomatoes. Spoon a dollop of Tapenade in each tomato and garnish it with parsley. Serve them as a quick first course.

Baked Beans with Bourbon and Apple Cider

SERVES 6 TO 8

There are certain foods that seem to be constant companions. I can't imagine eating barbecued spare ribs without their counterpart—baked beans. In this recipe white beans, cooked until just firm, are accented with an old-fashioned sauce of tomato, molasses, bourbon, and apple cider. These beans are also a nice addition to barbecued chicken, hamburgers, and baked ham.

1 pound navy beans or large white northern beans

1 medium onion, finely chopped

Sauce

¼ cup molasses

2 tablespoons brown sugar, preferably light

1 tablespoon dry mustard

1 tablespoon Worcestershire sauce

½ cup apple cider

2 tablespoons bourbon

½ cup tomato sauce

½ teaspoon salt

¼ teaspoon pepper

½ pound smoked ham pieces, cut into ¼-inch chunks

1. Soak the beans overnight in cold water; or use a quick soak method by bringing them to a boil in water to cover, boiling 2 minutes, covering, and letting them stand for 1 hour.

2. Drain the soaked beans and put them in a large saucepan with the chopped onion. Add enough water to cover generously. Bring to a boil and simmer partially covered until very tender, 1½ to 2 hours.

3. Combine all the sauce ingredients except for the ham in a medium mixing bowl. Mix well. Taste for seasoning and set aside.

4. Drain the beans and onions in a colander over a large mixing bowl or pan to catch the liquid. Reserve 2 cups of the bean liquid.

5. Preheat oven to 350°F. Pour the beans and onion into a medium ovenproof casserole, earthenware if possible. Pour the sauce over the beans and mix well. Add the ham and 2 more cups of bean liquid and mix to incorporate.

6. Cover the casserole and bake for about 35 minutes. Remove the cover, turn up the oven to 400°F, and continue to cook until liquid is almost gone, 45 minutes to 1 hour. Serve immediately.

ADVANCE PREPARATION: This may be prepared up to 3 days ahead and refrigerated. Remove from the refrigerator 1 hour before reheating. Reheat before serving in a 350°F oven for ½ hour.

Cuban Black Beans

SERVES 6 TO 8

Long-simmered whole black beans are flavored with a purée of onions and red pepper and seasoned with rich balsamic vinegar. The flavor of these beans actually improves if refrigerated overnight after cooking. Emmy Smith, who gave me this recipe, suggests serving Cuban Black Beans with Tomato-Papaya-Mint salsa for a sensational combination of flavors.

> 1 pound black beans, carefully chosen and cleaned
> 2 medium onions, halved
> 2 green peppers, halved
> 1 tablespoon fresh finely chopped oregano or 1 teaspoon dried
> 1 large hamhock (about 1 pound)
> 3 whole garlic cloves
> 2 teaspoons salt
> 3 tablespoons safflower oil
> 1 large onion, finely chopped
> 1 large sweet red pepper, seeded and finely chopped
> 2 medium garlic cloves, minced
> 4 tablespoons balsamic vinegar
> Pinch cayenne

1. Soak beans overnight in cold water; or use a quick soak method by bringing them to a boil in water to cover, boiling 2 minutes, covering, and letting stand 1 hour.
2. Drain the soaked beans and put them in a large casserole. Add enough water (about 2 quarts) to cover generously. Add the halved onions and green pepper, oregano, hamhock, garlic, and salt. Bring to a boil and simmer until mixture is slightly thickened and beans are cooked, 1½ to 2 hours.
3. Remove all the large pieces of vegetables and the hamhock. Drain, reserving about ½ cup bean liquid, and pour the beans into a medium casserole.
4. Heat the oil in a medium skillet over medium heat. Add the onions and sauté until slightly soft, about 3 minutes. Add

the red pepper and sauté 3 more minutes. Add the garlic and sauté another minute.

5. Place the onions, peppers, and garlic in a food processor with the reserved bean liquid and purée. Add the mixture to the black beans and then add the balsamic vinegar and cayenne pepper to taste. Mix to combine. Refrigerate overnight.

6. When ready to serve, reheat the beans in a 350°F oven for ½ hour. Serve immediately.

ADVANCE PREPARATION: This may be prepared 3 days in advance and refrigerated. Remove from the refrigerator 1 hour before reheating. Reheat before serving in a 350°F oven for ½ hour.

Eggplant, Tomato, and Mushroom Tart

SERVES 6

This main course pie uses tomatoes and eggplant to their full advantage. The pie crust stays dry because it is painted with Dijon mustard, and then Gruyère cheese is melted on top. This is a great dish to take to an outdoor concert or on a boat cruise. Serve with Garden Salad with Goat Cheese Thyme Dressing and Herbed Garlic Cheese Bread. Finish with Chocolate Pecan Torte with Espresso Crème Anglaise.

Filling

1¼ pounds eggplant, peeled and cut into ¼-inch dice
6 tablespoons olive oil
2 medium shallots, finely chopped
½ pound mushrooms, sliced
1 small red pepper, seeded and diced
2 medium garlic cloves, minced
1 teaspoon salt
¼ teaspoon black pepper
6 slices of bacon
3 eggs
1 cup crushed tomatoes
2 tablespoons finely chopped fresh parsley
2 tablespoons finely chopped basil
1 teaspoon finely chopped fresh thyme leaves
1 teaspoon finely chopped rosemary leaves
2 tablespoons freshly grated Parmesan cheese

Pie Shell

1 prebaked 11-inch tart shell or 9-inch prebaked pastry crust (see page 363)
3 tablespoons Dijon mustard
2 tablespoons Gruyère cheese, grated

Garnish

Yellow or red cherry tomato halves
3 tablespoons freshly grated Parmesan cheese

1. Place eggplant in colander and sprinkle with salt. Leave to drain for 15 minutes. Rinse and pat dry.
2. Heat the olive oil in a large skillet over medium heat. Add shallots and sauté until soft and transparent.
3. Add the eggplant, mushrooms, and red pepper and sauté until the eggplant is almost a purée and the mushrooms and pepper are soft, about 20 minutes. Add the garlic and continue to cook for another minute. Add the salt and pepper. Place in a medium bowl and set aside.
4. Preheat the oven to 375°F. Clean the skillet and return to

the stove. Fry the bacon over medium-high heat until crisp. Drain on paper towels, then cut into 1-inch pieces.

5. In a small bowl beat the eggs lightly and then add the crushed tomatoes and herbs. Add the bacon, eggplant mixture, and Parmesan cheese.

6. Using a pastry brush, paint the prebaked pastry crust with Dijon mustard. Sprinkle with the Gruyère cheese.

7. Place the crust in the oven and bake until the cheese just begins to melt, 5 to 7 minutes. Remove from the oven. Pour the eggplant mixture into the crust. Garnish with halved red or yellow cherry tomatoes, cut side up, and sprinkle on the additional 3 tablespoons Parmesan cheese, making sure the center is well covered. Put in the upper third of the oven and bake until the cheese is melted and the filling is set, for 25 to 30 minutes. Remove from the oven and cool before serving at room temperature.

ADVANCE PREPARATION: Eggplant mixture may be prepared 1 day in advance and refrigerated. The crust may be prepared 1 day in advance, covered, and refrigerated.

NOTE: The tart may also be served warm.

Vegetable Brochettes

SERVES 8

Of all the many ways to cook vegetables in the summer, this is my favorite. Grill these brochettes alongside your main course and your kitchen will stay cool. The squash and onions need to be blanched before grilling because they are much firmer. Allow the vegetables to marinate for at least 4 hours. Grilling with hardwoods such as mesquite or alderwood will give the brochettes a truly distinctive flavor. Serve these as an accompaniment to Grilled Halibut in Lemon Mustard Tarragon Marinade or Grilled Roast Beef with Sour Cream Herbed Sauce.

2 medium zucchini, cut into 16 round slices in total

2 medium yellow crookneck squash or yellow zucchini, cut into 16 round slices in total

16 small boiling onions

2 small Japanese eggplants, cut into 16 small slices in total

1 large sweet red pepper, seeded and cut into 16 pieces

16 small mushrooms, cleaned

Marinade

2 tablespoons fresh lemon juice

1 tablespoon sherry vinegar

2 medium garlic cloves, minced

2 tablespoons finely chopped basil leaves

1 teaspoon finely chopped fresh thyme leaves, or a pinch of dried

2 tablespoons finely chopped parsley leaves

2 teaspoons Dijon mustard

½ cup olive oil

¼ teaspoon salt

¼ teaspoon black pepper

1. Immerse the zucchini and summer squash in a medium pan of boiling water for 2 minutes. Drain and rinse with cold water to stop the cooking. Drain and place in a large mixing bowl.

2. Immerse the onions in a medium pan of boiling water for 10 minutes. Remove from the water, cool, and peel. Place in the mixing bowl with the squash.

3. Add the eggplant, red pepper, and mushrooms to the cooked vegetables.

4. In a small mixing bowl combine all the marinade ingredients and blend well. Taste for seasoning. Pour over the vegetables and stir well, coating all the vegetables. Marinate for at least 4 hours and up to 24 hours.

5. Soak 8 bamboo skewers in cold water for at least 1 hour. This will prevent them from burning when grilled. You may also use metal skewers.

6. Remove the vegetables from the marinade; reserve the marinade for basting.

7. Thread each skewer with 1 onion, 1 slice zucchini, 1 slice summer squash, 1 slice eggplant, 1 piece red pepper, and 1 mushroom. Repeat in the same order for each skewer.
8. Prepare the barbecue for medium-heat grilling. Place the brochettes on the grill and baste each side with the remaining marinade. Grill until the vegetables are tender, 7 to 10 minutes on each side.

ADVANCE PREPARATION: This may be prepared 1 day in advance through step 4 and refrigerated. The vegetables can be threaded on the skewers up to 4 hours in advance and refrigerated until grilling.

Tri-Color Vegetable Terrine

SERVES 4 TO 6

This versatile terrine can be a first course, side dish, or vegetarian main course. The light carrot-mushroom cheese custard is divided by a layer of sautéed spinach leaves. Serve this chilled, warm, or at room temperature. Try it with Grilled Orange-Cured Salmon or Grilled Turkey Breast in Orange Honey Mustard Sauce.

2 pounds carrots, peeled and sliced ¼-inch thick
4 tablespoons (¼ cup) unsalted butter
½ pound mushrooms, sliced
1½ pounds fresh spinach (about 2 bunches), cleaned, dried, and stemmed
4 eggs
½ cup half-and-half
2 cups grated Gruyère cheese
1½ teaspoons salt
½ teaspoon black pepper
⅛ teaspoon nutmeg, preferably freshly grated

1. Steam the carrots in a steamer basket over boiling water until al dente, 5 to 7 minutes. In a food processor fitted with a steel blade finely chop the carrots into small dice using the on/off pulse. Remove to a mixing bowl.

2. Melt 3 tablespoons butter in a medium skillet over medium heat. Add the mushrooms and sauté for 3 minutes. Drain well. In the food processor finely chop them into small dice using the on/off pulse. Add to the carrots.

3. Melt the remaining 1 tablespoon butter in the same skillet. Sauté the spinch over medium heat until soft but still bright green, 3 to 4 minutes. Place the spinach in a strainer and squeeze out all the liquid by pushing down with a spoon. Coarsely chop in the food processor using the on/off pulse. Set aside.

4. Preheat oven to 400°F. In a medium mixing bowl combine the eggs, half-and-half, and cheese. Add the carrots and mushrooms and combine thoroughly. Add the salt, pepper, and nutmeg and taste for seasoning.

5. Butter generously an 8 × 4 × 3-inch baking pan (or use a disposable loaf pan). Fill it with half of the carrot mixture. Spread the spinach evenly over the top with the remaining carrot mixture.

6. Place the loaf pan in a large pan filled halfway up the sides with hot water. Bake for 45 minutes until set, or until top is browned. Allow to rest for at least 15 minutes. Unmold onto a heated platter and serve warm.

ADVANCE PREPARATION: This may be prepared up to 1 day in advance, refrigerated, and served cold, or reheated at 350°F for 20 minutes.

Chilled Asparagus with Red Pepper Vinaigrette

SERVES 4

Springtime signals the arrival of fresh asparagus, to be enjoyed through-out the summer season. Chilled asparagus is especially refreshing for a luncheon or a casual dinner. I am always experimenting with different variations on vinaigrette and this one was created especially for slender asparagus spears. A purée of sweet red pepper is added to the dressing to give it a distinctive color and taste. Toasted pine nuts and chopped red pepper garnish the finished dish. Serve this on a buffet table or as a first course. For a main course try Crispy Roast Chicken with Spinach Pesto Cream or Spicy Citrus Grilled Swordfish.

Vinaigrette

    2 medium garlic cloves
    1 medium shallot
    3 tablespoons finely chopped sweet red pepper, seeded
    2 tablespoons red wine vinegar
    1 tablespoon balsamic vinegar
    2 teaspoons fresh lemon juice
    1 tablespoon whipping cream
  ¼ teaspoon salt
  ⅛ teaspoon finely ground pepper
    1 tablespoon finely chopped basil leaves
  ½ cup olive oil

    1 pound asparagus (preferably thin), peeled

Garnish

    2 tablespoons pine nuts
    2 tablespoons finely chopped, seeded, sweet red pepper, or diced roasted sweet red pepper (see page 362)

1. In a food processor fitted with a steel blade, process the garlic, shallot, and red pepper until minced. Add the vinegars, lemon juice, whipping cream, salt, pepper, and basil.

Process until combined. With the motor running, slowly add the olive oil. Taste for seasoning. Set aside.

2. Peel the asparagus and cut off 1 inch from the bottom of each stalk. Bring a large sauté pan of salted water to a boil and add the asparagus. Boil until just tender, about 5 minutes. Remove carefully with a slotted spoon and set on paper towels to drain.

3. Arrange the asparagus on a rectangular serving platter. Cover and refrigerate until chilled (about 3 hours) and ready to serve.

4. Preheat the oven to 350°F. Toast the pine nuts until lightly browned, about 5 minutes. Set aside.

5. When ready to serve, pour the vinaigrette evenly over the asparagus. Sprinkle the diced red pepper and toasted pine nuts on top and serve immediately.

ADVANCE PREPARATION: This may be prepared 8 hours ahead through step 4 and kept in the refrigerator until ready to serve. Garnish just before serving.

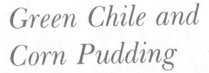

Green Chile and Corn Pudding

SERVES 4 TO 6

This is an extremely moist and flavorful custardy pudding. Inspired by a dish at San Francisco's Greens Restaurant, my version adds roasted chilies and plenty of sharp Cheddar cheese. Serve this with Grilled Veal Chops with Jalapeño Chutney and Grilled Japanese Eggplant for a perfect summer dinner. It is also excellent served as an entrée for lunch with a medley of salads such as Cherry Tomato and Hearts of Palm Salad and Green Bean, Mushroom, and Walnut Salad.

2 medium Anaheim chilies or ½ cup peeled and diced
canned green chilies, rinsed
4 cups corn kernels (about 8 medium ears)
½ cup half-and-half or milk
¾ cup whipping cream
5 large eggs
1¾ cups shredded sharp Cheddar cheese
1 teaspoon salt
¼ teaspoon white pepper

1. To peel the chilies, place on a broiler pan and broil approximately 6 inches from the heat until blackened on all sides. Use tongs to turn.
2. Close tightly in a brown paper bag. Let rest for 10 minutes.
3. Remove chilies from the bag, drain, and peel. Make a slit in each and open it up. Core and cut off the stem. Scrape out the seeds and ribs and finely chop the flesh. Set aside.
4. Preheat the oven to 350°F. Place all but 1 cup of the corn in a food processor fitted with a steel blade. Add the half-and-half or milk and purée until smooth.
5. Pour into a medium mixing bowl and whisk in the cream and eggs. Add the remaining 1 cup corn, finely chopped chilies, 1½ cups cheese, salt, and pepper and whisk until well combined.
6. Pour the mixture into a buttered 2-quart soufflé dish. Sprinkle the remaining cheese on top. Place the soufflé dish in a large ovenproof dish with enough hot water to reach halfway up the sides.
7. Bake until the top is golden brown and appears firm, 50 to 60 minutes. Remove from the oven and let rest 10 to 15 minutes before serving. It will become firmer as it cools.

ADVANCE PREPARATION: This may be prepared up to 4 hours in advance through step 5, covered, and kept at room temperature. Whisk again before pouring into the soufflé dish.

Grilled Corn on the Cob with Ancho Chile Butter

SERVES 6

Corn on the cob, grilled in the husk on the barbecue, is an earthy change of pace. If you're having an informal party it's fun to use the peeled-back husks to hold the corn. If this is too rustic for you, detach the husks and use corn holders. Ancho chile butter takes this grilled corn to another level altogether. Serve with Barbecued Ribs or Grilled Steaks, California Style and salad or coleslaw.

    2 tablespoons Ancho Chile Paste (see page 360)
    ½ cup (1 stick) unsalted butter, at room temperature
    ½ teaspoon salt
    6 whole ears of white or yellow corn, husks left on

1. *To make the chile butter:* Combine the ancho chile paste, butter, and salt in a small bowl. Beat together until thoroughly blended.
2. Pull back the husks, being careful not to break them off. Remove all the silk inside.
3. Soak the corn in a large bowl or sink full of cold water for ½ to 1 hour.
4. Drain and pat the corn dry. Rub with some of the ancho chile butter. Replace husks.
5. Prepare the barbecue for medium-heat grilling. Grill the ears for 10 to 15 minutes, depending on their size, turning to cook evenly.
6. Remove from the grill and, using a pot-holder glove, remove the husks.
7. Serve immediately with more ancho chile butter.

ADVANCE PREPARATION: The corn may be prepared 4 hours ahead through step 4 and kept at room temperature.

CHILIES

It's a common misconception that chilies are used in cooking simply to add hotness. In fact, their flavors add depth and complexity to a dish, and they can play a significant role in summer cooking. Different chilies have completely different properties and will add their own distinctive spirit. In all chilies, the fire is concentrated in the seeds and the ribs or veins, the little strips running down the inner surface of the chile. Here's a quick primer on some favorite chilies:

- Anaheim: This is also called the New Mexico chile, the chile verde, and the mild green chile. It's the chile to use when you want a mild chile taste. It is also excellent for stuffing. The Anaheim is medium light green turning to dark bright green and is 6 to 7 inches long. It must be roasted and peeled before using, and is available canned, whole, or diced.
- Poblano: The poblano has a distinctive, almost triangular shape and is about 5 inches long. This dark green chile has a deep, rich flavor and must be roasted and peeled. Its hotness can vary from mild to fairly hot, so taste the chile to make sure it will not overwhelm your dish. The poblano is good added to soups, salsas, and sauces.
- Jalapeño: This is bright to dark green and extremely hot. It is short and stubby, about 2 inches long. The jalapeño is also available canned and may be used when fresh ones are unavailable. It is excellent in salsa, sauces, dressings, and marinades. It does not need to be roasted and peeled, but be sure to seed it.
- Serrano: This skinny little pepper has a rich and spicy character and can be eaten dark green or scarlet red. It does not need to be roasted and peeled, but it must be seeded. It's great with salsa, sauces, main dishes, and as a garnish for dishes that contain it.

- Ancho: This wrinkled-looking chile is large (4 to 5 inches long) and has a triangular shape and mahogany red color. The ancho is the ripened, dried version of the poblano chile. This mildly hot chile is available in Mexican specialty stores or in the specialty section of supermarkets. For maximum flavor it should be toasted over high heat in a skillet until it begins to puff up. Pour boiling water over it to soften it before using.
- Crushed Red Pepper Flakes: This is dried hot pepper that has been crushed with the seeds inside, which means that it's very hot and should be used sparingly.
- Fresh chilies will keep refrigerated in the crisper in a plastic bag for a week. They are excellent in marinades, salsas, vegetables, rice, soups, and egg dishes.
- Dried chilies may be kept almost indefinitely. Make sure you toast them before using.

Green Corn Tamales with Sour Cream Tomatillo Sauce

SERVES 8 TO 12

These spectacularly good tamales are the dish to make at the peak of the corn season. If you're lucky enough to find white corn, you will have the sweetest, most delicate tamales imaginable. Just a touch of fresh jalapeño chile is added to the corn mixture for a subtle bite. Sour Cream Tomatillo Sauce is served on the side for a refreshing accompaniment. Since this is one of those elaborate dishes that requires lots of time and help, invite your friends who love to cook. Split up the jobs of husking and shucking the corn so that everyone can get involved. Filling the tamales and folding them into neat little packages takes a bit of experience so don't get discouraged if your first few aren't perfect—they'll still taste good. Serve this as a first course followed by Grilled Sea Bass with California Salsa or as a light main course with plenty of sliced tomatoes on the side. This vegetarian combination is summer eating at its best. You won't believe how many you can eat!

　30　ears fresh corn, unhusked
　　2　pounds Monterey Jack or mild Cheddar, shredded
　　1　cup corn meal
　　1　jalapeño chile, seeded and finely chopped*
　　1　tablespoon salt

Sauce
　　2　cups sour cream
　¾　cup Tomatillo Sauce (see page 348)

1. Clean the corn: With a large sharp knife, cut off the stem. Cut off extra long and straggly husks. The husks should just hug the corn.
2. Cut a line into the corn husks about ¼-inch up the ear, cutting just through the husks and not the corn. Remove the husks one by one. They will roll up and look like rolled paper. Discard the husks that are torn or too small—usually the outer and innermost leaves.
3. With a small knife cut the corn kernels off the cob. To do this, hold the ear in a very large mixing bowl and scrape the kernels off the cob into the bowl. Discard the cobs.
4. In a food processor fitted with a steel blade process 4 cups of the corn kernels with a handful of cheese until completely puréed. Pour into a large mixing bowl. Continue processing the corn meal with the rest of the cheese until all has been puréed. Add the corn meal, chile, and salt.
5. Lay 2 husks on a work surface with the 2 wide ends overlapping about 2 inches. Spoon about ¼ cup corn mixture in the center. Be careful not to overfill. The amount of filling may vary according to the size of the husks. Take the side nearest to you and roll it in the opposite direction, encasing the filling. Fold over the two long ends to completely encase and secure the filling. Push the filling toward the center as you fold the ends over. Place seam side down on a platter.

6. When ready to cook pour in enough water to come 2 inches up the sides of a 6-quart dutch oven. Place a steaming rack into the pot. Line the sides of the dutch oven vertically with husks. Transfer a layer of tamales to cover the bottom of the steaming rack and then top with additional layers until the pot is full. Fold over the husks from the sides of the pot to cover the tamales. Flatten additional husks over the top to completely cover the tamales. Repeat the process in a second dutch oven with the remaining tamales.

7. Place over high heat, cover, and steam until the filling is just firm enough to hold its shape, about 30 minutes.

8. While the tamales are cooking, combine the sour cream and Tomatillo Sauce in the food processor and process until puréed. Taste for seasoning. If you like it really spicy, add another finely chopped jalapeño chile.

9. When the tamales are cooked, transfer them to a serving platter and serve the sour cream–tomatillo sauce on the side. Don't forget a large bowl for the discarded husks.

ADVANCE PREPARATION: Although this is best made and cooked right before serving, the tamales may be steamed up to 3 hours ahead and kept warm in the pot. The husks will keep them warm.

*When working with chilies, always wear rubber gloves. Wash the cutting surface and knife immediately afterward.

Green Corn Tamales with Sour Cream Tomatillo Sauce

CORN

One of the joys of summer is choosing fresh corn, just picked, with the husk still attached so you can enjoy its garden-fresh sweetness. Although it's difficult to go wrong this time of year in selecting corn, remember these tips:

- Look for fresh green husks and tender milky kernels that are plump and leave no space between the rows.
- Don't buy ears with gigantic kernels.
- Store corn very cold and for only a short time, since it does not keep well and its delicious sugar will quickly turn to starch (an ice chest filled with ice will keep the corn at its best for a few hours).
- If at all possible, eat corn the same day it is picked.

Some varieties of corn read like new ice cream flavors:

- Butterfruit: crunchy yellow and sometimes white and yellow; great used raw in salads
- How Sweet It Is: white with crispy kernels
- Early Extra Sweet: tender yellow kernels that are especially sweet
- Kandy Korn: a yellow, starchy, sweet corn
- Tendertreat: yellow with creamy rather than crunchy kernels
- Peaches and Cream: sweet and juicy yellow and white kernels; good for eating raw
- Early Sunglow: among the sweetest and tenderest corn
- Silver Queen: sometimes called the queen of corn, this one boasts white, tender, crisp sweet kernels.
- Butter and Sugar: white and yellow, very sweet corn

To cook corn, drop the ears in a large pot of boiling water and cook for 2 to 4 minutes. Remove the ears with tongs and serve immediately with plenty of unsalted butter.

You can also barbecue corn so that the kernels almost caramelize for a deep, rich flavor (see page 265).

Lemon-Herb Roasted Potatoes

SERVES 6

These red rose potatoes are roasted with simple seasonings to a crispy golden brown outside, while the potato stays moist and flavorful within. They'll highlight many main dishes without overpowering them. Serve with Scrambled Eggs with Three Cheeses, Sautéed Chicken with Tomato-Leek Sauce, or Grilled Veal Chops with Peach-Jalapeño Chutney.

2½ pounds small red or white rose potatoes, unpeeled
¼ cup olive oil
2 tablespoons fresh lemon juice
1 teaspoon salt
1 teaspoon fresh oregano, or ½ teaspoon dried
1 teaspoon fresh thyme, or ½ teaspoon dried
¼ teaspoon paprika
½ teaspoon finely ground pepper

1. Preheat the oven to 425°F. Wash the potatoes, rinse, and pat dry. Cut each into ¾-inch dice.
2. Combine the olive oil, lemon juice, salt, oregano, thyme, paprika, and pepper in a large bowl and mix well. Add the potatoes and toss.
3. Arrange on an oiled baking sheet and bake about 35 minutes, turning every 15 minutes, until tender and well browned. Taste for seasoning.
4. Turn into a serving dish and serve immediately.

ADVANCE PREPARATION: This may be prepared 2 hours in advance and kept at room temperature. Reheat in a 350°F oven for 10 to 15 minutes.

Herbed New Potatoes with Vermouth

SERVES 4

These dressed-up potatoes look particularly pretty with a strip peeled around the center. Steaming the potatoes brings out their innate sweetness. The mint, chive, and vermouth butter adds a gentle yet striking contrast. Serve with Grilled Halibut in Lemon Mustard Tarragon Marinade, Roasted Rosemary Lemon Chicken, or Grilled Marinated Flank Steak.

1½ pounds small new potatoes

2 tablespoons unsalted butter
2 tablespoons dry vermouth
2 teaspoons finely chopped chives
1 tablespoon finely chopped mint
¼ teaspoon salt
⅛ teaspoon white pepper

1. Scrub the potatoes and peel if desired, or just peel a ring around the center for a more decorative look. Put in the top of a steamer over boiling water. Cover and steam until tender, 15 to 20 minutes.
2. Heat the remaining ingredients in a small saucepan over medium heat until the butter is melted. Taste for seasoning.
3. Transfer the potatoes to a serving bowl and pour the vermouth herb butter over. Serve immediately.

ADVANCE PREPARATION: These may be kept warm in a double boiler over water on low heat for 1 hour.

Vegetable Lemon Rice

SERVES 4 TO 6

My friend Nydia, who comes from Nicaragua, has taught me a lot about cooking rice. She insists that for the best taste you must sauté the rice over high heat before adding hot water. When you try this technique, I think you will agree. This family favorite includes peas and carrots, which add color, and basmati rice, which gives it a sweet, nutty flavor. Add the lemon juice if you like, depending on what you are serving with it. Serve this as an accompaniment to Veal Chops with Peach-Jalapeño Chutney or Barbecued Lamb with Orange-Tahini Peanut Sauce.

   2 tablespoons olive oil
   1 onion, finely chopped
1½ cups basmati rice
   2 medium carrots, peeled and finely diced (about 1 cup)
   3 cups hot water
   ¼ cup fresh lemon juice (optional)
   1 cup frozen tiny peas, defrosted
   1 teaspoon salt
   ¼ teaspoon pepper

1. Heat the olive oil in a medium saucepan on medium heat. Sauté the onion until slightly soft, 3 to 4 minutes.
2. Turn up the heat to high and add the rice. Brown for about 3 minutes, stirring constantly.
3. Reduce the heat to medium, add the carrots, and continue to stir another minute.
4. Add the hot water and lemon juice, if desired, to the rice, stir with a fork, and bring to a boil. Reduce the heat.
5. Cover and simmer 20 to 25 minutes. Add the peas at about the last 3 minutes of cooking and continue cooking until all the liquid has been absorbed and the rice is tender.
6. Add the salt and pepper and taste for seasoning. Serve immediately.

ADVANCE PREPARATION: This may be prepared 2 hours in advance and kept at room temperature. Add the peas just before reheating. Reheat carefully in the top of a double boiler over hot water on medium heat for 10 minutes.

Grilled Red Potatoes with Pesto and Cheese

SERVES 4 TO 6

If you can't find tiny potatoes for this recipe, use larger ones that have been cut into 1½-inch pieces. When cooked in aluminum foil, the potatoes steam while the pesto and cheese form a crispy outer coating. As you open the foil packages, their fragrance fills the air. You'll get nearly the same results if you'd rather bake them in the oven. Serve these as a side dish with simple grilled chicken or fish.

   1½ pounds baby red potatoes (about 18 potatoes)
    2 tablespoons Spinach Pesto (see page 351)
    1 tablespoon Parmesan cheese

1. Scrub the potatoes and immerse them in a large pan of boiling water for 10 minutes on medium-high heat. Remove from heat and pour into a colander. Cool.
2. Cut six 6 × 6-inch pieces of aluminum foil.
3. Place 3 potatoes on each piece of foil. Spoon 1 teaspoon of Spinach Pesto on the potatoes and then sprinkle with ½ teaspoon of Parmesan cheese.
4. Wrap each package until it is tightly closed.
5. Prepare the barbecue for medium-heat grilling (or preheat oven to 425°F).
6. Grill the potato packages 3 inches from the flame for 6 to 8 minutes per side (or place on a baking sheet and bake 25 to 35 minutes, depending on size of potatoes).
7. Place the potato packages on a serving platter and open them just before serving.

ADVANCE PREPARATION: May be prepared 8 hours in advance through step 4 and refrigerated. Remove from the refrigerator ½ hour before grilling.

Crispy Grilled Potatoes

SERVES 4

These potatoes are my choice when I am barbecuing the entrée and want a simple potato side dish. Partial cooking in advance will guarantee a crisp outer crust and a moist center when they are grilled. They make a nice addition to Grilled Swordfish with Red Pepper Hollandaise Sauce or Grilled Lamb Chops with Wine-Mint Marinade.

> 1½ **pounds baking white or red rose potatoes**
> 2 **tablespoons unsalted butter**
> 1 **medium garlic clove, peeled**
> ¼ **teaspoon salt**
> ⅛ **teaspoon black pepper**

1. Scrub and peel the potatoes. Immerse potatoes in a medium saucepan of boiling salted water for 8 to 10 minutes, depending on their size. Drain and cool. Cut the potatoes into 2-inch-thick chunks. Skewer the potato pieces onto metal skewers.
2. In a small saucepan combine the butter and garlic and bring to a simmer over medium heat. When the butter is completely melted, add the salt and pepper. Remove the garlic clove.
3. When ready to grill, prepare the barbecue for medium-heat grilling. Place potatoes on the grill and baste with the melted butter. Grill 6 to 8 minutes on each side. The potatoes should be crispy. Serve with more salt and pepper, if desired.

ADVANCE PREPARATION: This may be prepared 1 hour in advance through step 2 and kept at room temperature.

Crispy Grilled Potatoes

Spicy Potatoes Gratinée

This is the dish to make on one of those cool, cloudy summer days when the wind begins to blow. These potatoes are so addictive that I have sometimes made an entire meal of them—an indulgence, to say the least. Adapted from a dish served at the famed Troisgros Brothers' restaurant in Roanne, France, these potatoes are distinguished by the addition of fresh chilies. The potatoes are extra-delicious because milk and cream are absorbed into them in a two-step cooking process. Sautéed mild or hot chilies are layered between the potatoes for a colorful contrast. It takes just a few minutes to broil and peel the chilies, and they make a big difference to the delicacy of the dish. Serve as a side dish with Grilled Veal Chops with Fresh Corn and Tarragon Sauce. You can also serve these potatoes in individual gratinée dishes as a first course.

> 4 medium Anaheim or poblano chilies*
> 1 tablespoon unsalted butter
> 2½ pounds red rose potatoes
> 1¼ cups milk
> 1 cup whipping cream
> 1 teaspoon salt
> ⅛ teaspoon freshly ground pepper
> 1 tablespoon unsalted butter

1. To roast and peel the chilies, place them on a broiler pan and broil approximately 6 inches from the heat until blackened on all sides. Use tongs to turn the chilies.
2. Put the chilies in a brown paper bag and close it tightly. Let rest for 10 minutes.
3. Remove the chilies from the bag, drain them, and peel off the skins. Make a slit in each chile and open it up. Core each chile and cut off its stem. Scrape out the seeds and ribs. Cut the flesh into ¼-inch dice.
4. In a medium skillet, sauté the diced chilies in the butter until slightly softened, 3 to 5 minutes. Set aside.
5. Peel the potatoes. Slice into ⅛-inch or thinner slices (the

food processor works well for this, especially the fine slicing disk). Wrap the potatoes in a dish towel and wring out any excess water.

6. Heat the milk over a medium flame in a *heavy*, large, deep saucepan. Add the potatoes, separating the slices as you drop them into the milk and bring it to a boil. Cover, lower the heat, and simmer until most of the milk has been absorbed, 10 to 15 minutes. Watch carefully or the bottom of the pan may burn.

7. Add the whipping cream, salt, and pepper and again bring to a boil. Reduce the heat and simmer, covered, until almost all of the cream has been absorbed, about 15 more minutes. Don't let the bottom of the pan burn. Taste for seasoning.

8. Generously butter a medium (at least 9 inches in diameter and at least 2 inches deep) ovenproof baking dish. With a large spoon, transfer half of the potato mixture into the baking dish. Layer the chilies evenly on top. Cover with the remaining potatoes.

9. Preheat the broiler to medium-high heat. Place the potatoes about 4 inches from the heat and broil until nicely gratinéed, about 10 minutes. Watch carefully—the potatoes burn easily.

ADVANCE PREPARATION: This may be prepared 8 hours in advance through step 8 and refrigerated. Remove from the refrigerator 1 hour before broiling.

* When working with chilies, always wear rubber gloves. Wash the cutting surface and knife immediately afterward.

Spicy Potatoes Gratinée

Breads

Toasted Pita with Parmesan

SERVES 4

These tasty pita bread triangles are versatile and easy to make. They can accompany either soups, such as Golden Summer Soup or Yellow Squash Soup, or salads, especially Marinated Lentil Salad or Chicken Salad with Roasted Garlic Mayonnaise.

> 2 pita breads, sesame or plain
> 2 tablespoons olive oil
> 2 tablespoons freshly grated Parmesan cheese

1. Preheat the broiler, if necessary. Split each pita in half by tearing the top half from the bottom; put the halves together again and cut in 8 triangles. Arrange on a baking sheet, crust side down.
2. Brush the triangles with the olive oil and sprinkle with the Parmesan cheese.
3. Broil until browned. Serve hot.

ADVANCE PREPARATION: These may be prepared 8 hours in advance and served at room temperature.

VARIATION: Use small tortillas instead of the pita bread.

Use single-layer circles of pita bread or tortillas (corn or flour) cut into 6 to 8 triangles. Try some of these different topping ideas and run the triangles under the broiler just until they turn golden brown.

- Spread with Roasted Garlic Mayonnaise and sprinkle freshly grated Parmesan cheese on top
- Spread with Basil Shallot Mayonnaise and sprinkle aged, grated goat cheese on top
- Brush with avocado oil and sprinkle with crumbled fresh goat cheese and finely chopped thyme
- Spread with Ancho Chili Mayonnaise
- Brush with melted unsalted butter, chopped fresh herbs, salt and pepper

Crisp Tortilla Chips

SERVES 6

Although these chips are not deep-fried, they have all the taste and crunch of their greasy and less healthy cousins.

6 corn tortillas, cut into triangles
Salt
Pepper

1. Preheat the oven to 400°F. Place the triangles on a baking sheet. Heat in the oven until crisp, about 10 minutes.
2. Remove from the oven and place in a bowl. Season with salt and pepper and serve immediately.

Corn Tortillas

Tortillas bought packaged at the market tend to be full of preservatives and almost tasteless. If you've never had freshly made tortillas, you'll be surprised at how delicious and moist they can be. Best of all are the ones made with masa dough from a good tortilleria. See if they'll sell you some fresh dough. Tortillas are also surprisingly easy to make, especially with the right equipment. You can find a tortilla press at most cookware stores. These can accompany Tequila Lime Grilled Shrimp or Cuban Black Beans.

   2 cups masa harina
1½ cups warm water

1. Have ready 24 7-inch squares of wax paper. Combine the flour and warm water in a medium bowl. Blend the mixture with a fork until it forms a smooth ball, then divide the dough into 12 pieces. Form each piece into a ball 3 inches in diameter and cover the balls with an inverted bowl.
2. Put a wax-paper square on the bottom half of a tortilla press and place a dough ball on it, opposite the handle and slightly off center toward the edge of the press. Flatten the ball slightly and cover it with another wax-paper square. Lower the top of the press onto the wax paper and press down firmly on the lever until the tortilla measures 6 to 6½ inches in diameter. Repeat the process with the remaining dough.
3. Heat griddle on highest setting until hot. (A drop of water will bounce.) Carefully peel off the top wax paper from a tortilla and invert the tortilla onto the griddle. After 5 seconds, peel off the remaining wax paper. Cook the tortilla for 1 minute, turning it over for about 1 minute or until it looks dry and flecked with golden specks. Transfer to a plate. Cook the remaining tortillas in the same manner. Stack the tortillas between sheets of wax paper and, if not to be used immediately, wrap them in plastic wrap.

ADVANCE PREPARATION: These tortillas may be kept up to 1 day in the refrigerator. Reheat in foil in a 350°F oven for 10 minutes.

NOTE: If you're using fresh (or frozen and defrosted) masa dough, form it into 3-inch balls as in step 1 and proceed with the recipe.

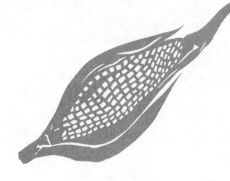

Fresh Fig Bread

MAKES 1 LOAF

This dense, moist tea bread takes advantage of the abundant crop of figs we enjoy each summer. The purée gives a fresh fig flavor to the dough, while the diced dried figs provide a burst of similar taste, along with a satisfying change of texture. Serve for breakfast or as a light dessert with fresh fruit. The bread is particularly delicious toasted and spread with softened cream cheese.

    6 medium-sized fresh figs
    2 cups all-purpose flour
    ½ teaspoon baking soda
    1 teaspoon baking powder
    ½ teaspoon salt
    ½ teaspoon ground ginger
    ¼ cup safflower oil
    1 egg, beaten
    ½ cup dried figs, coarsely chopped
    ¾ cup sugar
    ½ cup coarsely chopped walnuts

1. Peel the fresh figs and purée in a blender or food processor fitted with a steel blade. Measure out 1 cup purée.

2. Preheat the oven to 350°F. Butter and flour an 8 × 4-inch loaf pan.

3. Sift together the flour, baking soda, baking powder, salt, and ginger.

4. Combine the oil, egg, 1 cup fig purée, and chopped figs in a medium bowl. Slowly whisk in the sugar until well blended.

5. Add the sifted dry ingredients and mix well with a wooden spoon. Fold in the walnuts.

6. Spoon into a pan and bake until a cake tester inserted into the bread comes out clean, about 1 hour.

7. Cool 30 minutes in the pan and then turn out onto a rack. Serve warm or at room temperature with softened butter.

NOTE: This bread tastes best on the day it is baked.

Herbed Garlic Cheese Bread

SERVES 8

This is the perfect accompaniment for many barbecued dishes. It's also a nice way to begin your evening while awaiting dinner. Using freshly grated Parmesan cheese makes this version of the American classic a stand-out. Try it with Pasta Shells with Peppers, Mushrooms, and Sausages or Grilled Whole Bluefish with Lemon Dill Butter.

½ cup unsalted butter, at room temperature
3 medium garlic cloves, minced
½ cup freshly grated Parmesan cheese
1 tablespoon finely chopped basil
½ teaspoon finely chopped thyme
⅛ teaspoon fresh oregano, or a pinch of dried oregano
¼ teaspoon salt
⅛ teaspoon white pepper

1 large loaf French or sourdough French bread

1. Combine the butter, garlic, ¼ cup Parmesan cheese, basil, thyme, oregano, salt, and pepper in small mixing bowl. Blend well.
2. Preheat the oven to 400°F. Slice the bread in half lengthwise and spread each side with half of the mixture. Sprinkle the two halves with the remaining Parmesan cheese.
3. Slice the bread halves into 2-inch-thick slices about ¾ of the way through. Make sure that you haven't cut all the way through and that the crust is still holding the bread together. Wrap each half tightly in aluminum foil.
4. Place the loaves on a cookie sheet and bake for 10 to 15 minutes. Remove from the foil wrap and serve immediately.

ADVANCE PREPARATION: This may be prepared 4 hours ahead through step 3 and refrigerated. Remove from the refrigerator ½ hour before baking.

Barbecued Pizza with Leeks, Mozzarella, Tomatoes, and Pancetta

MAKES 2 MEDIUM PIZZAS;
SERVES 2 TO 4 AS A MAIN COURSE;
6 TO 8 AS AN APPETIZER

I've often thought that grilled pizza would be the ultimate summer recipe. One day, I was cooking at the Parkway Grill in Pasadena, California, and I told the chef, Hugo Molina, about my idea. Since the Parkway is renowned for its pizza, Hugo couldn't wait to try it. The result was a wonderful surprise. The pizza had a delightful smoky taste, the grill-marked crust was crispy, and the toppings were perfectly cooked. I was so enthusiastic I experimented with an assortment of pizzas on my home grill that night. A grill with a lid works best. This combination is my favorite. If pancetta, the Italian dry-cured bacon, isn't available, substitute thickly sliced bacon.

Topping
- ½ pound ripe plum (Roma) tomatoes
- 3 tablespoons olive oil
- 3 medium leeks, white and light green parts, cleaned and thinly sliced
- ¼ teaspoon salt
- ⅛ teaspoon pepper
- ½ pound pancetta, cut into 1-inch pieces
- ¼ cup olive oil

- 1 recipe Pizza Dough (see page 288)

- 1½ cups shredded mozzarella cheese
- ¼ cup finely chopped basil

1. *To make the topping:* Slice the tomatoes crosswise. Drain the slices in a colander for ½ hour to remove any excess liquid.
2. Heat the olive oil in a deep sauté pan over low heat. Add the leeks and mix thoroughly. Cover and cook over very low heat, stirring often, until tender, about 20 minutes. If any liquid remains in the pan, uncover and continue cooking, stirring, until it evaporates. Add the salt and pepper and taste for seasoning.
3. In a medium skillet, cook the pancetta over medium-low heat until crisp and slightly brown. Remove to paper towels and drain.
4. Place the pancetta, leeks, and mozzarella in separate small bowls. Reserve.
5. When ready to barbecue, prepare the barbecue for medium-high-heat grilling. (If your barbecue has no cover, improvise one out of aluminum foil.)
6. Oil 2 round baking sheets or pizza pans. Knead the dough again briefly and divide it into 2 equal parts. Put each on a baking sheet. With oiled hands, pat each piece of dough into a 9-inch circle. You may also roll out the dough on a

floured surface, using a rolling pin, and transfer the pizzas to the baking sheets.

7. Brush the tops of the pizzas with olive oil. Using a large spatula, transfer the pizzas to the center of the grill and cook until the dough begins to puff and there are grill marks on the bottom, about 2 minutes.

8. Using a large spatula, turn the pizzas over and move them to the coolest part of the grill. Brush the grilled top of the pizza with the remaining olive oil. Divide the leek mixture between the two pizzas, spreading them with it evenly. Sprinkle ¾ cup of the mozzarella cheese over each pizza. Divide and arrange the pancetta pieces on top, then divide and overlap the tomato slices in an attractive pattern. Sprinkle with the basil.

9. Move the pizzas into the center of the grill and cover the barbecue for 3 minutes. Check the pizzas and rotate them. Cover the grill and cook 2 to 3 minutes more. Watch carefully so that they do not burn on the bottom. The cheese should be completely melted. (If you want them hotter on top, you can place them under a preheated broiler for a minute or two.) They should be slightly charred. Place on platters and cut into wedges with a pizza wheel. Serve immediately.

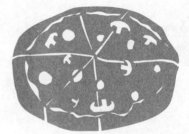

Barbecued Pizza with Leeks, Mozzarella, Tomatoes, and Pancetta

Pizza Dough

You can usually buy pizza dough from a good pizzeria and that may be the solution for the summer cook. Purists will want to make their own, though, and this food processor method is really very easy.

Pizza dough

> 2 ¼-ounce envelopes dry yeast or 2 (⅗-ounce) cakes of
>   fresh yeast
> 1 cup lukewarm water
> 3 cups all-purpose flour
> 1½ teaspoons salt
> 2 tablespoons olive oil

1. Sprinkle the dry yeast or crumble the fresh yeast over ¼ cup water in a small bowl and leave for 10 minutes. Stir to dissolve the yeast.
2. In a food processor fitted with a steel blade, process the flour and salt briefly. Add the remaining water and olive oil to the yeast mixture. With blades turning in the food processor, gradually pour in the yeast-liquid mixture. If the dough is too dry to hold together, add 1 tablespoon of water and process again. Process for 1 minute to knead the dough.
3. Transfer the dough to a clean bowl and sprinkle with a little flour. Cover with a damp cloth and let rise in a warm place for about 1 hour or until doubled in volume.
4. Punch the dough down and knead again briefly on a floured surface until smooth. Return to the bowl and cover.
5. Let the dough rise 30 to 45 minutes or until doubled in volume.
6. Shape according to the individual recipe.

ADVANCE PREPARATION: The dough may be prepared up to 8 hours ahead through step 4 and refrigerated. To continue, remove from the refrigerator and let rise 20 to 30 minutes. Then shape according to individual recipe.

Thinking up toppings for pizza is fun—the possibilities are almost endless. I tend to prefer simple combinations, but every now and then I want one with the "works," like the Mexican-style pizza. Here are some of my favorites:

- Plum (Roma) tomato, mozzarella, and basil
- Pesto sauce, Italian fontina, and cooked shrimp
- Goat cheese, arugula, and cooked chicken
- Goat cheese and black olives
- Grilled eggplant, tomato, Parmesan cheese, and thyme
- Mexican style: sautéed onion, roasted chilies, tomatoes, Cheddar cheese, and cilantro, topped with avocado and sour cream
- Roasted garlic, sun-dried tomatoes, and goat cheese
- Mascarpone, smoked salmon, and caviar
- Three Onion Relish with Niçoise olives, garlic, and anchovies
- Yellow and red cherry tomatoes, red onion, cooked sweet and hot sliced sausage, and Parmesan cheese

Desserts

Poached Peaches in White Zinfandel with Fresh Raspberry Sauce

SERVES 6

I created this recipe when my first crop of Babcock peaches turned out to be larger than I had ever expected. The Babcock peach is distinctive because of its creamy white fruit streaked with red. Fresh red raspberry sauce is lovely spooned on top of the poached peach halves. Serve these in your largest wineglasses and add a sprig of mint.

    6 medium Babcock or other white peaches, slightly firm
    3 cups white Zinfandel
    1 cup sugar
    2 cinnamon sticks
   10 sprigs fresh mint (preferably pineapple mint)

Raspberry Sauce
    1 pint fresh or 12 ounces frozen unsweetened raspberries
    1 tablespoon fresh lemon juice
    2 tablespoons powdered sugar

Garnish
    Fresh mint leaves (preferably pineapple mint)

1. In a large saucepan bring water to a boil. Immerse the peaches in the water for about 20 seconds and then remove immediately.
2. Peel the peaches and then cut in half, removing the pit.
3. In a large nonaluminum dutch oven or heat-proof casserole combine the wine, sugar, cinnamon sticks, and mint. Over medium heat bring the mixture to a simmer, making sure that the sugar dissolves.
4. Add the peach halves carefully. Cover and poach until tender but still firm, about 10 minutes. (Timing will depend

on the ripeness and size of the peaches.) Turn the peaches at least once while poaching to obtain an even color.

5. Remove the peaches from the syrup, place in a glass bowl, and cool. Cool the syrup, remove the mint leaves, and then drizzle on about ½ cup over the peaches.

6. *To prepare the raspberry sauce:* If using frozen raspberries, defrost and drain them. Purée the berries in a blender or a food processor fitted with a steel blade. Add the lemon juice and powdered sugar and process until smooth. Press the purée through a nylon strainer and refrigerate until needed.

7. *To serve:* Arrange 2 peach halves in each individual glass bowl. Pour over a tablespoon or so of the syrup and then spoon on some of the raspberry sauce. Garnish with fresh mint leaves.

ADVANCE PREPARATION: This may be prepared 8 hours in advance through step 6 and refrigerated.

VARIATION: The peaches can be poached whole. Increase the cooking time slightly and serve with a knife and fork, since the pit has not been removed.

NOTE: Babcock peaches and other white peaches cook faster than the yellow varieties.

Summer Fruit Compote

SERVES 6

In this compote bright summer fruits are gently poached together in a Johannesberg Reisling syrup. I like to use this wine because of its semidry, fruity character. You can vary the fruits you poach, but make sure that they are all about the same size. Slightly undercook them since they continue to cook while cooling. Accompany the compote with a plate of Almond Cookies with Lemon and Port.

6 medium peaches, slightly underripe
6 medium plums, slightly underripe
6 medium apricots, slightly underripe
3 cups Johannesberg Reisling
1 cup sugar
2 thick lemon slices

Garnish

Fresh mint leaves
Crème Fraîche (see page 369) (optional)
Amaretto Cream (see page 335) (optional)
Whipped cream (optional)

1. Immerse the peaches in a large pan of boiling water for 20 to 30 seconds. Remove immediately and cool. Peel, cut in half, and remove the pit. Place in a medium bowl.
2. Immerse the plums in a large pan of boiling water for 1 to 1½ minutes. Remove immediately and cool. Peel and place in the bowl with the peaches.
3. In a large saucepan combine the wine, sugar, and lemon slices and bring to a boil over high heat. Reduce to a simmer over medium-low heat.
4. Place all of the fruit in the syrup and simmer, turning occasionally. Cover the pan. The apricots may be done before the other fruit, so watch carefully. Remove the fruit as it becomes done and place it in a large glass bowl. The fruit should be slightly resistant when cut. Remember that it will continue to cook a few minutes more after being removed from the heat.
5. Reduce the syrup over high heat by one half. Remove the lemon slices and let the syrup cool.
6. Pour the cooled syrup over the fruit and refrigerate for 4 to 6 hours.
7. To serve, garnish the bowl with fresh mint leaves. Serve Crème Fraîche, whipped cream, or Amaretto Cream on the side.

ADVANCE PREPARATION: This may be prepared 1 day ahead and refrigerated.

CHEESE AND
FRUIT COMBINATIONS

Fruit and cheese platters can be a stunning ending to a simple meal or an elegant buffet. I always use a wicker cheese tray or other low baskets and accent the cheeses with edible flowers from the garden. Here is the one place I think flowers belong with food, nasturtiums or roses especially. A few wonderful fruit and cheese combinations follow. And of course you can mix any of the combinations.

- Nectarines with Explorateur or Brillat-Savarin
- Apricots with Mascarpone
- Pears with Gorgonzola
- Figs with St. André
- Peaches with frômage blanc
- Red and green seedless grapes with fresh goat cheese
- Granny Smith apples with aged Monterey Jack
- Melon slices with Brie
- A basket of mixed nuts in their shells with any combination of cheese and fruit

Summer Fruit Compote

Lemon-Orange Sponge Pudding

SERVES 4 TO 6

This is a light and citrusy one-dish dessert that is easy to make and refreshing to eat. The mixture bakes up into a sponge cake on top with pudding underneath. When serving, spoon the pudding sauce over the cake.

⅔ cup sugar
2 tablespoons unsalted butter, at room temperature
1 teaspoon lemon zest
1 teaspoon orange zest
3 eggs yolks
3 tablespoons all-purpose flour
2 tablespoons strained fresh lemon juice
2 tablespoons strained fresh orange juice
1 cup half-and-half
3 egg whites
⅛ teaspoon cream of tartar
½ cup whipping cream, whipped (optional)

1. Preheat the oven to 350°F.
2. In a medium bowl beat the sugar, butter, and citrus zests together until creamy and well blended. Add the egg yolks and beat into the mixture.
3. Stir in alternately the flour, citrus juices, and half-and-half until well blended.
4. In a medium bowl, with an electric mixer, beat the egg whites with the cream of tartar until stiff enough to hold a peak.
5. Fold the egg whites into the egg yolk mixture until just incorporated and pour into a 1-quart soufflé dish. Set the dish in a larger baking pan. Pour enough water into the pan to reach halfway up the sides of the dish. Bake until set, about 45 minutes. Serve hot with whipped cream or with a cold strawberry sauce, if desired.

NOTE: This dish should be prepared right before serving.

Mixed Berries with Mint

SERVES 4 TO 6

I like to serve this simple dessert on its own for a light ending to lunch or dinner. It's also great spooned on top of Pink Honeydew Melon Sorbet.

    ½ pint blackberries
    ½ pint raspberries
    ½ pint blueberries
    ½ pint small strawberries, hulled
    2 tablespoons Sugar Syrup (see page 335)
    1 tablespoon finely chopped mint

Garnish
    Whole mint leaves

1. In a large bowl, carefully mix the berries together, using a large spoon. Pour the Sugar Syrup over the berries and add the chopped mint. Mix the mint in carefully, taking care not to break up the berries. Garnish with fresh mint leaves.

Mocha Mousse

SERVES 6

This dessert is superrich with chocolate and sweet butter. The Crème Fraîche cuts the sweetness and smooths the texture.

    8 ounces semisweet chocolate, cut into pieces
    1 cup (2 sticks) unsalted butter, cut into pieces
    1 tablespoon strong coffee
    ¼ cup Crème Fraîche (see page 369)
    3 egg yolks
    6 egg whites
       Pinch cream of tartar

Garnish

> ½ cup whipping cream, whipped
> Chocolate coffee beans

1. In the top of a double boiler set over medium heat, combine the chocolate and butter and melt slowly. When completely melted remove the mixture from the heat and add the coffee, stirring to combine. Let cool.
2. In a small bowl, combine the Crème Fraîche with the egg yolks and blend well. Add to the cooled chocolate mixture.
3. In a large mixing bowl, with an electric mixer, beat the egg whites with the cream of tartar until very stiff.
4. Add half the chocolate mixture to the egg whites and fold to incorporate. (This will lighten the chocolate mixture.) Fold in the remaining chocolate mixture carefully, making sure that there are no lumps. Pour into a 1-quart serving bowl and chill at least 2 and up to 4 hours. The mousse should be set.
5. To decorate, fit a small star tube to a pastry bag and pipe the whipped cream along the rim of the serving bowl. Garnish with the chocolate coffee beans. If you don't have a pastry bag, decorate each serving with a dollop of whipped cream and chocolate coffee beans.

ADVANCE PREPARATION: This can be prepared 1 day in advance and refrigerated.

Almond Zabaglione with Strawberries

SERVES 4

Zabaglione is one of those quick last-minute desserts that is always well received. Amaretto is substituted for marsala in this variation on the classic zabaglione. Pour the hot almond custard over red, ripe straw-berries and garnish with toasted almonds or tiny amaretti cookies (amarettini).

2 tablespoons blanched sliced almonds

4 egg yolks
2 tablespoons sugar
2 tablespoons Amaretto
2 tablespoons whipping cream

2 pints strawberries, hulled and sliced in half

1. In a 350°F oven, toast the almonds for 7 to 10 minutes, watching carefully so they do not burn. Set aside.
2. In a zabaglione pan* or a medium-size double boiler add the egg yolks, sugar, and amaretto and beat until well blended.
3. Place the pan or double boiler over medium heat and whisk vigorously until mixture becomes foamy and begins to thicken. Remove from the heat, add the cream, and whisk until incorporated. The consistency should be thick and custard-like.
4. Pour on top of strawberries that have been placed in individual serving bowls. Sprinkle with the toasted almonds and serve immediately.

ADVANCE PREPARATION: The almonds may be toasted 2 hours before serving and kept at room temperature.

VARIATION: Hazelnuts may be substituted for the almonds and hazelnut liqueur may be substituted for the amaretto. Any summer berries may be used.

* A traditional Zabaglione pan is a round-bottomed copper pot, about 6½ inches in diameter, with a long handle.

Apricot Mousse

SERVES 6

This recipe has evolved over many years from an original by Perla Meyers. Although there are a number of steps, it's not actually complicated or difficult. Serve this dessert in your fanciest glass dessert bowls. The mousse makes a nice ending to a heavier meal, such as Barbecued Lamb with a Mustard Sage Crust, and a refreshing dessert to follow simple grilled chicken or fish.

1½ pounds fresh apricots, halved and pitted
1 cup sugar
1 cup half-and-half
4 egg yolks
1 teaspoon vanilla
3 egg whites
   Pinch cream of tartar
1 envelope or tablespoon gelatin
3 tablespoons apricot or peach liqueur
1 cup whipping cream

Garnish
½ cup whipping cream
3 small apricots

1. In a food processor fitted with a steel blade process the apricots until puréed. You may have to push the apricots down with a rubber spatula once or twice. Press through a fine sieve into a medium mixing bowl. Add ½ cup sugar and mix well. Set aside.
2. Scald the half-and-half in a medium saucepan over medium heat. Remove from the heat and cover.
3. In a medium mixing bowl, with an electric mixer, beat the egg yolks until frothy. Add the remaining sugar and beat the mixture until thick and pale yellow colored. Gradually add the scalded half-and-half, whisking until blended.

4. Pour back into the saucepan over medium heat and whisk until a thin custard forms. It should lightly coat the back of a spoon. Stir in the vanilla and remove from the heat. Strain through a fine sieve into a large mixing bowl.

5. Sprinkle the gelatin into a small saucepan and pour the liqueur over. Let the gelatin soften in the liqueur for about 5 minutes and then dissolve over low heat. Pour into the custard mixture and stir until completely blended.

6. Whip the egg whites with cream of tartar in a separate mixing bowl until stiff.

7. With an electric mixer, whip the cream in a medium mixing bowl until stiff peaks form.

8. Fold the apricot purée into the custard mixture. Next, carefully fold in the egg whites and whipped cream until the color is uniform.

9. Spoon into individual glasses or parfait dishes, cover, and chill at least 4 hours or overnight.

10. When ready to serve, prepare the garnish. With an electric mixer, whip the cream in a medium mixing bowl until stiff peaks form. Spoon into a piping tube fitted with a star tip.

11. On the top of each mousse pipe rosettes ½ inch apart along the edge.

12. Cut the apricots in half and remove the pits. Slice into ⅛-inch slices and place between the rosettes. Serve immediately.

ADVANCE PREPARATION: This may be prepared through step 9 up to 1 day ahead and refrigerated. Garnish just before serving.

Passion Fruit Caramel Custard

The dull, crinkly exterior and abundance of little seeds inside passion fruit belies its sensual, exotic flavor. Both California and New Zealand supply the United States with this unusual fruit so it is almost always available. Passion fruit tastes somewhere between an orange, a banana, and a mango with definite tropical overtones. Cut each passion fruit in two and use a small juicer to get all the nectar out of each half. This contemporary version of the classic caramel custard is a fitting finale to a Southwestern or Mexican-style menu. If you want to take Passion Fruit Caramel Custard on a picnic, make it in individual disposable aluminum cupcake rounds. Cook these for only half the time of the larger version.

Caramel
- ½ **cup sugar**
- 2 **tablespoons water**

Custard
- 2½ **cups half-and-half**
- 3 **eggs**
- 3 **egg yolks**
- ½ **cup sugar**
- ¼ **cup passion fruit juice (about 4 medium ripe passion fruit, juiced)**

1. Preheat the oven to 350°F.
2. *To make the caramel:* Combine the sugar and water in a small, heavy saucepan. Do not use a dark colored pan, or you will not be able to see the color of the caramel. Dissolve the sugar in water over low heat. Turn up the heat and continually swirl the pan over the flame. The mixture will be bubbly. If sugar crystals form on the sides of the pan, cover it for 1 minute to dissolve them. Boil until the mixture turns a golden brown color. Watch carefully, as caramel can burn easily.
3. When the mixture turns golden brown, remove it from the

heat. Pour the caramel into a 1½-quart porcelain baking dish. Rotate the dish to spread the caramel evenly over the bottom. Don't worry if it is not perfectly even; it will distribute itself during baking.

4. *To make the custard:* In a small saucepan scald the half-and-half over medium-high heat.

5. In a 3-quart mixing bowl, beat the eggs and egg yolks until frothy. Slowly add the sugar and beat until light, thick, and lemon colored.

6. Continue beating while pouring in the warm half-and-half in a thin stream. Stir in the passion fruit juice. Strain the mixture through a fine sieve into the caramel-lined mold.

7. Set the mold in a larger baking pan. Add enough hot water to the pan to reach halfway up the sides of the mold.

8. Reduce the oven temperature to 325°F. Transfer the mold in its water bath to the bottom third of the oven. Be sure to regulate the oven so the water in the pan never comes above a simmer. Bake until a tester inserted into the custard 1 inch from the outside edge comes out clean, about 1 hour.

9. Cool to room temperature. Refrigerate for at least 2 hours.

10. To unmold, run a knife carefully between the custard and the edge of the mold. Place a serving dish upside down over the mold, quickly invert the two, and remove the mold from the custard.

ADVANCE PREPARATION: The custard may be prepared 1 day in advance through step 9 and refrigerated.

VARIATION: Omit the passion fruit and add 1 teaspoon vanilla. Spoon berries over the cooled custard.

Strawberry Shortcake with Raspberry Custard Sauce

SERVES 8

These cream shortcake biscuits melt in your mouth. The chunky sauce of puréed and sliced strawberries is spooned over the biscuits. A cool, soothing custard enriched with whipped cream and raspberry liqueur replaces the customary whipped cream topping. Any combination of berries or fruits may be substituted for the strawberries.

Sauce

    8 egg yolks
    ¼ cup sugar
    ¼ cup framboise or kirsch
  1¼ cup whipping cream

Filling

    4 pints strawberries, hulled and sliced thickly
    ¼ to ½ cup powdered sugar, depending on sweetness of berries
    1 tablespoon framboise

Shortcake

    2 cups flour
    1 tablespoon baking powder
    ½ teaspoon salt
    2 tablespoons sugar
    6 tablespoons unsalted butter, chilled and cut into ½-inch pieces
    1 cup whipping cream

1. *To make the sauce:* In a zabaglione pan (see page 299) or a medium-size double boiler combine the egg yolks, sugar, and framboise or kirsch and beat until well blended.
2. Place the pan or double boiler over medium-low heat and whisk vigorously until mixture becomes foamy and begins to thicken. Remove from the heat. Add ¼ cup cream and

whisk until blended. Remove from the heat and pour into a medium bowl to cool.

3. *To make the strawberry filling:* Purée 2 cups of the strawberries and place them in a medium mixing bowl. Add the remaining strawberry slices, powdered sugar, and framboise. Mix gently to avoid bruising the strawberry slices. Set aside.

4. Whip the remaining cream in a medium bowl until stiff. Fold into the cooled custard mixture. Refrigerate until serving.

5. *To make the shortcake:* Preheat the oven to 425°F. In a food processor fitted with a steel blade, combine the flour, baking powder, salt, and sugar.

6. Add the butter using the pulse on/off motion until the mixture resembles bread crumbs. With the motor running, slowly pour in the cream, processing until the mixture becomes a soft dough.

7. Place the dough on a floured board. Knead with the heel of your palm and then roll it out into a ½-inch thickness.

8. Cut the dough into 3-inch squares or rounds.

9. Place the shortcakes at least 2 inches apart on an ungreased baking sheet. Bake until the tops are just light brown, 10 to 12 minutes. Cool on racks.

10. To assemble, split the shortcakes and place the halves, cut sides up, on a dessert plate. Place 2 tablespoons of the strawberries on top and then pour about 2 tablespoons of the custard over the strawberries. Serve immediately. Pass the extra custard sauce.

ADVANCE PREPARATION: The shortcakes are best if made no more than 2 hours before serving. The strawberry filling may be prepared up to 8 hours in advance and refrigerated. The custard may be prepared up to 1 day in advance and refrigerated.

QUICK FRUIT DESSERTS

- Sliced strawberries with balsamic vinegar
- Sliced figs with Crème Fraîche
- Peeled, sliced peaches with amarettini cookies
- Blueberries and diced nectarines with a sauce of mixed yogurt and sour cream, dusted with mace
- Sliced melon with a garnish of diced candied ginger and mint

Raspberry Pound Cake

SERVES 10 TO 12

This light, moist coffeecake is an especially nice addition to a weekend brunch. If you want to serve it as a dessert, spoon some Almond Zabaglione or Raspberry Custard Sauce over each slice, with extra raspberries for a garnish. Heavy bundt pans bake unevenly, so use a lightweight one for perfect results.

    5 eggs
    1 cup plus ⅔ cup sugar
 1¼ cups (2½ sticks) unsalted butter, at room temperature
        and cut into pieces
    2 tablespoons kirsch, framboise, or other fruit liqueur
 2½ cups all-purpose flour
    1 teaspoon baking powder
   ½ teaspoon salt
    3 cups fresh raspberries, not overripe*

Garnish
        Powdered sugar

1. Butter and flour a 9-inch lightweight bundt pan.
2. Preheat oven to 325°F.
3. In a large mixing bowl, blend the eggs and sugar with an electric mixer on medium speed. Add the pieces of butter and liqueur and blend with the mixer until fluffy. Add 2 cups plus 6 tablespoons of the flour, the baking powder, and salt and mix well.
4. In a separate bowl, toss the raspberries with the remaining 2 tablespoons flour, coating them evenly. Gently fold them into the cake mixture.
5. Pour into the prepared pan. Bake until a toothpick inserted in the center comes out clean, about 1 hour.
6. Cool 20 to 25 minutes in the pan. Remove the cake from the pan, invert onto a serving plate, and let cool thoroughly. Dust with powdered sugar.

ADVANCE PREPARATION: This may be prepared 8 hours in advance, covered in aluminum foil or plastic wrap, and kept at room temperature.

*The cup measurement is important here. It will be approximately 1½ pints.

AFTER DINNER COFFEE AL FRESCO

It may seem to be the most unlikely picnic beverage but, even if it's sizzling and you're sitting at the beach, there's nothing like a perfect cup of coffee to finish a meal. It's easy to pack up your espresso cups and a thermos of freshly brewed espresso. Whip some cream and store it in a container deep in the ice chest. To gild the lily, bring little containers of shaved chocolate, powdered cinnamon, and strips of lemon zest. Include miniature (airline size) bottles of liqueur. And don't forget the sugar.

Blueberry Nectarine Buckle

SERVES 6 TO 8

A buckle is one of those early American country desserts like a pan-dowdy, grunt, or cobbler that combines fruit with cake or biscuits. This buckle, made with sweet berries and tangy nectarines, tastes like a spiced cake. It's covered with a toasted pecan streusel topping. This is good served after dinner, at brunch, or with afternoon tea.

Topping
- ½ cup coarsely chopped pecans
- ½ cup all-purpose flour
- ½ cup dark brown sugar
- ¼ cup sugar
- ½ teaspoon cinnamon
- Pinch freshly grated nutmeg
- Pinch powdered ginger
- ½ cup (1 stick) unsalted butter, cut into small pieces

Cake
- ½ cup (1 stick) unsalted butter
- ¾ cup sugar
- 1 large egg
- 2 cups all-purpose flour
- 2 teaspoons baking powder
- ¼ teaspoon freshly grated nutmeg
- ¼ teaspoon ground ginger
- ½ cup milk
- 1 pint fresh blueberries, cleaned and picked over
- 2 medium nectarines, peeled, pitted, and cut into ¼-inch pieces

1. *To make the topping:* In a 350°F oven place the pecans on a baking sheet and toast until lightly browned, 7 to 10 minutes. Cool.
2. In a medium mixing bowl combine the cooled toasted pecans, flour, brown and white sugar, cinnamon, nutmeg, and

ginger. Add the butter and mix together until the mixture is crumbly. Set aside.

3. *To make the cake:* Butter and flour a 9-inch-square baking dish. Preheat the oven to 350°F.

4. In a large bowl combine the butter and sugar and cream together until the mixture is light and fluffy. Beat in the egg.

5. Sift together the flour, baking powder, nutmeg, and ginger and then add alternately with the milk to the butter mixture, blending the ingredients well.

6. Pour the batter into the prepared baking dish, spreading it evenly. Sprinkle the blueberries and the nectarine pieces over the batter in an even layer.

7. Sprinkle the nut mixture over the fruit and bake until the top is golden brown and bubbling, about 45 minutes. Serve with French vanilla ice cream or Amaretto Cream (see page 335), if desired.

ADVANCE PREPARATION: This may be prepared 8 hours in advance and kept at room temperature until serving.

Almond Peach Clafouti with Amaretto Cream

SERVES 6

This is a variation on the traditional peasant dessert from the Limousin district of France. There it is made with cherries rather than peaches. A custardy pancake-like batter is cooked with the fruit in a quiche or porcelain pan so that the batter bubbles up and cooks around the fruit. The Amaretto Cream is the perfect finishing touch.

Almond Peach Clafouti with Amaretto Cream

3 medium peaches (about 1½ pounds)
¼ cup sugar
¼ cup amaretto
¼ cup sliced almonds
1 large egg yolk
2 large eggs
½ cup sugar
½ cup (1 stick) unsalted butter, at room temperature
1 cup all-purpose flour
1 cup milk
¼ teaspoon almond extract

Sauce

Amaretto Cream (see page 335)

1. In a large saucepan bring water to a boil. Immerse the peaches in the water for about 30 seconds and then remove immediately.
2. Peel the peaches and cut in half. Remove the pits and cut each half into ¼-inch slices.
3. In a medium mixing bowl combine the sugar and amaretto. Add the sliced peaches and marinate about ½ hour.
4. Preheat the oven to 350°F. Place the almonds on a baking sheet and toast until they are light brown, 7 to 10 minutes.
5. To prepare the batter, combine the egg yolk, eggs, and sugar in a food processor fitted with a steel blade. While the machine is on add the butter and flour and mix for about 30 seconds. Add the milk, almond extract, 3 marinated peach slices, and the marinating liquid from the peaches. Blend until the batter is smooth, about 30 more seconds.
6. Generously butter a 9-inch baking dish or pie plate.
7. Preheat the oven to 375°F. Lay the peaches, overlapping, in the dish and sprinkle with the toasted almonds. Cover the peaches and almonds with the batter.
8. Bake for 15 minutes in the bottom third of the oven, then move to the center of the oven and bake until puffed and nicely browned, about 30 minutes longer. Sprinkle with powdered sugar and serve with Amaretto Cream while still warm.

ADVANCE PREPARATION: This may be prepared 4 hours in advance through step 6 and kept at room temperature.

Peach Brown Butter Tart

SERVES 6

With more than 130 varieties of peaches available at the peak of their season, it may be a bit confusing to select the right peach for this dessert. Pick any peach that appeals to you, has a rich peach color, and is perfectly ripe. In this tart, the pastry shell is layered with a nutty brown butter filling. Fresh sliced peaches are placed on top and then brushed with a peach glaze. This tart makes an excellent choice for a dessert buffet.

Pastry

- 1 cup all-purpose or white pastry flour
- Pinch salt
- 1 tablespoon powdered sugar
- 6 tablespoons (¾ stick) unsalted butter, frozen and cut into small pieces
- 1 egg yolk
- 2 tablespoons ice water

Filling

- 12 tablespoons (1½ sticks) unsalted butter
- 3 large eggs
- 1 cup sugar
- 3 tablespoons all-purpose flour

Topping

- ½ cup Peach Glaze (recipe follows)
- 2 medium peaches
- 2 tablespoons sliced almonds, lightly toasted

1. Place the flour, salt, and powdered sugar in a food processor fitted with a steel blade. Add the butter, egg yolk, and water and process until the mixture reaches a crumb-like texture, 5 to 10 seconds.
2. Preheat the oven to 375°F. Roll the dough out onto a pastry board sprinkled with flour. Mold into a ball for easy

rolling. Roll into an 11-inch circle. Drape the dough over a 9-inch removable flan ring, pie pan, or quiche pan.

3. Fit the dough into the flan ring or pan with your fingers. Raise and flute the edges ¼ to ½ inch above the top of the flan ring or pie pan by squeezing the dough from opposite sides using your index fingers.

4. Drape parchment paper or tin foil over the pastry and place baking beads, rice, or beans in an even layer on top. Bake for 15 minutes and remove from the oven. Remove the baking beads and paper and prick with a fork. Return to the oven and bake until light brown, 5 to 7 minutes more. Remove from the oven.

5. Place the butter in a small saucepan and melt over high heat. Watch carefully until the butter is dark brown and then remove from the heat. Pour through a strainer lined with a double thickness of cheesecloth into a small saucepan. Keep warm. There should be no black specks in the butter.

6. In a medium mixing bowl, beat the eggs together until frothy. Thoroughly beat in the sugar. Sprinkle in the flour and whisk until well combined and no lumps remain. Add the warmed brown butter and mix again.

7. Reduce the oven to 350°F. Place the pie shell on a baking sheet and pour in the filling. Bake for 20 to 25 minutes. The filling should be dark brown, set in the center, and move just slightly when pan is moved. Remove from the oven and let cool. When the tart is cool, remove it from the pan and place on a serving platter. Brush with Peach Glaze.

8. Immerse the peaches in boiling water for about 30 seconds and remove immediately. Peel and cut into thin slices and arrange decoratively around the outside rim of the tart shell. Arrange another concentric circle of peach slices in the center.

9. Brush the tart with the Peach Glaze and let it set. Sprinkle the tart with almonds and refrigerate until serving.

ADVANCE PREPARATION: This may be prepared 8 hours in advance and refrigerated. Remove it from the refrigerator ½ hour before serving.

1 12-ounce jar peach preserves
2 tablespoons fresh lemon juice

1. In a small saucepan bring the preserves and lemon juice to
   a boil.
2. Strain through a fine-meshed nylon strainer.
3. When ready to use, heat the glaze just to a boil. Brush on
   the fruit.

NOTE: Store the unused glaze in the refrigerator in a jar
for up to 2 months.

Lattice Crust Pie with Rhubarb, Peaches, Strawberries, and Plums

SERVES 6 TO 8

*Simple one-fruit summer pies are good; mixed fruit pies are even better.
Rhubarb, peaches, strawberries, and plums are baked together in this
pie but still retain their individual texture and flavor. The juices of
these four fruits cook into a thick syrup that is sweet yet tangy. The
lattice crust design gives it a fresh country look. Serve this with French
vanilla ice cream.*

Pie Crust
2 cups all-purpose flour or pastry flour
½ teaspoon salt
½ cup (1 stick) unsalted butter, chilled and cut into
   small pieces
3 tablespoons shortening, chilled
1 egg
1 tablespoon fresh lemon juice
3 to 4 tablespoons ice water

Lattice Crust Pie with Rhubarb, Peaches, Strawberries, and Plums

Filling

  1½ cups rhubarb, cut into ½-inch slices

    2 medium peaches, cut into ½-inch slices (peeled or unpeeled)

    2 cups (1 pint) strawberries cut into ½-inch slices

    2 medium purple plums, cut into ½-inch pieces

   ¾ cup granulated sugar

   ¼ teaspoon nutmeg, preferably freshly grated

   ½ teaspoon cinnamon

   ⅓ cup all-purpose flour

    3 tablespoons fresh lemon juice

Egg Glaze

    1 large egg

    1 tablespoon water

1. *To make the pastry:* Combine the flour and salt in a food processor fitted with a steel blade. Process a few seconds to blend. Add the butter and shortening and process until the mixture resembles coarse meal, 5 to 10 seconds.

2. With the motor running, gradually add the egg, lemon juice, and water until the dough just begins to come together and will hold a shape when pressed. Wrap in wax paper or plastic wrap and refrigerate for 2 to 4 hours. (It is best to separate the dough into two rounds and wrap slightly flattened to make it easy to roll out the pie crust.)

3. Prepare the filling by combining all the fruit in a medium mixing bowl. Add the sugar, nutmeg, cinnamon, flour, and lemon juice and stir until the fruit is evenly mixed with the dry ingredients and lemon juice.

4. Roll out one of the pie crust rounds until it is 11 inches in diameter. Ease the crust over a 9-inch pie plate and then work the pastry into the pie plate, crimping the edges about ½ inch above the rim of the pie plate. Water-proof the pie crust by brushing the sides and bottom of the pie crust with the egg glaze, made by beating the egg and water together until frothy.

5. Spoon the fruit into the pie, heaping it in the center.

6. Roll out the other dough round and cut it into strips, about 1 inch wide.

7. Preheat the oven to 425°F. Brush the edge of the pie crust with the egg glaze. Place a row of the dough strips ¾ inch apart across the pie, pinching the ends so they stick to the pie crust. Take the remaining strips and place in the opposite direction on top of the pie so the strips (when touching) are at right angles. Brush the strips with the egg glaze.

8. Bake the pie on a baking sheet for 10 minutes and then reduce the heat to 350°F. Continue baking for 35 to 45 minutes. Check the crust once to make sure it is not browning too quickly.

9. Remove from the oven and let cool. Serve with Amaretto Cream or French vanilla ice cream.

ADVANCE PREPARATION: This may be prepared 8 hours in advance and kept at room temperature until serving.

Hazelnut Plum Tart

SERVES 8 TO 10

You don't have to peel the plums for this French-style tart. The plum slices retain their shape and add a biting counterpoint to the sweet hazelnut filling. This is a gorgeous dessert you'll be proud to serve because of its highly professional appearance. I like to offer a big bowl of Crème Fraîche on the side.

Pastry
1¼ cups all-purpose flour
1 tablespoon powdered sugar
   Pinch of salt
½ cup (1 stick) unsalted butter, frozen and cut into small pieces
1 egg yolk
2 tablespoons ice water

Hazelnut Filling

   1½ cups sliced or chopped hazelnuts
   ¾ cup sugar
   ¼ cup (½ stick) unsalted butter
   2 tablespoons all-purpose flour
   ¼ cup hazelnut liqueur
   2 eggs

Plum Topping

   1¼ pounds purple plums, pitted and thinly sliced
   2 tablespoons unsalted butter
   2 tablespoons sugar

Garnish

   2 tablespoons sliced or chopped hazelnuts

1. *To make the pastry:* Combine the flour, sugar, and salt in a food processor fitted with a steel blade. Process a few seconds to blend. Add the butter and process until the mixture resembles coarse meal, 5 to 10 seconds.
2. With the processor running, add the egg yolk and then gradually the water. Process until the dough is just beginning to come together and will hold a shape when pressed.
3. Transfer the dough to a floured pastry board or work surface. Press into a round shape for easy rolling. Roll out a circle large enough to fit a 10-inch tart pan (one with a removable bottom). Drape the dough circle over the rolling pin and fit it into the pan. Roll a rolling pin over the top edge of the tart pan with moderate pressure to remove the excess dough. Place the tart pan on a baking sheet. Preheat the oven to 400°F.
4. Press the pastry with your fingers so it adheres to the sides of the pan. If using a tart pan with straight edges, raise the edges of the pastry ¼ to ½ inch above the rim of the pan by squeezing the dough from both sides, using your index fingers.
5. *To make the hazelnut filling:* Finely grind the hazelnuts in a food processor fitted with a steel blade.
6. Add the sugar, butter, flour, and hazelnut liqueur. Pulse

the machine on and off until a meal-like paste is formed. Add the eggs and process for 10 seconds to incorporate.

7. Spread the mixture in an even layer in the lined pan.
8. *To make the plum topping:* Arrange the plum slices in overlapping concentric circles on the filling. Be sure to fit them tightly together. Arrange 2 concentric rows of the plum slices in the center of the tart.
9. Dot the plums with the butter and sugar and bake until the tart is brown on top, about 1 hour. Remove from the oven and cool.
10. Garnish with hazelnut slices and serve with Crème Fraîche or French vanilla ice cream.

ADVANCE PREPARATION: The tart may be prepared 8 hours in advance through step 6, covered, and kept in the refrigerator overnight. The finished tart may be kept up to 6 hours in the refrigerator. Remove it from the refrigerator 1 hour before serving. It is best served at room temperature.

Chocolate Pecan Torte with Espresso Crème Anglaise

SERVES 6

This is the cake of choice among my confirmed chocoholic friends. It contains no fruit that might interfere with the intensity of the chocolate experience. This European-style torte is almost a cooled chocolate-pecan soufflé. It's covered with a chocolate glaze and decorated with chocolate-dipped pecans. The chilled coffee custard sauce provides a refreshing counterpoint. Just before serving, spoon a pool of sauce on a dessert plate and place a slice of cake in the center.

Glaze and Decoration

 6 ounces semisweet chocolate
 ½ cup (1 stick) unsalted butter
 ½ teaspoon safflower oil
 1 tablespoon light corn syrup
 20 large pecan halves

Torte

 6 ounces semisweet chocolate
 ¾ cup (1½ sticks) unsalted butter
 4 eggs
 ¾ cup sugar
 3 tablespoons all-purpose flour
 3 tablespoons ground pecans

Garnish

 Espresso Crème Anglaise (recipe follows)

1. *To make the glaze:* Slowly melt the chocolate and butter in the top of a double boiler over low heat, stirring until smooth. Stir in the oil and corn syrup. Remove from heat and let cool. It should be room temperature to glaze the cake.

2. *To prepare the pecans:* Preheat the oven to 350°F and place the pecans on a baking sheet. Bake until slightly browned, about 10 minutes. Cool. Dip half of each pecan into the glaze and place on a baking sheet lined with wax paper. Refrigerate until set. Reserve the remaining glaze. (Keep the glaze at room temperature; don't let it harden. If it does harden, gently soften it over a double boiler until it is tepid.)

3. *To make the torte:* Cut a circle of wax paper to fit an 8-inch round cake pan. Place the paper in the bottom of the pan and butter the pan and paper generously.

4. Combine the chocolate and butter in the top part of a double boiler over medium-low heat and melt slowly, stirring occasionally. Remove from the heat and let cool.

5. In an electric mixer, whisk the eggs until frothy. Gradually

add the sugar and beat until the mixture is pale lemon-colored, about 5 minutes.

6. Preheat the oven to 375°F. Fold the chocolate mixture into the egg mixture and blend well. Stir in the flour and the ground pecans until well combined.

7. Pour the mixture into the cake pan. Bake until the outside is firm and the inside is slightly soft but not runny, 25 to 30 minutes. A tester should come out of the torte slightly wet. Cool the torte in the pan, then unmold it onto a cake rack placed on a cookie sheet lined with wax paper.

8. Pour the glaze over the cooled torte, tilting it so that the glaze runs down the sides. Use a long spatula to touch up the sides if there are any unglazed areas.

9. When the glaze is set, carefully place the glazed pecans in a border circle on top of the torte.

10. Slide a spatula under the torte and lift it onto a cake platter lined with a doily. Serve with Espresso Crème Anglaise.

ADVANCE PREPARATION: The torte may be kept up to one day either at room temperature or refrigerated. Remove from the refrigerator 1 hour before serving.

Espresso Crème Anglaise

MAKES 6 SERVINGS

1⅓ cups half-and-half
½ vanilla bean, split open*
3 egg yolks
⅓ cup sugar
2 tablespoons strong espresso coffee

1. In a small saucepan, combine the half-and-half and vanilla bean. Bring to a simmer over medium-high heat. Turn off the heat and cover the pan. Let the vanilla bean steep for 20 minutes.

2. Place the egg yolks in the top of a double boiler over medium heat. Add the sugar and whisk until thick and lemon-colored.

3. Remove the vanilla bean and pour in the hot half-and-half slowly, whisking constantly. Add the espresso and continue whisking until the mixture reaches a custard-like consistency. It should coat the bottom of a wooden spoon. *Do not let boil or the custard will curdle.*

4. Immediately remove the sauce from the heat and pour it through a fine meshed sieve into a bowl. Put the bowl over ice water and stir until the sauce is cooled. Cover and store in the refrigerator until needed.

*If a vanilla bean is unavailable, use 1 teaspoon vanilla extract and add it to the sauce when you add the espresso.

ADVANCE PREPARATION: This may be made 1 day in advance and refrigerated until ready to serve.

Cherry Amaretti Crisp

SERVES 8 TO 10

Pitting cherries, like peeling grapes, is clearly a labor of love; it's well worth it, however, to make this contemporary version of a classic American dessert. You can prepare this the night before a dinner party and pop it into the oven just before serving. Almonds and cherries have a natural affinity, heightened here by subtle spicing and lemon zest. If you don't have time to make a custard sauce, serve this with a large bowl of Crème Fraîche or big scoops of French vanilla ice cream.

Crust

- 1 cup oatmeal
- 1 cup amaretti (Italian almond kernel cookies), coarsely chopped (about 16)
- ½ cup chopped almonds
- ⅓ cup light brown sugar
- 1 teaspoon cinnamon
- ½ teaspoon allspice
- ¼ teaspoon ginger
- ½ cup (1 stick) unsalted butter, cut into small pieces

Filling

- ⅓ cup sugar
- 3 tablespoons Amaretto
- 2 tablespoons fresh lemon juice
- 1 teaspoon minced lemon zest
- ½ teaspoon cinnamon
- 3 tablespoons cornstarch
- 6 cups sweet cherries, pitted (about 3 pounds)

1. *To make the crust:* Combine the oatmeal, amaretti, almonds, brown sugar, cinnamon, allspice, and ginger together in a medium mixing bowl. Knead the butter into the dry mixture with your fingers until evenly distributed. Set aside.

2. Combine the sugar, amaretto, lemon juice, lemon zest, cinnamon, and cornstarch in a large saucepan over low heat. Whisk to dissolve the cornstarch and cook about 3 minutes, whisking constantly. Add the cherries, stirring to coat them with the sauce. Cook about 2 more minutes.

3. Preheat the oven to 350°F. Butter a 2-quart soufflé dish. Pour the cherry mixture into the dish and let cool a few minutes. Spoon the cookie mixture over the cherries.

4. Place the dish on a baking sheet and bake for 45 minutes. Watch carefully after 30 minutes; you may need to cover it with aluminum foil if it starts getting too brown. Remove from the oven and cool.

ADVANCE PREPARATION: This may be prepared 1 day in advance through step 3 (except for preheating the oven), covered, and refrigerated. Remove it from the refrigerator ½ hour before baking.

Cherry Amaretti Crisp

Fudgy Brownies

MAKES 24 2 × 2-INCH BROWNIES

These rich, fudgy brownies are a variation on my good friend Clau-
dette Einhorn's recipe. For her catering business in Indianapolis,
Claudette prepares these by the hundreds, adding orange liqueur to the
batter. I like my chocolate "straight," so I add vanilla instead; it
intensifies the chocolate flavor. Either way, these brownies are winners.

　¾ cup (1½ sticks) unsalted butter
　4 ounces unsweetened chocolate
　4 large eggs
　2 cups sugar
　1 teaspoon vanilla or ¼ cup orange liqueur
1¼ cups all-purpose flour
　½ teaspoon baking powder
　½ teaspoon salt
　1 cup chopped almonds, walnuts, or hazelnuts

Garnish
　　Powdered sugar (optional)

1. Grease a 9 × 13-inch baking pan. Preheat the oven to 350°F.
2. Place the butter and chocolate in the top of a double boiler. Over medium heat slowly melt the chocolate and butter. Cool.
3. Place the eggs in a medium mixing bowl and beat in the sugar until the mixture is thick and pale lemon-colored.
4. Stir in the vanilla and the cooled chocolate and butter mixture. Mix until color is uniform.
5. Carefully mix the flour, baking powder, and salt into the chocolate mixture. Stir in the nuts.
6. Pour the batter into the prepared pan and bake until a toothpick tester comes out slightly fudgy, 25 to 30 minutes. Remove from the oven, cool, and slice into 2 × 2-inch bars. Sprinkle powdered sugar on the brownies, if you like.

ADVANCE PREPARATION: These may be prepared 1 day in advance and stored in an airtight container.

Almond Cookies with Lemon and Port

MAKES 40 COOKIES

These Italian-inspired light cookies are best eaten as soon as you take them out of the oven, when they are most crispy. Almonds, lemon, and port are a sublime combination. The lemon tempers the sweet port while the almonds provide the essential taste. These go well with a small glass of port; you can then dip the cookies in the port.

- 1 cup finely chopped almonds
- ½ cup unsalted butter, softened to room temperature
- ½ cup sugar
- 2 egg yolks
- ⅓ cup port (Tawny or other sweet style)
- 1 teaspoon vanilla
- 2 teaspoons finely chopped lemon zest
- 1 cup all-purpose flour

Garnish
  Powdered sugar

1. Preheat the oven to 350°F. Place the almonds on a baking sheet and toast about 3 minutes. Cool.
2. In a medium mixing bowl, beat the butter with the sugar until it is creamy and fluffy.
3. Add the egg yolks, port, vanilla, and 1 teaspoon lemon zest and stir to combine.
4. Stir, slowly adding the flour until completely absorbed.
5. Drop teaspoons of the cookie dough 1 inch apart on an ungreased cookie sheet. (You will need 2 cookie sheets.) Sprinkle a pinch of lemon zest on top of each cookie.
6. Bake until golden brown, 12 to 15 minutes. Cool on cookie racks. When cool, sprinkle the cookies with powdered sugar.

NOTE: These are best made and eaten the same day. If there are any left over, store them in an airtight container.

SUMMER FRUIT
SALADS AND PLATTERS

Fruit salad is often the answer to what to serve on the hottest days. It is one of the few dishes appropriate for breakfast, brunch, lunch, and dinner. Mixing peak-of-the-season fruits in a large bowl and tossing them together with a little lemon juice to preserve their color is the everyday way to make fruit salad. Here are a few more elaborate suggestions:

- Using a melon baller, make melon balls from watermelon (red and yellow, if possible), crenshaw, and orange honeydew melons. Flavor the mixed melon salad with a sweet liqueur—passion fruit liqueur is especially good, but the orange-flavored ones also work well. Serve the salad in a big glass bowl decorated with mint sprigs. A good creamy dressing to serve on the side is plain yogurt blended with Crème Fraîche and flavored with a few drops of the same liqueur.

- Slice peeled Babcock peaches in half and remove the pit. The flesh of this delicious peach is creamy white with red streaks running through it. Fill the centers of the peaches with raspberries and finish with a dollop of Crème Fraîche and a sprig of mint.
- Combine peeled and diced papaya with diced avocado and dress with lemon juice. In the Caribbean, the papaya seeds are served with the papaya and much enjoyed for their peppery taste. Add them to the mixture for an interesting change.
- Combination fruit platters can be beautiful to look at as well as wonderful to eat. Here's just one idea, meant for a large party, to inspire you.

Arrange very thinly sliced triangles of red and yellow watermelon with the rind along the edge of one part of the platter. Continue the border of fruit, using other thinly sliced melons, such as honeydew, crenshaw, cantaloupe, and Persian. In the center of the platter, alternate yellow and white sliced peaches, brushed with lemon juice. Slice purple and yellow plums and arrange them in an informal pattern. Wedges of nectarines, papaya, and mango, also brushed with lemon or lime juice, complete the sliced fruits. Between each variety of fruit place berries—red raspberries around the peaches, strawberries around the plums, and blueberries around the mangos and papaya. Lemon and camellia leaves can be used to garnish the edge of the platter.

Toasted Hazelnut Cookies

MAKES 25 2-INCH COOKIES

Hazelnuts, or filberts, are now available in packages, peeled and sliced. Toasting the hazelnuts brings out their full character. These buttery nut cookies go wonderfully with Crushed Strawberry Ice Cream or Frozen Peaches and Cream.

¾ cup sliced or chopped hazelnuts
½ cup unsalted butter, at room temperature
½ cup dark brown sugar
1 teaspoon vanilla
1 large egg
¾ cup all-purpose flour

Garnish
Powdered sugar (optional)

1. Preheat the oven to 350°F. Place the hazelnuts on a baking sheet and toast until light brown, 3 to 5 minutes. Remove from the oven and let cool.

2. In a medium mixing bowl, combine the butter and brown sugar and mix with an electric mixer until well blended. Add the vanilla and egg and then slowly incorporate the flour. Carefully stir in the toasted hazelnuts.

3. Increase the oven to 375°F. Drop teaspoons of the batter 1 inch apart on 2 ungreased cookie sheets. Bake until the cookies are light brown, about 8 minutes. Place the cookies on cooling racks. Sprinkle cookies with powdered sugar, if desired.

NOTE: These are best made and eaten the same day. If there are any left over, store in an airtight container.

Frozen Praline Mousse

SERVES 6

I love this dessert—it's like making ice cream without an ice cream maker. Using sugar syrup rather than granulated sugar gives this dish its creamy consistency. The mousse is easy to make and can be kept frozen for up to 2 weeks, so it's perfect to have on hand in your freezer for last-minute entertaining. Just before serving, heat Bittersweet Hot Fudge Sauce to pour on top. Of course, the hot fudge sauce is optional, but why not go all the way?

⅓ cup sugar
2 tablespoons water
6 egg yolks
1 teaspoon vanilla
1 cup whipping cream
¾ cup Pecan Praline (see page 336)

Garnish
- ½ cup whipped cream
- ½ cup Pecan Praline (see page 336)
- 1 cup Bittersweet Hot Fudge Sauce (see page 334) (optional)

1. Brush an 8 × 4 × 2-inch loaf pan or any 3- or 4- cup mold with vegetable oil. Line the mold with plastic wrap, leaving enough excess to fold over the top later.
2. To make the sugar syrup, dissolve the sugar in the water in a small saucepan over low flame until clear.
3. Place the egg yolks and vanilla in a medium mixer bowl. Using an electric mixer, add the sugar syrup slowly while mixing on low speed. Continue beating the egg yolks and sugar syrup until thick and pale lemon-colored.
4. In a separate bowl, beat the whipping cream until stiff.
5. Fold the egg yolk mixture into the whipped cream until the color is uniform. Fold in the praline, making sure it's evenly distributed. Pour into the prepared mold and cover with the plastic wrap. Freeze for at least 6 hours.
6. *To serve:* Unmold the mousse, remove the plastic wrap, and slice. Place the slices on individual dessert plates and decorate with additional whipped cream and praline. Serve with Bittersweet Hot Fudge Sauce.

ADVANCE PREPARATION: The mousse may be prepared up to 2 weeks in advance and frozen. Remove it from the freezer for 15 minutes before slicing.

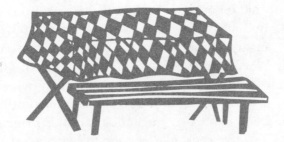

Frozen Praline Mousse

Crushed Strawberry Ice Cream

MAKES 2 QUARTS

This dessert has a double taste of strawberries, both crushed and sliced. It is clearly a cut above the often tasteless varieties of strawberry ice cream usually available. The new frozen canister ice-cream makers that require little churning and only 20 minutes of freezing time may have taken the old-fashioned "charm" out of ice-cream making, but they have certainly made it easier. If your ice cream maker holds less than 2 quarts, divide this recipe in half. Try it with Almond Cookies with Lemon and Port.

¼ cup sugar
2½ pints strawberries, hulled and sliced in half
2 cups whipping cream
1 cup milk
4 eggs
¾ cup sugar
2 teaspoons vanilla
1 tablespoon fresh lemon juice

1 cup finely chopped strawberries

1. Finely chop 1 cup of the sliced strawberries and set aside. Sprinkle the sugar over the remaining strawberries in a medium mixing bowl. Let stand for 30 minutes and then process the strawberries in a food processor fitted with a steel blade until completely smooth. Pour it through a fine sieve, if you prefer no seeds.
2. Combine the cream and milk in a medium saucepan and scald on medium-high heat. Remove from the heat.
3. In a mixing bowl, beat the eggs until frothy. Slowly add the sugar and vanilla and beat until thick and pale lemon-colored.
4. When the cream and milk are scalded, gradually whisk 1 cup into the egg mixture. Whisking, gradually pour the egg mixture back into the cream and milk in the saucepan.
5. Cook slowly over medium-low heat, stirring constantly, until the mixture is thick enough to coat a wooden spoon, 5 to 10

minutes. Do not overcook or the mixture will curdle. Remove from the heat, strain into a medium mixing bowl, and cool.

6. Add the puréed strawberries to the custard and mix well.
7. Pour the custard mixture into a chilled ice cream machine and churn, following the instructions, until the ice cream begins to thicken. While the machine is running, add the finely chopped strawberries. At this point the ice cream will be firm but not hard. Either put it in the freezer to harden or serve it immediately.

ADVANCE PREPARATION: This may be prepared 8 hours in advance through step 6 and kept in the refrigerator.

NOTE: This recipe may be halved to make 1 quart.

White Chocolate Terrine with Strawberries and Praline

SERVES 6 TO 8

White chocolate contains sugar, cocoa butter, dry milk solids, and usually vanilla flavoring. It has the cocoa butter from the bean but not the chocolate liquor, which gives chocolate its very distinctive flavor and rich, dark color. White chocolate can be difficult to melt, so follow the directions carefully. Tobler Narcisse, also called Tobler White, is my choice because of its pure flavor and easy melting quality.

This is one of my favorite summertime desserts. A thin layer of puréed strawberries is sandwiched between crunchy praline in the center of the white chocolate mousse. This dessert makes a luxurious presentation when cut into slices and arranged on plates, each slice surrounded by a pool of ruby-red strawberry sauce.

1 plus ¼ cups whipping cream
6 ounces white chocolate, cut into 1-inch squares
⅓ cup sugar
⅓ cup water
6 egg yolks
2 tablespoons fresh lemon juice
1 teaspoon finely chopped lemon zest

Filling

½ pint strawberries, hulled and finely puréed
1 cup Pecan Praline (see page 336)

Garnish

1 cup fresh Strawberry Sauce (see page 337)
Whole strawberries with stems on
½ cup Pecan Praline (see page 336)
Mint leaves

1. Brush a 9 × 5 × 2-inch loaf pan with vegetable oil. Line it with plastic wrap, leaving enough excess to cover the pan later.
2. Whip 1 cup cream in a medium mixing bowl until it forms soft peaks. Don't overbeat. Refrigerate.
3. Melt the white chocolate slowly in the upper part of a double boiler over medium-low heat, making sure the water does not touch the upper pan. Watch carefully as it tends to burn easily. Make sure no water or steam touches the white chocolate or it may become very stiff. Whisk the remaining ¼ cup cream into the chocolate. The mixture should be thick and almost cheese-like, but lump-free. Turn the heat down to low and keep warm, stirring occasionally.
4. Combine the sugar and water in a small saucepan over medium heat. Bring to a simmer, stirring until the sugar is dissolved. It should be very hot.
5. Place the egg yolks, lemon juice, and lemon zest in a medium mixing bowl. Slowly add the hot sugar syrup and beat with an electric mixer for 8 minutes.
6. Beat in the *warm* white chocolate. Fold in the whipped

cream until completely blended. The mixture should be mousse-like and uniform in color. Pour into a 5- or 6-cup measuring cup with a spout.

6. Pour half the mousse into the terrine. Keep the other half in the refrigerator. Put the terrine in the freezer until frozen, about 2 hours. Then sprinkle ½ cup of the praline over the frozen mousse. Spoon the strawberry purée on top and then sprinkle the remainder of the praline on top. Pour the remaining mousse over the praline and strawberries and cover the terrine with the plastic wrap. Place in the freezer for at least 6 hours.

7. *To serve:* Spoon a thin layer of strawberry sauce in the center of each dessert plate and slide the plate around to cover it completely with the sauce. Unmold the mousse and remove plastic wrap. Cut the mousse into 1-inch slices and place a slice in the center of each plate. Sprinkle with praline. Garnish with a fresh whole strawberry with the stem left on and a fresh mint leaf.

ADVANCE PREPARATION: This can be prepared 2 weeks in advance and kept in the freezer. Remove it from the freezer 15 minutes before slicing.

Frozen Peaches and Cream

MAKES 2 QUARTS

The crunchy sweetness of praline and a rich peachiness are the hallmarks of this summer ice cream. Frozen Peaches and Cream has an intense flavor due to the high ratio of peach to custard base. Make sure to buy medium-size peaches since they are more flavorful and tend to be less watery than the large ones. While the ice cream is great on its own, adding fresh raspberries and raspberry sauce turns it into an incomparable fruit sundae.

3 pounds ripe peaches
1 cup milk
2 cups whipping cream
5 egg yolks
1 cup sugar
2 teaspoons vanilla
1 cup Pecan Praline (see page 336)

1. Immerse the peaches in a large pan of boiling water for 30 seconds. Remove and peel the skin off the peaches and pit them. Coarsely chop 1 pound of the peaches in a food processor fitted with a steel blade and reserve. Process the remaining peaches until puréed and set aside.
2. Combine the milk and the cream in a medium saucepan and scald over medium-high heat.
3. In the bowl of an electric mixer beat the eggs until frothy. Slowly add the sugar and vanilla, beating until thick and pale lemon-colored.
4. Whisk 1 cup of the cream mixture into the eggs and then add the rest of the cream. Transfer the mixture back to the saucepan. Stir the custard mixture with a wooden spoon over medium-low heat until the custard thinly coats the back of a spoon, 5 to 10 minutes. Do not overcook or the mixture will curdle. Remove from the heat and pour through a fine sieve into a medium mixing bowl.
5. Add the puréed peaches to the custard and mix well.
6. Pour the custard mixture into a chilled ice cream machine and churn, following the manufacturer's instructions, until the ice cream begins to thicken. While the machine is running, add the coarsely chopped peaches and praline. The ice cream will be firm but not frozen. Either put it in the freezer to harden or serve it immediately.

ADVANCE PREPARATION: This may be prepared 8 hours in advance through step 5 and kept in the refrigerator.

NOTE: This recipe may be halved to make 1 quart.

Pink Honeydew Melon Sorbet

MAKES ABOUT 1 QUART

The "pink" honeydew is really more orange in color, but it cannot be mistaken once you take a taste. This sorbet is unusually light and refreshing. Try serving it with Mixed Berries with Mint.

3½-pound pink honeydew melon or 1½ pounds flesh or 3
    cups purée
  1 tablespoon fresh lemon juice
 ½ cup sugar syrup (see page 335)

1. Process the melon pieces, lemon juice, and sugar syrup together in a food processor or blender until completely puréed.
2. Pour into a chilled ice cream maker and follow the manufacturer's instructions. Churn until the melon mixture is firm, 15 to 20 minutes, and serve immediately or freeze.

ADVANCE PREPARATION: Although this is best served right out of the ice cream maker, it can be made 1 week in advance and frozen. Remove it from the freezer 30 minutes before serving.

VARIATION: Other melons may be used, such as white honeydew, cantaloupe, or crenshaw.

Bittersweet Hot Fudge Sauce

MAKES 1½ CUPS

I prefer a Belgian bittersweet chocolate for this recipe. The blend of butter, cream, and chocolate makes the sauce harden just slightly when it hits the cold ice cream. This delectable sauce is perfection with Frozen Praline Mousse or plain ice cream.

> 8 ounces (½ pound) bittersweet chocolate (preferably Belgian), coarsely chopped
> ½ cup (1 stick) unsalted butter, cut into small pieces
> ¼ cup whipping cream

1. In the top part of a double boiler over medium heat, combine the chocolate and butter and melt slowly. When melted, whisk in the cream.
2. Pour over ice cream and serve immediately.

ADVANCE PREPARATION: This may be prepared 4 hours in advance and kept *barely* warm in the top of a double boiler. It also can be prepared up to 1 week in advance and refrigerated. Reheat slowly in a double boiler.

Amaretto Cream

MAKES 2 CUPS

This refreshing, quick sauce made from soft ice cream and whipping cream is delicious spooned over fruit desserts. Try it on Blueberry Nectarine Buckle, Cherry Amaretti Crisp, or Almond Peach Clafouti.

½ pint whipping cream
½ pint French vanilla ice cream, softened
2 tablespoons amaretto

1. In a medium mixing bowl whip the cream until just stiff. Beat in the softened ice cream. Add the amaretto and blend. Serve within the hour.

Sugar Syrup

MAKES 2 CUPS

Keep this preparation in your refrigerator to use in sorbets, fruit salads, mousses, or ice creams. Make sure that the syrup is cold before you use it.

2 cups water
2 cups sugar

1. Place the water and sugar in a medium saucepan. Over medium heat, bring to a simmer, stirring until the sugar is dissolved.
2. Let the syrup cool to room temperature. Refrigerate it in a sealed jar.

ADVANCE PREPARATION: The syrup may be kept up to 1 month in the refrigerator.

Pecan Praline

MAKES 1½ CUPS

Toasting brings out the full flavor of the pecans before they are coated with a golden brown caramel. When hardened, the praline is chopped into a coarse powder. Sprinkle this delicious confection on ice cream or use it in Frozen Praline Mousse, Frozen Peaches and Cream, or White Chocolate Terrine with Strawberries and Praline.

 1 cup pecan pieces
⅔ cup sugar
 3 tablespoons water

1. Preheat the oven to 350°F. Toast the pecans for 5 to 7 minutes, watching to see that they do not burn. Chop coarsely in a food processor and set aside.
2. Oil a baking sheet well.
3. Combine the sugar and water in a small, heavy saucepan. Do not use a dark-colored pan, as you will not be able to see the color of the caramel. Dissolve the sugar in the water over low heat. Turn up the heat and continually swirl the pan over the flame. The mixture will be bubbly. If sugar crystals form on the sides of the pan, cover it for 1 minute and they will dissolve. Boil until the mixture turns a golden brown color. Watch carefully as caramel can burn easily.
4. When the mixture turns golden brown, remove it from the heat. Add the pecans and mix together well, coating the nuts with the caramel.
5. Pour onto the greased baking sheet and let cool.
6. When cooled, coarsely chop the praline in a food processor, pulsing on and off.
7. Place the powder in an airtight container and freeze.

ADVANCE PREPARATION: This may be prepared in advance and kept up to 2 months in the freezer.

Strawberry Sauce

Using a nylon strainer ensures that the strawberries won't pick up a metallic taste from a metal one. Serve this with White Chocolate Terrine with Strawberries and Praline, over Crushed Strawberry Ice Cream, or with Lemon Orange Sponge Pudding.

    1 pint fresh strawberries, hulled
    1 tablespoon fresh lemon juice
    2 tablespoons powdered sugar

1. Process the berries in a food processor fitted with a steel blade or in a blender until puréed. Add the lemon juice and powdered sugar and process until blended.
2. Strain the purée through a nylon strainer, using one spatula to push the sauce through and another to push the sauce off the underside of the strainer.
3. Refrigerate until needed.

ADVANCE PREPARATION: This may be kept up to 5 days in the refrigerator. Remove from the refrigerator ½ hour before serving.

Sauces, Relishes and Basic Recipes

SAUCES

Summer Vinaigrette

MAKES 1 CUP

This vinaigrette is chock-full of fresh herbs that will liven up any variety of salad greens, fresh vegetables, cold seafood, chicken, or pasta salads.

 1 medium shallot, finely chopped
 1 medium garlic clove, minced
 1 tablespoon finely chopped parsley
 1 tablespoon finely chopped chives
 1 teaspoon finely chopped basil
 1 teaspoon Dijon mustard
 1 tablespoon fresh lemon juice
 3 tablespoons red wine vinegar
 ¾ cup olive oil
 ½ teaspoon salt
 ¼ teaspoon black pepper

1. Combine the shallots, garlic, parsley, chives, basil, Dijon mustard, lemon juice, and red wine vinegar in a medium bowl and whisk until well blended. (Or place in a food processor fitted with a steel blade and process until well blended.)

2. Slowly pour in the olive oil, whisking continuously (or processing) until blended. Add the salt and pepper and taste for seasoning.

ADVANCE PREPARATION: This may be prepared and kept up to 1 week in the refrigerator. Whisk before using.

Buttermilk Garden Herb Dressing

MAKES 2 CUPS

This garden-fresh dipping sauce is an all-American classic. If you can't find burnet, a cucumber-flavored herb, add extra parsley. Delicious with raw vegetables, fresh lettuce greens, or tomatoes.

    1 cup Basic Homemade Mayonnaise (see page 344)
    1 cup buttermilk
    1 medium garlic clove, minced
    1 teaspoon Dijon mustard
    2 teaspoons finely chopped burnet
    2 tablespoons finely chopped chives
    1 tablespoon finely chopped dill
    1 tablespoon finely chopped parsley
    ¼ teaspoon salt
    ¼ teaspoon white pepper

1. Combine all the ingredients in a medium mixing bowl and whisk until completely blended. Taste for seasoning.

ADVANCE PREPARATION: This may be prepared 5 days in advance and refrigerated.

FLAVORED MAYONNAISE

An interesting mayonnaise can easily spice up simple dishes. The following ingredients can be added to basic mayonnaise to turn it into a real asset. Make sure that these additions are finely chopped or minced to add the fullest flavor.

- Anchovies
- Ancho Chile Paste
- Basil and shallots
- Lemon and chives
- Roasted pepper purée
- Mango chutney and curry powder
- Watercress, dill, and spinach with fresh lemon juice

Tapenade

MAKES 1½ CUPS

Tapenade is to Provence what pesto is to Italy. This basic strongly flavored olive paste is excellent as a dipping sauce for raw vegetables. It's also delicious for spreading on a cracker, seasoning a sauce, and flavoring chicken or fish.

    20 oil-cured black olives
     2 medium garlic cloves, minced
     2 tablespoons capers, well drained
     4 anchovy fillets, drained
     2 teaspoons Dijon mustard
     2 tablespoons fresh lemon juice
     2 tablespoons finely chopped basil
    ¼ cup finely chopped Italian parsley
    ⅛ teaspoon cayenne pepper
     1 egg yolk
    ½ cup olive oil

1. Place the olives on a wooden board. With the back of a heavy cleaver, smash them, separating the pit from the olive. Remove the pits.
2. Combine all the ingredients except for the egg yolk and olive oil in a blender or a food processor fitted with a steel blade. Process the ingredients until puréed. Use a rubber spatula to occasionally push down the ingredients if necessary.
3. Add the egg yolk and, with the motor running, slowly add the olive oil until it is completely absorbed. Taste for seasoning. Cover in an airtight container and refrigerate until needed.

ADVANCE PREPARATION: This may be prepared up to 1 week ahead and refrigerated.

VARIATION: Add 1 6½-ounce can drained tuna to the tapenade in step 2.

Basic Homemade Mayonnaise

MAKES 1½ CUPS

Basic but not ordinary, this sauce is used as a dressing for salads and as a dip for vegetables. Spruce it up by adding Ancho Chile Paste, Tapenade, or roasted garlic (see following recipe).

>   2 eggs or 1 whole egg and 1 egg yolk
>   2 tablespoons fresh lemon juice
>   2 teaspoons Dijon mustard
>   Pinch cayenne pepper
>   Pinch white pepper
>   1 to 1½ cups safflower oil
>   Salt (optional)

1. Combine the eggs, lemon juice, mustard, cayenne pepper, and white pepper in a blender or a food processor fitted with a steel blade. Process for 5 to 10 seconds.

2. With the blades turning, add the oil in a slow, steady stream. Process until smooth, scraping the sides of the bowl occasionally. Taste for seasoning.

3. Refrigerate in an airtight container.

ADVANCE PREPARATION: This may be made up to 3 days in advance and refrigerated.

Roasted Garlic Mayonnaise

MAKES 1½ CUPS

Roasting garlic gives it a subtle, sweet, nutty taste. This variation on the classic aioli is good on salads, cold chicken, smoked fish, cold seafood, or used as a dipping sauce for vegetables.

>   2   medium heads of garlic
>   1½ cups Basic Homemade Mayonnaise (see previous
>   recipe)
>   1   tablespoon fresh lemon juice

1. Preheat the oven to 425°F. Place the garlic in aluminum foil and wrap tightly. Place on a baking sheet and bake for 1 hour. Remove from the oven and let cool.

2. When cool, squeeze the soft garlic pulp out of the cloves by pushing hard on the garlic head. (You should have about 2 heaping tablespoons.) Place in a small bowl. Add the mayonnaise and lemon juice, whisking to combine.

3. Refrigerate in an airtight container.

ADVANCE PREPARATION: May be made 3 days in advance and refrigerated.

Roasted Garlic Mayonnaise

Tomato Basil Sauce

MAKES 1½ CUPS

This sauce is actually a mild version of a Mexican tomato salsa. Basil replaces the usual hot chilies, while crushed red pepper flakes add just a touch of hotness. Tomato Basil Sauce requires no cooking and is excellent on pasta. Try adding a little vinaigrette to this sauce and tossing it with cooled pasta and vegetables for a garden pasta salad. It also makes an appetizing garnish for simple vegetable soups.

4 medium tomatoes, peeled, seeded, and coarsely chopped
1 medium red onion, finely chopped
2 garlic cloves, minced
6 tablespoons fresh basil, finely chopped
3 tablespoons Italian parsley, finely chopped
2 tablespoons olive oil
¾ teaspoon salt
¼ teaspoon pepper
¼ teaspoon crushed red pepper flakes (optional)

1. Combine all the ingredients in a medium bowl and mix well. Cover and refrigerate. Taste for seasoning.

ADVANCE PREPARATION: This sauce may be prepared 1 day in advance and refrigerated.

Fresh Tomato Sauce

MAKES 5 CUPS

At the height of the tomato season try making this fresh tomato sauce. Double or triple it and keep some in your freezer for fall, after the ripe tomatoes are gone. It is lighter than a marinara sauce and can be used in place of canned crushed tomatoes in soups, sauces, or pasta.

  3 tablespoons olive oil
  1 medium onion, finely chopped
  1 medium carrot, finely chopped
  1 celery stalk, finely chopped
  4 pounds ripe red tomatoes, peeled and crushed
  2 large garlic cloves, minced
  3 tablespoons finely chopped parsley
  ½ bay leaf
  1 tablespoon finely chopped fresh oregano
  2 tablespoons finely chopped basil
    Salt
    Pepper

1. Heat the olive oil in a large nonaluminum casserole over medium heat. Add the onion, carrot, and celery and cook until soft, stirring frequently to avoid burning.
2. Add the tomatoes, garlic, and herbs. Partially cover and reduce the heat to medium low. Simmer for 1½ hours, stirring occasionally. Remove the bay leaf.
3. Purée the mixture in a blender or a food processor fitted with a steel blade and then press the sauce through a strainer or a food mill. Pour back into the saucepan and boil until reduced to about 5 cups.
4. Season to taste with salt and pepper. Serve hot.

ADVANCE PREPARATION: This sauce may be kept up to 5 days in the refrigerator. It also may be frozen in small containers for up to 2 months.

Tomatillo Sauce

MAKES 2½ CUPS

Tomatillos are the foundation of this light, spicy green sauce. If fresh tomatillos are unavailable, you can substitute canned, drained tomatillos with a pinch of sugar; however, you won't need to cook them. Use Tomatillo Sauce to flavor a vinaigrette, or sour cream, or as a salsa on grilled meat or fish. It's also great on eggs and fresh corn tortillas.

¾ cup chicken stock (see page 366)
1 small onion, coarsely chopped
1 pound tomatillos, husked and quartered
1 or 2 jalapeño chilies, seeded and finely chopped*
2 medium garlic cloves, minced
3 tablespoons finely chopped cilantro
¼ teaspoon ground cumin seed
½ teaspoon salt
1 tablespoon fresh lemon juice

1. In a large skillet, heat the chicken stock over medium heat. Simmer the onion in the chicken stock for about 5 minutes, covered.
2. Add the tomatillos and cook another 5 minutes, covered.
3. Pour the contents of the skillet into a blender or a food processor fitted with a steel blade and process until coarsely chopped. Add the chilies, garlic, cilantro, cumin, salt, and lemon juice. Taste for seasoning. Pour into a storage container and cool. Refrigerate until using.

ADVANCE PREPARATION: This sauce can be made 5 days ahead and refrigerated in an airtight container.

*When working with chilies, always wear rubber gloves. Wash the cutting surface and knife immediately afterward.

Red Pepper Tomato Sauce

MAKES 2½ CUPS

This sauce is especially easy because there's no need to peel the tomatoes or roast the peppers. Red Pepper Tomato Sauce is excellent on pasta with the addition of poached chicken or shellfish. Or use it on steamed vegetables with a sprinkle of grated Parmesan cheese.

> 3 tablespoons unsalted butter
> 1 medium onion, finely chopped
> 4 large sweet red peppers, seeded and thinly sliced
> 2 large tomatoes (about 1 pound), peeled, seeded, and finely chopped
> 1 medium bunch basil, coarsely chopped
> 1 teaspoon salt
> ¼ teaspoon pepper

1. In a large nonaluminum saucepan melt the butter over medium heat. Add the onion and sauté until softened, 3 to 4 minutes.
2. Add the peppers, tomatoes, and basil and cook, partially covered, over medium-low heat until soft, about 20 minutes. Remove from the heat.
3. Pour the vegetables into a blender or a food processor fitted with a steel blade and process until puréed, about 1 minute. Press through a fine strainer over a medium bowl.
4. Season with salt and pepper. Taste for seasoning.

ADVANCE PREPARATION: This may be prepared 2 days in advance and refrigerated. Reheat before serving.

Tomato Cucumber Salsa

MAKES 2½ CUPS

This chunky-style salsa is full of crunchy cucumber. Try it on grilled seafood, with avocado soup, or as a dip for tortilla chips.

    2 large tomatoes (about 1 pound), peeled, seeded, and
       finely chopped
    ½ cup peeled, seeded, and finely chopped European
       cucumber
    1 medium jalapeño chile, seeded and finely chopped*
    1 tablespoon finely chopped cilantro
    1 tablespoon fresh lemon juice
    1 medium garlic clove, minced
    ½ teaspoon salt

1. Combine all the ingredients in a medium mixing bowl and mix well. Taste for seasoning. Cover and refrigerate.

ADVANCE PREPARATION: May be kept up to 3 days in the refrigerator. Remove it from the refrigerator ½ hour before serving.

VARIATION: Canned jalapeño chilies may be used if fresh are not available. If using the canned variety, omit the lemon juice.

*When working with chilies, always wear rubber gloves. Wash the cutting surface and knife immediately afterward.

Spinach Pesto

MAKES 1 TO 1½ CUPS

Spinach combined with basil yields a milder version of pesto. It is sometimes used without the cheese, as in the Pesto-Cucumber Sauce for poached salmon. I prefer to add the cheese right before serving so that I can use the sauce either way. Spinach Pesto is excellent as a flavor enhancer for soups, dressings, and sauces and as a glaze for tomatoes.

2	medium garlic cloves
1¼	cups fresh basil (about 1 medium bunch)
1	cup fresh spinach
¼	cup parsley
3	tablespoons pine nuts
½	cup olive oil
¼	teaspoon black pepper
½	cup freshly grated Parmesan (optional)

1. In a food processor fitted with a steel blade, process the garlic cloves until puréed.
2. Add the basil, spinach, and parsley and process until finely chopped. Add the pine nuts and finely chop.
3. With the blades turning, slowly pour in the olive oil in a fine stream and process until the oil is absorbed. Add the pepper.
4. If using Parmesan, add it just before serving and process until well blended. Taste for seasoning.
5. Refrigerate in a tightly covered container until ready to use.

ADVANCE PREPARATION: This pesto may be prepared 1 week in advance through step 3 and kept in the refrigerator. Add the cheese just before serving.

Tomato-Béarnaise Sauce

MAKES 1½ CUPS

This variation on the traditional Béarnaise is particularly good on fish, steaks, chicken, and poached eggs. It is quite easy to prepare and can be kept warm in a small thermos for half an hour before serving.

2 tablespoons white wine vinegar
2 tablespoons dry white wine
2 teaspoons chopped fresh tarragon, or 1 teaspoon dried
2 medium shallots, finely chopped
4 egg yolks
½ teaspoon salt
½ teaspoon cracked pepper
1 tablespoon tomato paste
1 cup (2 sticks) unsalted butter

1. Pour boiling water into a 1-pint wide-necked thermos jar to warm it. (Omit this step if you're serving the sauce just after it's made.)
2. In a small saucepan, heat the first four ingredients until almost all the liquid is absorbed.
3. Place the shallot mixture in a blender or food processor fitted with a steel blade. Add the egg yolks, salt, pepper, and tomato paste and blend for 20 seconds.
4. Heat the butter in the same pan until sizzling but not browned. This is important to enable the sauce to thicken properly.
5. With the motor running, slowly pour the hot butter into the blender or food processor in a thin stream until completely incorporated. Taste for seasoning.
6. If preparing ahead, drain and dry the thermos jar and immediately pour the hot sauce into it. This will keep the sauce hot for up to ½ hour. Serve warm.

Tomato-Papaya Mint Salsa

MAKES 2 CUPS

Papaya and tomato may seem like an unlikely combination but not so. Tropical and refreshing, this salsa goes well with grilled seafood, chicken, or black beans.

    2 large tomatoes (about 1 pound) peeled, seeded, and diced
    1 cup peeled, seeded, and diced ripe papaya (about ½)
    1 jalapeño chile, seeded and finely chopped*
    1 shallot, finely chopped
    3 tablespoons finely chopped mint
    2 tablespoons fresh lime juice
    ½ teaspoon salt

Combine all the ingredients in a medium mixing bowl and mix well. Refrigerate covered until ready to serve.

ADVANCE PREPARATION: This salsa may be prepared in the morning and refrigerated until ready to serve.

VARIATION: Canned jalepeño chilies may be used if fresh are not available, but omit the lemon juice in the recipe.

*When working with chilies, always wear rubber gloves. Wash the cutting surface and knife immediately afterward.

RELISHES

Three-Onion Marmalade with Fresh Thyme

MAKES ABOUT 3 CUPS

This relish goes well with just about any grilled dish. Chicken, veal, beef, vegetables, and grilled sausages all benefit from this caramel thyme-scented marmalade. Package any extra in pretty containers for gifts.

¼ cup (½ stick) unsalted butter
2 medium leeks, white part only, cleaned and finely chopped
1 large red onion, finely chopped
1 large yellow or Maui onion, finely chopped
¾ cup red wine
¼ cup balsamic vinegar
1 tablespoon sugar
1 teaspoon finely chopped thyme leaves
¼ teaspoon salt
⅛ teaspoon white pepper

1. Melt the butter in a large nonaluminum casserole over medium-high heat. Add the leeks and onions and sauté until very soft, 10 to 15 minutes. Stir frequently.

2. Add the wine, balsamic vinegar, and sugar to the onions and simmer over low heat until almost all of the liquid has evaporated. The onions should be very tender and slightly caramelized. Add the thyme, salt, and pepper. Taste for seasoning. Cool and serve at room temperature.

NOTE: This may be stored in the refrigerator in an airtight container for up to 1 month. Heat the marmalade with a small amount of water and then let it come to room temperature before serving. You may need to adjust the seasoning and add more fresh thyme.

Apricot-Plum Sauce

MAKES 4 CUPS

I often double this recipe and bring it to friends as a house gift. Apricot-Plum Sauce is particularly good with pork, chicken, quail, and game hens. Dilute it with wine or nectar to use it as a marinade.

    1 large onion, coarsely chopped
    4 garlic cloves, minced
  ¼ cup coarsely chopped fresh ginger
    2 limes, thinly sliced
    1 pound apricots, pitted and coarsely chopped
    1 pound plums, pitted and coarsely chopped
    1 cup cider vinegar
  ½ cup tawny port
    2 cups dark brown sugar
    1 teaspoon cinnamon
    1 teaspoon ground allspice
  ½ teaspoon cayenne pepper or crushed red pepper flakes
    1 teaspoon salt
  ¼ cup finely chopped cilantro

1. In a food processor fitted with a steel blade, process the onion, garlic, ginger, limes, apricots, and plums until puréed.
2. In a medium nonaluminum dutch oven or heavy pot, combine the puréed ingredients and all the remaining ingredients except the cilantro and bring to a boil over medium-high heat.
3. Lower the heat and simmer until slightly thickened, about 45 minutes. Stir frequently to avoid burning. Remove from the heat and cool. Add the cilantro and taste for seasoning. Pour the sauce into a large glass container and refrigerate.

ADVANCE PREPARATION: This sauce may be refrigerated in an airtight container for up to 2 months.

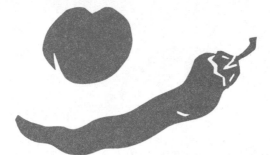

Fresh Pickled Red and Green Grapes

MAKES 6 12-OUNCE JARS

These wonderful little jewels are equally enjoyable as an appetizer all by themselves or served with cold turkey or chicken. This recipe adapts one of Mrs. Catherine Plagemann's as suggested by M.F.K. Fisher. Make extra jars for gifts; these unusual treats are unbelievably easy to make.

3 cups red seedless grapes, Red Flame preferred
3 cups green seedless grapes, thin-skinned preferred
3⅔ cups sugar
2⅓ cups white wine or white vinegar
6 cinnamon sticks

1. Prepare jars by putting them through hottest cycle in the dishwasher.
2. While the jars are still hot, place a cinnamon stick in each jar and spoon the grapes in, making sure that the colors are well mixed.
3. Combine the sugar and vinegar in a medium saucepan and bring to a boil. Reduce heat and simmer for 5 minutes.
4. Pour over the syrup, covering the grapes completely. Stir a bit, then cover jars. Let sit (in the dark) at least overnight, up to 4 days before eating. Keep in the dark (to keep color from fading) until opening. Refrigerate once opened.

Fresh Pickled Red and Green Grapes

Peach-Jalapeño Chutney

MAKES ABOUT 1 QUART

Bottled chutneys tend to be overly sweet with not much other flavor. In India, chutneys (from the Hindu word "chatni," meaning to lick or to taste) are reserved for special occasions. This version is a spicy cooked relish of sweet, ripe peaches, spices, and chilies. Serve this on grilled chicken, veal chops, or pork chops, or add it to sour cream for a dipping sauce. It's also great with melted sharp Cheddar cheese on brown bread. And, of course, it makes a wonderful gift.

2 pounds peaches, slightly soft
1 cup apple cider vinegar
1 cup dark brown sugar
2 medium garlic cloves, minced
1 small onion, finely chopped
2 small jalapeño chiilies, seeded and finely chopped*
1 teaspoon mustard seed
1 tablespoon fresh minced ginger
½ cup golden raisins
1 teaspoon cinnamon
1 teaspoon ground allspice
¼ teaspoon salt

1. Immerse the peaches in a large saucepan of boiling water for about 30 seconds and then remove immediately. Peel, pit, and cut into a coarse dice.
2. Place all the remaining ingredients in a medium non-aluminum dutch oven or heavy pot.
3. Bring the ingredients to a boil over medium-high heat. Lower the heat and let simmer, partially covered, for about

45 minutes. Stir the chutney frequently, making sure that it does not burn or stick to the bottom of the pan.

4. Remove from the heat and cool. Taste for seasoning.
5. When cool, pour the chutney into glass containers. Store in the refrigerator.

ADVANCE PREPARATION: This chutney may be refrigerated in an air-tight container for up to 2 months.

*When working with chilies, always wear rubber gloves. Wash the cutting surface and knife immediately afterward.

Peach-Jalapeño Chutney

BASIC RECIPES

Ancho Chile Paste

MAKES ¾ CUP

This rustic paste has an unusual, very rich taste. Garlic and the ancho chile are "toasted," which is a Mexican technique for intensifying their flavors. The chile is then softened and finally puréed into a thick paste. This is a wonderful condiment to have on hand. Try adding a spoonful to sour cream, mayonnaise, or butter. It's also a spicy coating for meat to be grilled or roasted.

>   2 large garlic cloves, unpeeled
>   6 large ancho chilies (about 3 ounces)
>   3 tablespoons olive oil
>   ½ teaspoon salt

1. Place the garlic in a small skillet over medium-high heat. Toast the garlic cloves by turning them as they begin to brown. When light brown in color, remove from the heat. Peel.
2. In the same skillet heat the chilies over medium heat until they begin to expand and the flesh becomes soft. The chilies should smell rich, but should not be charred. Remove from the heat. Cool.

3. Wearing rubber gloves, slit the chilies open and remove the seeds and any veins. Place the chilies in a small bowl, pour boiling water over them to cover, and let soften for 15 minutes. Remove from the water and drain well.

4. In a food processor fitted with a steel blade, process the chilies and garlic until puréed. Add the olive oil and salt and process until well combined. Taste for seasoning. Store in an airtight container in the refrigerator.

ADVANCE PREPARATION: This may be prepared and kept up to 1 month in the refrigerator.

Ancho Chile Paste

Roasted Peppers or Chilies

SERVES 6

Here's a recipe for perfectly roasted and peeled peppers or chilies. Actually the peppers and chilies are not roasted at all but rather broiled or grilled right on the barbecue to char them. Then they steam in a paper bag to make peeling them easier. Although you may think this is tedious the first time around, you'll find it actually takes little time and the delicious results are well worth the effort. Keep the peppers covered with oil if you are preparing them in advance. They are also excellent served alone, dressed with a light vinaigrette.

**Red, golden, green or purple bell peppers or
Anaheim or poblano chilies***

1. To peel the peppers or chilies, place them on a broiler pan or medium-high-heat grill and broil approximately 6 inches from the heat until blackened on all sides. Use tongs to turn the peppers or chilies.
2. Remove the peppers or chilies from the broiler or grill. Close them tightly in a paper bag. Let rest for 10 minutes.
3. Remove them from the bag. Drain and peel off the skins. Make a slit in each pepper or chile and open it up. Core and cut off the stem. Scrape out the seeds and ribs from the insides.
4. With a sharp knife or pizza wheel, cut the peppers into different shapes. If serving sweet peppers alone, place them in a serving dish and pour dressing over. Sprinkle with chopped basil and decorate with small Niçoise olives. Serve at room temperature or slightly chilled.

ADVANCE PREPARATION: This may be prepared 5 days in advance and refrigerated. Remove from the refrigerator ½ hour before using.

*When working with chilies, always wear rubber gloves. Wash the cutting surface and knife immediately afterward.

Prebaked Pastry Crust

MAKES 1 9-INCH SINGLE PIE CRUST
OR 1 11-INCH TART CRUST

We all need a good, basic, no-fail crust and this is it.

- 1 **cup all-purpose flour**
  Pinch salt
- 6 **tablespoons (¾ stick) unsalted butter, frozen, cut into small pieces**
- ¼ **cup ice water**

1. Combine the flour and salt in a food processor fitted with a steel blade. Process a few seconds to blend. Add the butter and process until the mixture resembles coarse meal, 5 to 10 seconds.
2. With the blades of the processor turning, gradually add the water until the dough is just beginning to come together and will hold a shape when pressed.
3. Transfer the dough to a floured pastry board or work surface. Press into a round shape for easy rolling. Roll out into a circle large enough to fit a 9-inch pie shell or an 11-inch tart pan with a removable bottom. Drape the circle of dough over the rolling pin and fit it into the pan. Roll the rolling pin over the tart pan with moderate pressure to remove the excess dough. Place the pan on a baking sheet.
4. Preheat the oven to 375°F. Prick the shell and then cover it with a large piece of parchment or wax paper. Place lima beans, rice, or baking beads on top. Distribute them evenly to prevent the shell from shrinking. Bake for 20 to 25 minutes. Remove from the oven, let cool, and remove the beans.

ADVANCE PREPARATION: The dough may be prepared through step 3, sealed in plastic wrap, and frozen until ready to use. Thaw before baking.

Veal Stock

MAKES 3½ QUARTS

Veal stock has a meaty richness, but is not as heavy as beef stock. Prepare a large quantity and divide it into small containers to keep in your freezer. Veal stock is primarily used in sauces and reductions.

> 2 pounds veal necks
> 1 pound veal bones
> 2 large carrots, cut into 2-inch slices
> 1 large onion, cut into 2-inch slices
> 2 leeks, cleaned and sliced into 2-inch chunks
> 1 bouquet garni*

1. Preheat the oven to 425°F. Place the necks and bones in a large roasting pan. Roast until browned, about 1½ hours.
2. Remove the pan from the oven and place on top of a burner. Remove the bones and necks and place in a 6-quart stockpot.
3. Add about 3 cups water to the roasting pan over medium-high heat. Stir, scraping any bits stuck to the bottom of the pan, and bring the water to a boil. The water should turn a rich brown color.
4. Pour the water into the stockpot and add enough more water to nearly cover the bones. Add the vegetables and bouquet garni.
5. Bring the mixture to a boil over medium heat, then turn down to the lowest heat possible. Simmer uncovered for 8 to 10 hours or overnight. Occasionally skim off the fat that rises to the top.
6. Turn off the heat and let cool. Remove the bones and pour the stock through a fine strainer (a conical strainer is excellent for this purpose) into a large bowl. Let cool to room temperature. Cover and refrigerate 2 hours.
7. With a large spoon, remove the fat that has come to the top and discard. The stock should be clear.
8. Line the strainer with cheesecloth and pour the stock

through again to make sure it is fat free. If not using immediately, pour into containers and refrigerate.

ADVANCE PREPARATION: If not used within 3 days, the stock should be frozen and then reboiled before using. Freeze it in small containers for convenient use.

VARIATION: For beef stock, substitute beef bones for veal bones.

*To make a bouquet garni, wrap a parsley stem, bay leaf, and sprig of fresh thyme in cheesecloth and tie with string.

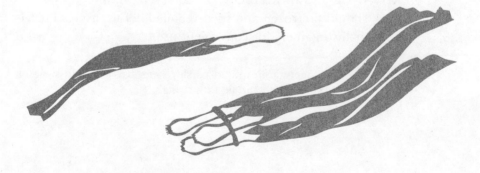

Chicken Stock

MAKES 3 QUARTS

There are enervating days in summer when even purists wouldn't dream of making chicken stock from scratch. Well-organized cooks make stock ahead and freeze it; this recipe is for them. For the faint-hearted, canned chicken broth is the answer. Look for brands with no sodium; they have the fewest additives.

4 pounds chicken necks and backs
3 celery stalks
3 medium carrots, peeled
2 medium onions, root ends cut off, cut into halves
2 medium leeks, green and white parts, cleaned and sliced
  Bouquet garni*
2 teaspoons salt

1. Combine all the ingredients except salt in a 6-quart stock-pot. Add enough cold water to fill the pot ¾ full. Bring slowly to a boil over medium heat, uncovered.
2. Turn down to the lowest possible heat and simmer for 3 hours uncovered. Add salt. Taste for seasoning.
3. Strain through a colander or strainer lined with cheesecloth. Let cool and refrigerate. With a large spoon remove the fat from the surface and discard.
4. If not using immediately, pour into containers and refrigerate.

ADVANCE PREPARATION: If not used within 3 days, the stock should be frozen and then reboiled before using. Freeze it in small containers for convenient use.

*To make a bouquet garni, wrap a parsley stem, bay leaf, and sprig of fresh thyme in cheesecloth and tie with string.

Hot Pepper Oil

MAKES 1 CUP

Use this spicy oil sparingly. It enlivens many dishes, from soups to salad dressings. And it will keep in the refrigerator almost indefinitely.

¼ **cup crushed hot red pepper flakes**
1 **cup safflower oil**

1. Combine the pepper flakes and oil in a small saucepan over medium heat. Bring to a boil and then immediately turn off the heat. Cool.
2. Strain into a small glass jar that can be sealed. Keep refrigerated.

VARIATION: Leave the pepper flakes in the oil. They will fall to the bottom and can be used in seasoning. The oil will become hotter as it stands.

Fish Stock

MAKES ABOUT 1 GALLON

  2 tablespoons safflower oil
  2 pounds heads, skin, bones, and flesh of fresh fish
  1 medium onion, peeled and thinly sliced
  2 medium carrots, unpeeled and cut into 2-inch pieces
  6 parsley stems
  2 celery stalks with leaves, cut into 2-inch pieces
  1 bay leaf
10 white peppercorns
  5 sprigs fresh dill
  1 lemon, thinly sliced

1. In a 6-quart stockpot, heat the oil and sauté the fish for 2 to 3 minutes over low heat. Do not brown.
2. Add the remaining ingredients to the pot and enough water to nearly cover them. Bring to a boil over medium heat. Reduce the heat and simmer uncovered for 45 minutes.
3. Strain through a colander or strainer lined with cheesecloth. Let cool. Remove the fat from the surface with a large spoon and discard.
4. If not using immediately, pour into containers and refrigerate.

ADVANCE PREPARATION: If not used within 2 days, the stock should be frozen and then reboiled before using. Freeze it in small containers for convenient use.

Crème Fraîche

MAKES 1 CUP

Crème Fraîche is a versatile substitute for whipping cream in sauces and desserts. You may want to sweeten it slightly when serving it with fresh fruit.

  1 **cup whipping cream, preferably not ultra-pasteurized**
  2 **tablespoons cultured buttermilk**

1. Combine the cream and buttermilk in a glass jar or crockery bowl (not metal) and whisk until well blended. Loosely cover the jar or bowl with aluminum foil, letting some air in. Leave in a warm place for at least 12 hours and up to 24 hours. The cream will become thick enough for a spoon to stand up in it and will have a sour, nutty taste.
2. Stir cream when thickened. Cover and refrigerate until ready to use.

ADVANCE PREPARATION: Crème Fraîche may be kept up to 1 week in the refrigerator.

Index